CW01064113

DOES ANYTHING REALLY MATTER?

Derek Parfit, 1942–2017
A life that mattered

DOES ANYTHING REALLY MATTER?

ESSAYS ON PARFIT ON OBJECTIVITY

EDITED BY PETER SINGER

OXFORD

UNIVERSITY PRESS

OXFORD
UNIVERSITY PRESS

Great Clarendon Street, Oxford, OX2 6DP,
United Kingdom

Oxford University Press is a department of the University of Oxford.
It furthers the University's objective of excellence in research, scholarship,
and education by publishing worldwide. Oxford is a registered trade mark of
Oxford University Press in the UK and in certain other countries

© the several contributors 2016

The moral rights of the authors have been asserted

Impression: 1

All rights reserved. No part of this publication may be reproduced, stored in
a retrieval system, or transmitted, in any form or by any means, without the
prior permission in writing of Oxford University Press, or as expressly permitted
by law, by licence or under terms agreed with the appropriate reprographics
rights organization. Enquiries concerning reproduction outside the scope of the
above should be sent to the Rights Department, Oxford University Press, at the
address above

You must not circulate this work in any other form
and you must impose this same condition on any acquirer

Published in the United States of America by Oxford University Press
198 Madison Avenue, New York, NY 10016, United States of America

British Library Cataloguing in Publication Data

Data available

Library of Congress Control Number: 2015953853

ISBN 978-0-19-965383-6

Printed in Great Britain by
Clays Ltd, St Ives plc

CONTENTS

PREFACE

When Derek Parfit's two-volume, 1,400-page *On What Matters* appeared in 2011, it was widely hailed as a work of lasting philosophical significance. Much of the ensuing discussion, however, focused on those sections of the book in which Parfit argued that the best versions of three major contending traditions in normative ethics—Kantianism, contractualism, and rule consequentialism—are in fundamental agreement, identifying the same acts as wrong. Underlying and supporting this original and important argument, however, is another, more fundamental claim, also defended at considerable length: that there are objective moral truths, and other normative truths about what we have reasons to believe, and to want, and to do.

Skepticism about objective truth in ethics is as old as philosophy. Plato's *Republic* is an early attempt to rebut skeptical challenges about ethics, and perhaps an indication that Socrates, too, saw the need to challenge ethical relativism and ethical subjectivism. In contemporary English-language philosophy, most ethical skeptics or subjectivists trace the roots of their view to the eighteenth-century Scottish philosopher David Hume. Hume assumes, and we commonly believe, that morality must be able to influence what we do. Otherwise, we may wonder, what is its point? But Hume also held that reason alone cannot move us to action. Our wants and desires determine our ultimate goals, and the role of reason is limited to telling us how best to achieve these goals. Reason applies to means, not ends. Hence, Hume famously held, it is not contrary to reason to prefer the destruction of the whole world to the scratching of my finger, and equally not contrary to reason to choose my own total ruin to prevent a trivial harm to a stranger. Even acting contrary to one's own interests—preferring "my own acknowledged lesser good to my greater" is, on Hume's view, not contrary to reason. What it is rational for me to do depends on what I want.

If Hume is right both in his assumption about the relation between morality and action, and about the role of reason in action, then there is an obvious problem for those who think that moral judgments can be objectively true. Moral judgments will only be able to influence our actions if they somehow connect with our desires, and my desires may differ from yours without either of us making a mistake. Wants and desires are neither true nor false. An objectively true moral judgment would have to be true for everyone, irrespective of what he or she most desires, but what reason for acting would it offer to those whose desires are not furthered by acting on it?

Something like this line of argument has led most of the leading moral philosophers of the past eighty years—figures like A. J. Ayer, C. L. Stevenson, R. M. Hare, J. L. Mackie, Christine Korsgaard, Bernard Williams, Simon Blackburn, and Allan Gibbard—to reject the idea that our ethical judgments can be objectively true or false. Under varying names—emotivism, prescriptivism, constructivism, irrealism, or expressivism—they have embraced some form of ethical subjectivism or skepticism.

Parfit's critique of the forms of subjectivism that draw on Hume's view of the limits of practical reason begins with a discussion of the role of reason in a situation relating to self-interest rather than morality. He asks us to imagine a man who cares, as most of us do, about what pleasures or pains he will experience in future, but with this difference: if they will happen on a future Tuesday, he doesn't care about them at all. If he is contemplating what will happen to him on a Monday, a Wednesday, or any other day, he would much rather experience slight discomfort now than agony on that day; but if the agony will be on a future Tuesday, he doesn't care about it, and so will choose it over slight discomfort now. This man is not under any illusion that pains on future Tuesdays are less painful than pains on other days, for he knows that when that future Tuesday becomes the present day, the agony will be as terrible as it is on a Monday or Wednesday. He also knows that—since it will then not be a *future* Tuesday—he will not be at all indifferent to the agony he then experiences. Nor does he believe in a strange deity who will reward him for his indifference to what will happen to him on future Tuesdays. He differs from us purely in what he desires. Surely, Parfit claims, this man's desires are irrational: "That some ordeal would be much more painful is a strong reason not to prefer it. That this ordeal would be on a future Tuesday is no reason to prefer it."

It is difficult to deny that such a man would be irrational, and the only possible source of this irrationality is his desires. But Hume's approach leaves no room for desires to be rational or irrational. Hume's followers may say that this a very odd set of desires to have, and that as far as we know no one has ever had this set of desires, but it remains conceivable that someone could have them, and that is enough to pose a problem for Hume's view. Moreover, many people have attitudes that are somewhat like future-Tuesday indifference. Many people put off going to the dentist, for instance, even though they are well aware that doing so will mean more pain overall than if they were to go to the dentist now. At least in extreme cases, these desires also seem to be irrational. But subjectivists about reason cannot, it seems, say that they are.

Similarly, subjectivists about reason cannot say that the fact that putting my hand in a flame will cause me agony is a reason not to put my hand in the flame. They must say that whether I now have a reason not to put my hand in the flame will depend on whether I now desire to avoid agony. Parfit thinks this is a mistake: desires do not give us reasons for acting. I may desire to experience agony, but that does not give me any reason to put my hand in the flame, since I have no reason to have this desire, and strong reason not to have it. Parfit grants that, on his view, reasons may not motivate us. Whether something will motivate me to act in a certain way is, he says, a psychological fact, and quite distinct from the normative fact that I have a reason to act in that way. I may have a reason to do something without being motivated to do it.

Since subjectivists deny that there are any objective, or object-given, reasons for acting, if Parfit is right that having a present desire for something does not give one a reason for acting, it would follow that on the subjectivist view we have no reasons for doing anything, and hence, though some things may matter to us, in a larger sense, nothing matters. Hence Parfit eschews any middle ground that would allow us to accept subjectivism but go on as if nothing much had changed. For him, if there are no ethical truths, nihilism awaits and his life has been wasted, as have the lives of others who have spent their time trying to work out what we ought to do. In several of the papers that follow, this striking claim is discussed, and the authors try to show Parfit that, even though there are no ethical truths, in the robust sense of "truth" that Parfit is using, his life is very far from having been wasted.

Parfit rejects not only ethical subjectivism, but also ethical naturalism. To say that we have reason to reduce suffering, other things being equal, is to make a substantive normative claim that Parfit believes to be true, but it is not something that we can deduce from the meanings of moral terms like "good" or "ought." Here Parfit agrees with Hume that we cannot deduce an "ought" from an "is," meaning that no set of natural facts implies, on its own, any normative truths. We cannot identify normative truths with facts about the natural world, whether about our biological nature, about evolution, or about what we would approve of under some set of specified conditions, or any other causal or psychological fact.

How then do we come to know normative truths? Like many of his objectivist predecessors—Richard Price in the eighteenth century, Henry Sidgwick in the nineteenth, and W. D. Ross in the early twentieth, Parfit is an intuitionist. "We have," he writes, "intuitive abilities to respond to reasons and to recognize some normative truths." But these intuitive abilities are not, for Parfit, some special quasi-sensory faculty, nor do we use them to discover some mysterious new realm of non-natural facts. Rather, we come to see that we have reasons for doing some things, in something like the way in which we come to see that two plus two equals four. This rubs against the widely held metaphysical view that the world can be fully explained by reference to the kind of facts that are open to investigation by the natural sciences. Rejecting this view seems to open the way to believing in all kinds of spooky entities, and hence many non-religious philosophers have accepted metaphysical or ontological naturalism. Parfit does not defend non-natural religious beliefs, but argues that without irreducibly normative truths, nihilists would be right, for nothing would matter.

It is, for example, an irreducibly normative claim that if we establish that the premises of a valid argument are true, then we have a decisive reason for believing the conclusion of the argument. Thus Parfit challenges metaphysical naturalists: if the position you defend were true, he says, we could not have any reason to accept it, for there would be no such reasons. It still might be true, but the only position we have any reason to hold is that metaphysical naturalism is false.

Some will object that even if we accept Parfit's arguments, it would be a pyrrhic victory for objectivism. He can overcome Hume's objections only by rejecting the assumption that morality must be capable of moving us to action. And what is the point of an objective morality, if we are not motivated to act in accordance with the moral truths it contains? Parfit could respond, like Kant, that insofar as we are rational beings, we will respond to the reasons that morality offers. And if we are not, well, the truths of morality would remain true even if no one were to act on them.

*

In 2010 I taught a graduate seminar at Princeton on the then-forthcoming *On What Matters*, using a draft that Parfit had made available for that purpose. In Part Six Parfit returns to the issue of objectivism in ethics that he had discussed in Part One, and criticizes, sometimes quite sharply, several prominent contemporary philosophers who defend contrary positions. Some of these philosophers were at Princeton or near enough to be able to visit Princeton during the semester, so I invited them to discuss Parfit's criticisms of their views. Harry Frankfurt, Frank Jackson, Mark Schroeder, and Simon Blackburn did so. The discussions we had with them shed light not only on Parfit's position, but also on the long-running debate about whether there can be objectively true normative statements. I thought if these discussions could include other philosophers with whom Parfit disagreed and be published, together with Parfit's responses, the resulting book would reinvigorate discussions of objectivism in ethics.

Not everyone I invited to contribute to this volume accepted my invitation, but many of them did, including leading advocates of expressivism, naturalism, and constructivism. To this I added two outstanding essays written by graduate students taking the class, Richard Chappell and Andrew Huddleston, as well as an essay by Bruce Russell, who supports intuitionist objectivism. The final chapter of this book, which I co-authored with Katarzyna de Lazari-Radek, was added at the urging of Peter Momtchiloff, Oxford University Press's editor for this book, and because Parfit thought that its inclusion would give him an opportunity, in his response, to clarify his views regarding the place of impartial reasons in morality.

The reader may already have noticed that Parfit's responses to the essays presented here are not to be found in this volume. That is because something unexpected happened. Peter Railton had suggested, in the last part of the defense of naturalism that he contributed to this volume, how he and Parfit might resolve their disagreements, and Parfit was delighted to accept this suggestion. Allan Gibbard, the quasi-realist expressivist, had previously claimed, in his *Meaning and Normativity*, that the best version of his expressivism would coincide, in its theses, with the best version of non-naturalism, if only non-naturalists would give up their belief that there are ontologically weighty non-natural normative properties—although, he added, the two views differ in the explanations they offer. Parfit claims in his response to Gibbard that non-realist cognitivism, which is the form of non-naturalism he defends, takes precisely the form that Gibbard said would coincide with his own view.

Parfit considered the prospect of resolving these meta-ethical disagreements to be of such significance that he wrote several chapters explaining why he thought this could be done, and invited both Railton and Gibbard to contribute additional essays presenting their views of the extent of this resolution. As a result, the essays by Railton and Gibbard that appear in this volume should be taken, not as their last word on the issues they are discussing, but as stages in a process that is all too rare in philosophy, in which defenders of positions that initially appear to be fundamentally opposed, instead of further entrenching their opposition, significantly reduce their meta-ethical disagreements. The additional contributions by Railton and Gibbard, however, added to Parfit's extensive discussions, meant that to publish everything in one volume would have made it unwieldy. Parfit and I therefore agreed that it would be better to publish the original critical essays on their own, as they now appear in this volume. Parfit's responses, together with the additional essays by Railton and Gibbard are appearing in a separate companion volume, to be published together with this, entitled *On What Matters, Volume Three*.

ACKNOWLEDGEMENTS

My greatest debt is to the authors of the following essays, without whom there would have been no book. I am grateful not only for their contributions to the book, but also for the patience they showed while Derek Parfit was writing, revising, and expanding his responses. My gratitude to Parfit is manifold, first for allowing me to use, as the basic text for my graduate seminar, a pre-publication draft of the initial two volumes of *On What Matters*; second for agreeing to respond to the essays in this book; and third for working extraordinarily hard to complete his responses in time for them to appear together with this book. Balancing deadlines against the very proper concern to produce the best work one can is never easy, but I am delighted with the way in which Parfit managed it, and I am sure readers of *On What Matters, Volume Three* will be equally appreciative of his achievement.

I thank Peter Railton, Allan Gibbard, and Derek Parfit for their suggestions regarding the wording to be used, in the final two paragraphs of the Preface, to describe the extent of their agreement. Some passages in the Preface draw on my review of *On What Matters* in *The Times Literary Supplement*, 20 May 2011.

At Oxford University Press, Peter Momtchiloff supported the proposal from the beginning and was always helpful as it took shape. Emily Brand saw it smoothly through production, and Timothy Beck did an outstanding job with the copy-editing.

Derek Parfit's unexpected death on the second day of 2017 came as a shock and a loss to all of the contributors to this book. For those of us who knew Derek well, the feeling is personal, and we miss him deeply. And for all of us, no matter how sharp our philosophical differences with him may have been, there is a sense that the world of philosophy has lost an extraordinary presence, and will be the poorer for his absence.

We regret, of course, that Derek could not see the publication of this volume and its companion, *On What Matters, Volume Three*. At least we have the minor consolation that our essays stimulated him to defend and further develop his views on objectivity in ethics. These volumes will now remain as the last exchange of ideas he was able to have in print. His work on them was complete. The last thing he did on the books was to approve the final proof of his spectacular photograph of storm clouds over St Petersburg's Palace Square that is on the covers. He cared a great deal about the photograph, and was not satisfied with the colours of the first proof that he was shown, insisting on further proofs, even though that meant a delay in the publication of the books. Looking at the covers now, we can see why he was so particular about getting them right.

Peter Singer
*University Center for Human Values, Princeton University
and School of Historical and Philosophical Studies,
University of Melbourne*

CONTRIBUTORS

Simon Blackburn, University of North Carolina at Chapel Hill; the New College of the Humanities; Trinity College, Cambridge

Richard Yetter Chappell, University of York

Stephen Darwall, Yale University

Allan Gibbard, University of Michigan, Ann Arbor

Andrew Huddleston, Birkbeck, University of London

Frank Jackson, Australian National University

Katarzyna de Lazari-Radek, University of Lodz

Peter Railton, University of Michigan, Ann Arbor

Bruce Russell, Wayne State University

Mark Schroeder, University of Southern California

Peter Singer, Princeton University and University of Melbourne

Michael Smith, Princeton University

Sharon Street, New York University

Larry S. Temkin, Rutgers University

1

HAS PARFIT'S LIFE BEEN WASTED? SOME REFLECTIONS ON PART SIX OF *ON WHAT MATTERS*

Larry S. Temkin

1. Introduction

It is my great pleasure to contribute to this volume of essays responding to Derek Parfit's *On What Matters*.[1] I have chosen to respond to Part Six, *Normativity*, which in my judgment is the book's most insightful and profound section, even as it is almost certain to be the most puzzling and infuriating for many readers. I have no doubt that this portion of the book alone will require and richly repay careful exploration and

[1] Oxford University Press, 2011. I would like to thank Peter Singer for inviting me to contribute to this volume, and for his useful feedback on an earlier draft. I would also like to thank Jeff McMahan, Frances Kamm, and Shelly Kagan for their many helpful comments. A special debt is owed to Derek Parfit, with whom I have had countless hours of extraordinarily fruitful discussions over the years about these and other topics. Finally, this essay was written while I was the Laurance S. Rockefeller Visiting Professor for Distinguished Teaching at Princeton's University Center for Human Values. I would like to thank everyone who helped make my visit to the Center possible and so enjoyable, especially Peter Singer and the Center's Director, Chuck Beitz.

analysis for generations to come. Accordingly, my hopes for this essay are quite limited. I merely want to call attention to a few of Parfit's claims that I find puzzling or worrisome, and give some sense for the source of my unease. Perhaps others will find it worthwhile to pursue some of the lines of inquiry that I can only broach here.

Before beginning, I'd like to start with a short story. Many years ago, when I was still a graduate student, I was attracted to the deepest problems of meta-ethics, and I tentatively planned to write a dissertation addressing those problems. One day, I was walking with Derek, and I asked him *his* views about meta-ethics. Derek looked at me, and very earnestly replied, "My views about meta-ethics? I don't do meta-ethics. I find it *much* too hard."[2] Being an individual who can (sometimes!) recognize and respond to reasons, I abandoned my plans to write a meta-ethics thesis on the spot. My reasoning was simple: "Too hard for Derek Parfit, too hard for me"!

Like Derek, I am a realist about reasons, and I believe that there are full-fledged normative *truths*. Here is an example of one such truth: the reasoning I engaged in when, as a graduate student, I abandoned my plan to write a thesis on meta-ethics was an example of *good* reasoning!

In any event, I was pleased when I learned, some years later, that Derek had changed his mind. He now thought that it *was* possible for him to make progress on some of the deepest meta-ethical issues. I think he was right, and that Part Six does exactly that. At the very least, I think that Derek greatly illuminates the differences between competing meta-ethical positions, and gives the strongest arguments yet on offer for the respectability of an approach to normativity that involves externalism, objectivity, realism, non-naturalism, and what he calls "irreducible normative truths."[3] Moreover, I find myself largely in agreement with most of his positive meta-ethical claims. Still, in the customary philosophical way (one, which I recognize, is not altogether healthy for the profession!), in this essay, I shall not focus on the many major points where I

---

[2] Given the passage of time, this may not be an exact quote. But it is pretty close, especially the last two sentences, which were especially memorable.

[3] Arguably, "externalism," "objectivity," "realism," "non-naturalism," and "irreducible normative truths" are all terms of art for Derek, but for my purposes, here, it is not necessary to delineate the distinctive ways in which he understands these notions.

find Derek's claims compelling. Instead, I want to focus on some claims that I find somewhat problematic. In doing this, I am acutely aware, and remind the reader, that for the most part those aspects of Derek's account that I find problematic pale in their significance in comparison with those aspects that I find congenial.

The remainder of the essay is divided into four sections. In Section 2, I suggest that we reject Parfit's claim that normative facts have no *causal* impact on the natural world. In Section 3, I argue that the gap between Parfit's favored externalist view and that of his internalist opponents is not quite as large as it may seem in reading Part Six. In particular, I note two internalist insights that externalists should accept; namely, that in an important sense practical reasons *do* depend on something internal to us, and that there is, indeed, an important and intimate connection between reasons and motivation. In Section 4, I dispute Parfit's contention that unless his meta-ethical view is correct, nothing matters, and his life has been wasted. In Section 5, I conclude the essay with a brief summary.

2. *On the Causal Efficacy of Normative Reasons*

Parfit claims that normative truths have no causal impact on the natural world.[4] I don't believe that a lot hinges on this claim, but I confess that I find it puzzling. Parfit begins Chapter 1 of *On What Matters* with the sentence, "We are the animals that can both understand and respond to reasons."[5] As the book unfolds, variations of this sentence and the idea it expresses prove to be one of the main mantras of the book.[6]

I agree that we (often) understand or, as I also like to put it, recognize and respond to reasons. But if, as Parfit claims, we often *respond* to reasons, why not add that in those cases where we *are* responding to reasons, those reasons have had a *causal* impact on our actions? I think that on both of the major philosophical accounts of causation—the counterfactual model and the deductive-nomological model—reasons would count as

---

[4] See, for example, *On What Matters* (henceforth, *OWM* in citations), II, 306, 497, 503, 510, 517–18, 532, 618.
[5] *OWM*, I, 31.
[6] See, for example, *OWM*, I, 32, 48, 51, 78, 100; *OWM*, II, 307, 310, 414, 423, 461, 497, 503, 510, 515, 528, 531, 540, 544, 547, and 620.

having a causal impact on our actions. Given this, I see no compelling reason to avoid claiming that reasons, or normative facts, can have a causal impact on us and, a fortiori, that they can have a causal impact, through us, on the world.

I don't want to get into all the tricky details of the metaphysics of causation, or all the many qualifications, and bells and whistles, that might be added in any *fully* adequate account of causation. Instead, let me just sketch the basis of my reasoning on a standard counterfactual account of causation, and leave the analogous sketch for the deductive-nomological model to the reader.

On a standard counterfactual (or "but for") account of causation, we say that in a typical example of causation (ignoring problems of overdetermination and such) A is a cause of B whenever it is the case that "but for" A, B wouldn't have occurred. Slightly more technically, we typically say that A is a cause of B whenever it is true that in the closest possible world in which A didn't occur, B didn't occur.[7]

Here is a simple example. A gust of wind arises, blowing a piece of paper from one end of the room to the other. We say that the gust of wind caused the paper to move across the room, if we think it is true that in the closest possible world in which the gust of wind didn't arise the paper would not have moved across the room.[8] Here is another simple example. I am driving along the road at fifty miles an hour when I put my foot on the brake, bringing the car to a stop. Here, we might say that my putting the foot on the brake caused the car to stop, because had I not done so the car wouldn't have stopped.

Importantly, there can be more than one cause of any given event— and in most cases there will, in fact, be an indefinitely large number of

---

[7] For the classic discussion of counterfactuals, and their implications for our understanding of causation, see David Lewis's *Counterfactuals* (Basil Blackwell and Harvard University Press, 1973).

[8] Recall that I am here ignoring the problem cases of overdetermination and their related cousins. So, if John was *just about* to pick up the piece of paper and carry it across the room when the gust of wind arose, we want to say that the gust of wind caused the paper to cross the room even though it looks as if the paper would have moved across the room even if the wind hadn't arisen. Various moves are available on a counterfactual account of causation to handle such cases, but since this is an essay on normativity, and not an essay on the metaphysics of causation, I shan't pursue them here.

causes. In the car example, it may also be the case that, *in addition to* my putting my foot on the brake, the light's turning red caused the car to stop. This is because "but for" the light's turning red I would have left my foot on the accelerator and continued driving along the road at fifty miles an hour.

Given that there can be many causes of any given event, it seems plain that when an event involves an *action* of a rational agent, *one* of the causes of the action can be *the reasons* that led the agent to perform that action. That is, recognizing and responding to the normative fact that I *ought* to stop—that is, to the reasons that there are for stopping in a country where the rules of the road require that drivers stop at red lights, and where the possible consequences of failing to stop can be dire—I put my foot on the brake, bringing my car to a halt. Had the reasons been different—for example, had stopping at the red light posed a grave threat to me or others, while running the red light would have been the safest course of action—then assuming that I was able to recognize and appropriately respond to the reasons that those natural facts give rise to, I would have *acted* differently and *not* stopped the car. Accordingly, "but for" my reasons to stop I would *not* have stopped, and so, on a counter-factual account of causation, we should *rightly* say that the normative fact that I had good reason to stop, or that I ought to have stopped, had a causal impact on my stopping.

The preceding type of story applies in countless cases to the actions of rational agents. Parfit recognizes that there might be normative facts, or truths, of the following sort: one ought to provide for one's own future well-being; one ought to provide for the well-being of one's children; or one ought to provide for the well-being of those less fortunate. Parfit also thinks that rational agents are capable of understanding and responding to such normative facts. Accordingly, it might well be that recognizing and responding to one normative truth, DP goes out of his way to have a yearly physical with his doctor; that responding to a different normative truth, LT spends ridiculous amounts of time filling out reimbursement forms so that he will have a larger nest egg to leave to his children; and that responding to yet another normative truth, PS writes a substantial yearly check to Oxfam. Accordingly, on Parfit's view it makes perfect sense to claim that, in each case, "but for" the normative truths in question the agents would have acted differently. That is, if Parfit is right that humans are often able to understand and respond to reasons, then it makes perfect sense to suppose that *if* the normative truths applying in any given choice situation had not been present—either because the context had changed so that different normative truths applied, or (*per impossibile*) because there were different normative truths or no normative truths—then the individuals would have acted differently. That is enough, I think, for us to rightly claim that reasons, or normative facts, can have a causal impact on the world, via the will and actions of the rational agents who recognize and respond to them.

Indeed, even an agent who merely *understands* or *recognizes* a reason as such, or a normative fact to be true, without ever *responding* to that fact in the sense of *acting* on the basis of it, will be in a brain state that she would have not been in "but for" the reason or fact in question. On a counterfactual account of causation, that is enough, I think, for it to be true that the reason or normative fact had a causal impact on the world.

Why might someone want to deny that normative facts of the sort Parfit believes in have a causal impact on the world? Several considerations might underlie such a view. First, one might hold such a position for terminological reasons, claiming that what we *mean* when we say that A causes B, entails that A is a natural event, and on Parfit's view normative facts are neither events nor natural. Second, one might claim that to have a causal impact on the world, or at least on the natural world, one must be a *part* of the natural world in the way that tables, chairs, balls, and the events involving such objects are a part of the world, and that Parfit's non-natural normative facts fail to meet this criterion. Third, one might think that we have a fairly good understanding of the mechanisms that explain how objects in the natural realm might have a causal impact on other objects in the natural realm, but absolutely *no* understanding of the mechanisms that would explain how non-natural entities might have a causal impact on natural entities, or even of how interaction between such utterly distinct realms *might* be possible, and this should be enough to make one suspicious as to the possibility that non-natural entities might have a causal impact on the natural world. Fourth, relatedly, one might suppose that the view that non-natural facts can have a *causal* impact on natural facts would be akin to the view of substance dualists, that immaterial substances can have a causal impact on material substances, and vice versa. Recognizing that the difficulty of understanding and explaining how the latter could be true ultimately led many to abandon substance dualism in favor of some form of substance monism—typically, some form of materialism—one might hope to avoid a similar fate for the view that there are both non-natural normative facts and natural facts, by denying that belief in the existence of non-natural normative facts commits one to believing that such facts have a *causal* impact on the natural world. Fifth, one might point out that *causes* of events in the natural world are the domain of science, but that non-natural normative facts are the domain of philosophy and not science, and hence that non-natural normative facts are not causes of events in the natural world (if they were, they would be studied by scientists, which they clearly are not!). Finally, one might think that accepting the view that non-natural normative facts can have a causal impact on the natural world commits one to a belief in the "supernatural," or the "occult," or the "mystical," which no right-thinking philosopher or scientist would want to do. Accordingly, one might think that even if one accepts, as Parfit does, that there *are* non-natural normative facts, one should avoid saddling such a position with the further view that such facts can have a *causal* impact on the natural world, so as to avoid the unwelcome implications that come with that further view.

Let me briefly respond to such concerns. First, although many people believe that causation is a relation that only obtains between *events*—so that if A causes B, A and B must both be events—this would not be sufficient reason to deny that normative facts can have a causal impact, or play a causal role in the world, on the grounds that normative facts are not events. After all, we routinely recognize that rocks are the sort of things that can have causal impact on windows (which are certainly part of the world!), even if we insist that, strictly speaking, it is not the rock, itself, that causes the window to break, but the event that consists in the rock's striking the window with sufficient force. The point is that were it not for the rock, the event that consists of the rock's striking the window would not have obtained, and that is sufficient for us to rightly claim that the rock played a causal role, or had a causal impact, on the world, when it struck the window, thereby causing it to break. Similarly, one might claim that even if it is true that, strictly speaking, it is not the normative fact that John ought to do *A*, itself, that causes John to do *A*, but rather it is John's understanding and appropriately responding to that normative fact, as long as it is true that were it not for the obtaining of that normative fact John would not have recognized and responded to it by doing *A*, that is sufficient for us to rightly claim that the normative fact played a causal role or had a causal impact on the world, when it led, via John's understanding and appropriately responding to it, to John's doing *A*.

Second, Parfit distinguishes between "narrow" and "wide" senses of "exist," allowing him to contend that possible objects, mathematical truths, and non-natural normative facts exist in the "wide" sense, even if they don't exist in the "narrow" sense in which tables, chairs, and other members of the "natural" world exist.[9] Accordingly, one might similarly contend that even if one grants the terminological point that there is *a* sense of "cause," a *narrow* sense, in which only *natural* entities can have a causal impact on the world, that is compatible with there being *another* sense of "cause," a *wide* sense, in which non-natural entities, including normative facts, can have a causal impact on the world. One might then add that a wide sense of cause is every bit as respectable as a narrow sense, given that it relies on the same fundamental account of causation (either a counterfactual account, as discussed above, or a deductive-nomological account).

Third, Parfit considers the possibility that there might have been a god of the sort that many theists believe in.[10] By hypothesis, such a god would have been an all-powerful being who existed outside of space and time—a non-natural, indeed, supernatural being who would have been capable of miraculously influencing the course of natural events merely through the exercise of her Divine Will. If we knew that such a god existed, and had commanded the Red Sea to part, and that as a result the Red Sea parted, I think virtually everyone would agree that god had *caused* the Red Sea to part. Since, by hypothesis, if god *hadn't* commanded the Red Sea to part it wouldn't have parted (at least not in the closest possible world), that would be sufficient reason for most people

---

[9] *OWM*, II, 469–70.
[10] *OWM*, II, 306–7.

to claim that god caused it to part (at least in a *wide* of sense of cause, assuming that there is, indeed, a *narrow* sense of cause which is restricted to merely natural events). But notice, most people would say this even granting that god isn't a part of the natural world, even granting that we have absolutely *no* understanding of the mechanisms that would explain *how* a non-natural entity like god could have a causal impact on the nat-ural realm, and even granting that god and her relations with the world are best studied by theologians and philosophers, rather than scientists.

Reflecting on the possible causal impact of a supernatural god on the natural realm casts doubt, I believe, on the cogency of the first, second, third, and fifth considerations, discussed previously, for denying that non-natural normative facts could have a causal impact on the natural world.

As for the fourth consideration, it isn't clear that the view that non-natural facts can have a *causal* impact on natural facts needs to be as (seem-ingly) intractable or problematic as the view that immaterial substances can have a causal impact on material substances, and vice versa. While many people have a hard time understanding what immaterial sub-stances are, or how there could be such *things*, few are puzzled about the claim that there are mathematical facts, like "2 + 2 = 4," or logical facts, like "all lemons are lemons," even though they recognize that such facts are non-natural, in the sense that they don't exist *in the world* in the way that tables, chairs, and electrons do, and are not subject to the laws gov-erning the natural realm which are studied by scientists. Likewise, few are puzzled about the claim that there are facts like "tables, chairs, and electrons exist in the world," even though such facts are *also* non-natural, in the sense that the *facts themselves* don't exist *in the world* in the way that the objects they refer to, or are about—namely, tables, chairs, and electrons—do, and in the sense that such facts are not *themselves* subject to the laws governing the natural realm which are studied by scientists. Similarly, many people can accept that there are normative facts, like "if you believe that *A* implies *B*, and you believe that *A*, then you *ought* to believe *B*," or "you ought to avoid senseless agony," even though such facts are *also* non-natural, in the sense that they don't exist *in the world* in the way that tables, chairs, and electrons do, and are not subject to the laws governing the natural realm which are studied by scientists.

Moreover, if one believes that we have evolved as beings with a faculty of, or capacity to, reason, so that as Parfit suggests, "We are the animals that can both understand and respond to reasons,"[11] then it needn't seem deeply puzzling or mysterious how non-natural facts could have a causal impact on the natural world. They could have such an impact when we, who are members of the natural world, employ our powers of reasoning to *discover* or understand or recognize such facts (which are *not* immaterial substances!), and when we then appropriately *respond* to such facts in forming or performing our beliefs, desires, or actions.

Moreover, my own view is that far from casting doubt on whether we should accept the possibility of there being non-natural normative facts, contending that non-natural facts can have a causal impact on the natural realm is part of the most plausible and coherent picture for believing that there are such facts. After all, if one believes that there are no causal connections between non-natural normative facts and the natural world, then presumably we could provide a *full causal* account of *all* of our beliefs, desires, and actions—which are, after all, part of the natural world—in terms of other features of the natural world. In that case, one need not appeal to non-natural normative facts to explain any features of our empirical world, and so, applying Ockham's Razor, it might seem perfectly reasonable to abandon our belief in non-natural normative facts, and to dispense with all talk about such facts. If, on the other hand, we believe that non-normative facts *can* have a causal impact on the natural world, we might continue to believe in, and correctly appeal to such facts, in order to best explain many observable facts in the natural realm.

Why did John believe, desire, or do what he did? In some cases, at least, it seems the correct answer to such a question is that he did so, in part, because he understood, or recognized, certain non-natural normative facts and *responded* to them appropriately! Had the non-natural facts been different, John would have believed, desired, or acted differently. That is enough, I think, to make it true that the relevant non-natural normative facts *caused* John to believe, desire, or do what he did (at least in a plausible, and natural, *wide* sense of "cause").

[11] *OWM*, I, 31.

Finally, as Parfit recognizes, there are many who believe that talk of "non-natural normative facts" or "irreducible normative truths" commits one to "supernatural," "occult," or "mystical" metaphysical and epistemological views that no right-thinking philosopher or scientist should accept. John Mackie held such a belief, and it formed the basis of his arguments from metaphysical and epistemological queerness which he offered in opposition to the kind of non-natural normative view that Parfit espouses.[12] Parfit rejects the arguments from queerness,[13] and I believe he is right to do so. But for now, the key point I want to make is that any worries about the "supernatural," "occult," or "mystical" nature of non-natural normative facts or irreducible normative truths arise *independently* of, and are not, I think, exacerbated or compounded by, the issue of how there could be a *causal* interaction between non-natural facts and the natural world. That is, I think the "mysteries," if there are any, concern how there could *be* such non-natural normative facts, or how we could ever come to be *acquainted* with such facts, if there are any. Once we "solve" such "mysteries," and come to understand the sense in which there can be such facts and how, through our reason, we can recognize and respond to them, I don't see that there would be any *further* "mystery" to be solved as to how such facts could have a causal impact on the natural world.

If, through our reason, we *can* discover, or understand, or recognize non-natural normative facts, and then respond to them appropriately, then such normative facts can influence our beliefs, desires, or actions. Accordingly, as we have argued, such facts will sometimes have a causal impact on the world in a perfectly straightforward and non-mysterious way—this will be so as long as it is true that *if* the non-normative facts had been different, our beliefs, desires, or actions would have been different.

Perhaps there is another reason why Parfit wants to deny the causal efficacy of non-natural normative facts. But I fail to see what it is. Indeed, as suggested previously, I think that it is harder to see why one should believe that there are non-natural normative facts, or that we have the

---

[12] See Mackie's *Ethics: Inventing Right and Wrong* (Penguin Books, 1977), Chapter 1.
[13] See *OWM*, II, Chapters 30–2.

capacity to understand and respond to them, if one grants that such normative facts have *no* causal impact on the natural world. In sum, given Parfit's beliefs, which I share, that there are non-natural normative facts and that we have the capacity to understand and respond to such facts, I think the most plausible and coherent view is that such facts *can* have a causal impact on the natural world. They do so whenever our beliefs, desires, and actions are shaped by them, via the appropriate use of our capacity to reason.[14]

3. Reducing the Distance between Internalism and Externalism

Much of Parfit's effort in *On What Matters* attempts to reduce the apparent distance between three major moral theories: Kantianism, Contractualism, and Consequentialism. Instead of discussing these theories solely in the terms by which they are typically understood and defended by their staunchest advocates, Parfit tries to develop what he regards as the best, most defensible, version of each type of theory. When he does so, he finds, or so he argues, that far from being incompatible with each other, each theory supports each other, and is part of a single, coherent, *Triple Theory*, that is the most acceptable, or true, moral theory. Echoing a thought he attributes to Mill, Parfit suggests that, on reflection, we can see that advocates of the three great moral theories have been "climbing the same mountain on different sides."[15]

Whatever one thinks of the ultimate success of Parfit's argument that there is one true moral theory that at the same time captures and expresses the most fundamental insights of Kantianism, Contractualism, and Consequentialism, it is hard not to be struck by the *spirit* with which he approaches this task. Instead of focusing solely on the many points of deep disagreement between the competing theories, Parfit seeks to find points of agreement or mutually supporting insights and arguments.

[14] Note, my discussion here is not intended to convince Parfit's opponents of the causal efficacy of non-natural normative facts. My aim is simply to suggest that for someone who holds a position like Parfit's, it makes more sense to accept than to deny that non-natural normative facts can have an effect on the natural realm.

[15] *OWM*, I, 419. See, also, *Reasons and Persons* (Oxford University Press, 1984), 114.

Curiously, however, this attitude, which I find both strikingly refreshing and deeply admirable, and which pervades much of the first five parts of the book, seems to largely disappear in Part Six.

Although Parfit continues to *express* the view that it is important, wherever possible, to reduce apparent areas of disagreement about meta-ethical issues, and even goes so far, in advocating this position, as to suggest that many of his meta-ethical opponents either don't have the same concepts of reasons or normativity that he, Parfit, has,[16] or that they often fail to understand, remember, or accurately reflect their own "actual" views,[17] in fact, as one reads Part Six, one has the overwhelming sense that the differences between Parfit's position and everyone else's are utterly unbridgeable, and that no insights of the opposing positions might usefully support or illuminate each other. That is, my own sense in reading Part Six is that Parfit offers his reader a stark either/or, all-or-nothing proposition: either accept the kind of externalist, objectivist position that he favors, according to which there are non-natural normative facts and corresponding irreducible normative truths, or be reduced to a bleak position akin to nihilism or skepticism about values, according to which nothing—absolutely nothing!—matters.[18]

For much of my life, I have thought about various competing meta-ethical views in much the same way as I have just portrayed them. Basically, I thought that one must either be an "objectivist" who believed in robust, full-fledged notions of Morality, Values, and Reasons (yes, with *capitals* M, V, and R!) or, however much one might *talk* about "morality," "values," and "reasons," one was merely a "subjectivist," at best, whose views were akin to skepticism about the normative realm (or Normative Realm, as I thought of it). And I confess, to a large extent, I continue to have great sympathy for a view of that kind. Yet, as I read Part Six, I kept thinking that despite the enormous substantive differences between them, the various competing meta-ethical views *couldn't* be, and *weren't*, quite as diametrically opposed as Parfit's tone suggested. So, in the conciliatory spirit that pervades most of Parfit's wonderful

---

[16] See, for example, *OWM*, II, 271–2, 293–4, 411, 434–9, 447–8, 552–3, 600, 603.
[17] See, for example, *OWM*, I, 70, 93, 96, 100; II, 456–7, 595, 603.
[18] See, for example, *OWM*, I, 107; II, 267, 275, 282, 291, 295, 310, 339, 368, 410, 419, 442, 453, 465, 601.

book, let me suggest two respects in which the contrast between Parfit's view and that of some of his opponents need not be quite so stark and seemingly all-or-nothing.

Parfit rightly notes that one of the central claims of many *internalists* is that there is a fundamental connection between the notion of a *reason* and the notion of *motivation*.[19] For most internalists, reasons must always be reasons *for* someone, and something can only be a reason *for* someone if it is capable of *motivating* or *moving* the agent (typically, to act). But, internalists argue, for something to actually motivate someone to act, it must somehow get a grip on them, or somehow get a "hook" in them, and this will only be the case if there is something *in* the agent or *about* the agent that enables this to happen. For someone like Williams, for something to be a reason *for* an agent, there must be something already *in* the agent's "subjective motivational set, *S*"—which may include the agent's beliefs, desires, dispositions, or other intentional states—which will explain how that reason can succeed in motivating the agent.[20]

Gil Harman argues for his social convention theory of morality largely on internalist grounds.[21] He claims that there could be a clear-thinking, fully-informed hit man from Murder, Incorporated, who wasn't motivated not to kill his innocent target, without thereby being in *any* way irrational.[22] Harman takes this as evidence that the hit man has no *reason* not to kill his innocent target, since, Harman thinks, if he *did* have a reason not to kill he *would* be motivated not to kill his target. From this, Harman concludes that the hit man has no moral obligation not to kill his victim, since he agrees that there is a connection between moral obligations and what one has a reason (and hence would be motivated) to do. Harman goes on to suggest that only if the hit man *accepted* a relevant social convention against killing the innocent, where such acceptance would involve developing the appropriate beliefs, desires, dis-

---

[19] See, for example, *OWM*, I, 75, 109–10; II, 268, 270–1, 277–8, 381, 421, 435–7, 441, 446, 449.
[20] See Williams's classic paper "Internal and External Reasons," reprinted as Chapter 8 in his collection of essays, *Moral Luck* (Cambridge University Press, 1981).
[21] See "Moral Relativism Defended" (*The Philosophical Review*, 84, 1975: 3–22), "Relativistic Ethics: Morality as Politics" (*Midwest Studies in Philosophy*, III, 1978: 109–21), and *The Nature of Morality: An Introduction to Ethics* (Oxford University Press, 1977).
[22] "Moral Relativism Defended," 5–6.

positions, and intentional states so that, to put it in Williams's terms, his motivational set, S, now included the elements that would motivate him to abide by the convention against killing the innocent, could we rightly say that he had a moral obligation and reason not to kill the innocent.

Parfit has much to say about the internalist position, but one of the key claims he makes is that by correlating the notions of *reason* and *motivation* in the way that they do, internalists show that they are concerned with a *psychological* notion of reason, rather than the *normative* notion of reason with which Parfit is concerned.[23] Parfit insists that in asking "What *ought* I to do?" he is asking for *advice*; he is asking what he has most, or decisive, or sufficient reason to do. For Parfit, the answer to the *normative* question of what a person ought, or should, or has reason to do, depends on what non-natural, and irreducible normative facts obtain, and these are external in the sense that they do not depend on the particular internal makeup of the person.[24] Parfit wants to know what, if anything, he is *justified* in believing, desiring, or doing, and he regards that as a normative question that is wholly distinct from the purely psychological question that he thinks the internalist is concerned with, namely, given a person's subjective motivational set, S, what factors and circumstances would motivate him to believe in, desire, or do certain things.

So, to note one example, for Parfit, undeserved suffering is bad, it is bad in all possible worlds, and its badness in no way depends on anyone's internal features or makeup. Accordingly, for Parfit, that I have reason to avoid undeserved suffering is true independently of what I happen to want or desire and, more generally, is true independently of whatever beliefs, desires, dispositions, or other intentional states make up my current subjective motivational set, S.

---

[23] *OWM*, I, 107–10; *OWM*, II, 268–71, 421, 429.

[24] Of course, a person's internal features may be relevant to what normative facts *apply* in any given situation, but not to what normative facts there are. For example, if my constitution is such that I enjoy chocolate ice cream but not vanilla, then that will be relevant to whether you ought to provide me with chocolate or vanilla ice cream in certain circumstances. But, for Parfit, the normative truth guiding you—roughly, that other things equal one should promote greater happiness—does not *itself* depend on my, or anyone else's, internal features.

Suppose one accepts, as I do, Parfit's view that irreducible normative facts are true in all possible worlds and, correspondingly, that such facts are "external" in the sense that their truth does not depend on the constituents of anyone's "internal" subjective motivational sets, or, for that matter, on there even *existing* any rational or sentient beings that even *have* "internal" subjective motivational sets. This is analogous to the view, shared by many, that such logical and mathematical facts as "A = A" and "2 + 2 = 4" are true in all possible worlds, and that such truths do not depend, in any way, on the "internal" contents of anyone's subjective motivational sets—that is, they do not depend for their truth on anyone's beliefs, desires, dispositions, or other intentional states—or that there even *exist* rational beings who are capable of *recognizing* such truths—that is, even in a universe in which there were no rational or sentient beings, it would still be true, and necessarily so, that "A = A" and "2 + 2 = 4." Still, even if one fully accepts such an *externalist* view, there is room to acknowledge that the *internalist* position reflects an important insight. Namely, for a normative fact to actually be a reason capable of *guiding our actions*—that is to say, a *practical* reason—there must be something about *us*—*an internal feature of our makeup*—capable of recognizing and responding appropriately to the normative fact; that is, *we* have to be able to understand and respond to the fact that there *is* a reason to believe, care about, or do certain things.

The point here is not deep, but it is important. We might usefully illuminate it by making a distinction between a normative fact being a ("mere") *reason* and a normative fact being a *reason for* creatures capable of recognizing and responding to reasons.[25] Internalists might plausibly contend that their concern is with *practical* reasons, and that it is only when and insofar as a reason is a *reason for* some creature that it is or can be a *practical* reason; and, moreover, that it is only because of some *internal* feature(s) that a being will be capable of recognizing and responding to a reason so that the reason will, indeed, be a *reason for* that being. On such a view, in a world devoid of rational beings one can claim all one wants that there are normative facts such as "undeserved

[25] I am grateful to Frances Kamm for urging that I clarify my view here, and to Frances, Jeff McMahan, and Shelly Kagan for their suggestions as to how best to do this.

suffering is *bad*," or "one *ought* to prevent undeserved suffering," and one can further claim, if one wants, that such normative facts are, or correspond to, *reasons*; but, the internalist will insist, in such a world such reasons will not be *practical*—and, indeed, there will be *no* practical reasons. The internalist position here might be roughly analogous to someone who granted that in a world devoid of sentient beings there might still be colored objects, but that in such a world colors would have *no practical* significance in the sense of being able to guide or influence the decisions or actions of an agent.[26] Thus, for an object's being blue to have *practical* significance, it must be blue *for* some agent capable of recognizing and responding to it as a blue object in the agent's deliberations.

Now, insofar as internalists might make such a claim—that reasons are only *practical* when there are beings that they are *reasons for*, and that there must always be something *internal* to a being which makes it possible for a reason to be a *reason for* that being—I think internalists would be claiming something which is both true, and important. After all, as we have already seen, Parfit notes at the very beginning of Chapter 1, "*We* are the animals that can both understand and respond to reasons" (emphasis added). *Snails* don't respond to reasons (we believe). Neither do trees or rocks. So, the normative fact that undeserved suffering is bad cannot be a *reason for* snails, trees, or rocks. Such a fact can *only* be a *reason for* creatures that are sufficiently like us. I suggest then, that internalists are *right* to insist that there is something internal to us, and to other creatures which are relevantly like us, that makes it possible for there to even *be* practical reasons in the sense in which *practical* reasons must always be *reasons for* creatures like us to believe, care about, or do certain things.

But then we can ask "what is it, exactly, which is *internal* to us that makes it possible for normative facts to provide practical reasons for us?" And here, we see that externalists like Parfit can suggest a rather different answer than internalists like Williams, Harman, and Hume. Parfit might simply claim that it is precisely that complex set of cognitive

---

[26] I grant that the analogy here is not perfect, hence my qualification "roughly," but I think it is close enough to be helpful.

abilities that most normal humans have that enables us to understand and respond to reasons! It is what once would have been called our "faculty of reason." This is a feature about us which is, as it were, "internal" to us, and which enables irreducible normative truths—whose truth is genuinely independent of anything internal to us—to provide *reasons for* creatures like us, *practical* reasons.

So, Parfit may be right that normative facts don't depend for their truth on anyone's subjective motivational sets. Accordingly, there may be good reason to be an "externalist" about normative facts as Parfit contends. Even so, I suggest that one can reduce the distance a *bit* between Parfit's view and that of his opponents, if one recognizes, as Parfit surely does, that it is in virtue of an *internal* cognitive capacity of ours that normative facts can provide *practical* reasons for animals like *us*, as opposed to snails, trees, and rocks.

All parties to the debate about the nature of normative facts would agree that entities lacking certain relevant cognitive capacities are utterly incapable of understanding and responding to reasons. Accordingly, for such entities we should grant that, in a fundamentally important sense, there simply *are* no *practical* reasons. This is, I believe, a plausible and important *internalist* position, even though it is distinct from the particular internalist position about the primacy of subjective motivational sets espoused by many of Parfit's opponents, and even though this version of internalism is fully compatible with the externalist tenets that Parfit defends.

Next, let us return to Parfit's contention that in asking what we ought to do, externalists are asking the *normative* question about what we are *justified* in doing, whereas internalists are asking the "merely" *empirical*, and presumably unrelated, *psychological* question of what we are, or would be, *motivated* to do given certain assumptions. Given our previous points, I believe that the gap between the normative question about justification, and the empirical psychological question about motivation, is not nearly as stark, and unbridgeable, as Parfit's discussion seems to imply. A fortiori, this is another respect in which I think the distance between the externalist and internalist positions is a *bit* narrower than one might surmise in reading Part Six.

If I am right that irreducible normative truths can cause us to believe, care about, or do certain things, and if I am right that this is in virtue of certain cognitive capacities that enable creatures like us to understand and appropriately *respond* to reasons, then it is reasonable to conclude that in *ideal* circumstances creatures like us *will be* psychologically motivated to believe, care about, or do what they are *justified* in believing, caring about, or doing. Now admittedly, there is much work to be done in spelling out what constitutes "ideal" circumstances, work that I shall not pursue in this essay. But the outlines of such a position are clear enough. If a creature were fully informed, clear thinking, and had sufficiently developed cognitive capacities to understand the reasons it had for believing, caring about, or doing certain things, then it *would* respond *appropriately* to such reasons, in the absence of distorting, interfering, or rival influences that prevented it from doing so.[27] Thus, for example, if there were *decisive* reasons to believe, care about, or do certain things, then, in ideal circumstances, a *fully* and *solely* rational being would understand and respond appropriately to the reasons that there are, which is to say that such a being would, in fact, be *motivated* to believe, care about, or do those things which he was *justified* in believing, caring about, or doing.[28]

---

[27] Importantly, to respond *appropriately* to the reasons that there are involves more than merely responding in a way that *conforms* to such reasons, it involves responding in the way that one does *for the sake* of the reason. The idea here parallels Kant's famous distinction between acting *from* duty versus acting in *conformity* with duty, where, roughly, in the former case one does what is right because one recognizes that it *is* right and one wills the action for that very reason, while in the latter case one does what is, in fact, right, but one wills the action to promote some (phenomenal) interest or desire, perhaps, for example, because one believes that doing the action will make one happy or rich, and one has a desire to be happy or rich. See Kant's famous discussion of the shopkeeper example in the first section of his *Grounding of the Metaphysics of Morals* (Hackett Publishing Company, 1981, translated by James W. Ellington, p. 10).

[28] Parfit, himself, recognizes and accepts this point. For example, he writes that "when it is true that (E) we have decisive reasons to act in some way, this fact makes it true that (F) if we were fully informed and both procedurally and substantively rational, we *would* choose to act in this way" (emphasis added, *OWM*, I, 63), and "If we are aware of facts that give us certain reasons for acting, and we are fully substantively rational, we *would* be motivated to act for these reasons" (emphasis added, OWM, II, 268). But rather than emphasizing the close connection between what his view implies and what internalists claim, Parfit emphasizes the difference between the two views, adding the following

Of course, as has long been recognized, we are not fully rational beings. And often we are not in ideal circumstances. So we will, as a matter of fact, often fail to be guided by reasons, even decisive reasons (that, according to externalists, there are for us) to believe, care about, or do certain things. Often, instead of being motivated by reasons, we will in fact be motivated by constituents of our subjective motivational set—including various appetites, passions, drives, or urges—that we have no *reason* to have. So, it is true that given our complex natures, which are neither fully nor solely rational, we will often be empirically motivated to do what we are not justified in doing according to the externalist view. But, as we have seen, this does not entail that the question of motivation for creatures like us is wholly distinct from the question of justification.

There *is* a connection between reasons and motivation as internalists have long insisted. But the connection isn't what many internalists have claimed it to be. The connection stems from the cognitive capacity that creatures like us have to understand and respond to reasons. In virtue of this capacity, which we can call our faculty of reason, even externalists should grant that in ideal circumstances we *would* be motivated, psychologically, to do what we *ought* to do, normatively. But, of course, cir-

---

sentence after the second of the preceding quotations, "But that does not imply that normativity in part consists in actual or possible motivational force" (*OWM*, II, 268). As my discussion makes plain, I think Parfit might have done more to emphasize the deep internalist insight that there is an important connection between reasons and motivation, even if he goes on to contend that the connection is not quite what most internalists have thought it to be.

Peter Singer rightly notes that my contention that a fully and solely rational being could be motivated to do anything at all, in the absence of some antecedent interests or desires, would be *denied* by Humeans, so that *if* Humeans are right, the gap between Parfit's view and the Humeans would remain wide. I agree, and to try to offer an argument that would convince Parfit's Humean opponents that my contention is right lies well beyond the scope of this essay. But my point here is that my contention is one that *Parfit* accepts, so that on his view the gap between his position and that of his opponents is not as stark as Parfit seemingly makes it out to be.

If this is right, there may be an interesting asymmetry between Parfit's position and that of his Humean opponents. Humeans might want to insist that there is a wide, unbridgeable, gap between their position and Parfit's, but Parfit should contend that the gap between his view and theirs is not, in fact, quite so wide and unbridgeable as his opponents think.

cumstances are rarely ideal, which explains why we often fail to be motivated to believe, care about, or do what we ought to.

There remain deep substantive differences between externalists like Parfit, and internalists like Williams or Harman. As noted above, Harman believes that the hit man from Murder, Incorporated, could be fully informed, clear thinking, and *fully* rational, and yet not be motivated to avoid killing his innocent victims. Accordingly, as we saw, for Harman, given the link between reasons and motivation, there is *no* reason for the hit man not to kill his victims. Parfit strenuously disagrees with Harman, and I think rightly so. But what Parfit needs to say in response to Harman is not that the question of normative justification is *independent* from the question of empirical motivation, but rather that Harman is *mistaken* in contending that the hit man from Murder, Incorporated, could be fully informed, clear thinking, and *fully* rational (where this includes being substantively as well as procedurally rational), and yet not be motivated to avoid killing his innocent victims. Assuming, on Parfit's view, that the hit man has decisive reason not to kill his victims, Parfit should insist that if the hit man *were* fully informed, clearly thinking, and *fully* rational, then he *would* be motivated not to kill his victims— for to be *fully* rational (or, perhaps, more cautiously, *fully* and *solely* rational) is to understand and respond appropriately to whatever reasons there are for a fully informed and clear-thinking agent.

I believe that the faculty of reason *is* a motivating faculty,[29] so that there is a connection between reasons (in the normative, justificatory sense) and motivation (in the empirical psychological sense) as internalists have long contended. But the faculty of reason is not the *only* motivating element for creatures like us.[30] As internalists have rightly recognized, we are also often psychologically motivated by various elements of our subjective motivational set and, as Parfit might put it, sometimes those elements may be non-rational or irrational. I conclude that externalists should grant, and even insist on, the importance of the

---

[29] As recognized in n. 28, I have not and cannot argue for that here, as to do so lies well beyond the scope of this essay.

[30] For a fascinating discussion of a host of issues related to this topic, in the context of addressing the problem of weakness of the will, see David Pears's *Motivated Irrationality* (Oxford University Press, 1984; St. Augustine's Press, 1999).

internalist insight that there is a link between reasons and motivation. I also think that externalists should grant that internalists are correct in believing that there is an important link between what people are often motivated to do, and the constituents of their subjective motivational set, S. But what the externalist needs to deny, as Parfit does, is that the link between reasons and the constituents of a person's subjective motivational set, S, is what internalists take it to be.

4. Has Parfit's Life Been Wasted?

No! Does anything follow from this? Not much, I think.

At various places in Part Six, Parfit claims that unless his meta-ethical view is correct, then his life, and those of certain other prominent ethicists who have devoted their lives to trying to figure out what they ought, normatively, to do, have been wasted.[31] This is an extremely interesting and provocative claim, but I find it *deeply* implausible. I shall not try to fully defend my view, but let me make several sets of observations in response to Parfit's claim.

First, underlying Parfit's claim is the contention that unless his kind of externalist view is correct, with its commitment to non-natural normative facts, or irreducible normative truths, *nothing matters*.[32] But if *nothing* matters, then it *can't* be true that Parfit's life was wasted, or that any other life was wasted for that matter, because "wasted" is a *normative* notion. That is, Parfit's life could only have been *wasted*, if there had been some *other* life available to Parfit that would have been *better*. But according to Parfit, unless his view is true, nothing matters, hence no alternative life *could* have been better, or worse for that matter! So, Parfit isn't entitled to claim that unless his view is true his life has been *wasted*. Instead, Parfit should simply claim that unless his view is true, no life is better or worse than any other, nor are any lives equally good. Lives are simply *different* (or not)—but they do not, and cannot, differ in any way with respect to their *value*. Parfit has spent much of his life trying to

---

[31] Parfit mentions Henry Sidgwick and David Ross in this regard, but no doubt he thinks it is true of many others, as well. See *OWM*, II, 303–4, 367.
[32] See *OWM*, I, 107; *OWM*, II, 267, 282, 295, 367–8, 419, 425, 433, 442, 453, 465, 601.

figure out how one ought to live. He might have spent it counting blades of grass. If nothing matters, it doesn't matter in any way that he chose to live the life that he did—but he couldn't have *wasted* his life in living it as he did.

We see, then, that there is nothing *special* about the fact that Parfit was consumed, throughout his life, with trying to determine how one ought to live one's life. If Parfit is right, then it would not only be *his* life which had no significance for good or bad—this would be true of *all* lives, human and otherwise.

This brings me to my second set of observations. Parfit seems to believe that *unless* his particular kind of external meta-ethical view is true, Shakespeare's life had no significance, neither did Albert Einstein's, nor Buddha's, Plato's, Mozart's, Newton's, Beethoven's, Harriet Tubman's, Charles Darwin's, Madame Curie's, Kant's, Lincoln's, Florence Nightingale's, Margaret Mead's, Helen Keller's, Gandhi's, Margaret Sanger's, Martin Luther King Jr's, and so on. This is hardly an *argument*, but I find such a claim *really* hard to believe.

Let me put this point differently. Short of embracing an extreme form of skepticism, one I see absolutely *no* convincing reason to embrace, I don't think there is, or could be, any reason to doubt the view that *at least one* of the many people named above lived a life of value and significance! In fact, I think virtually *all* of the people named above almost certainly lived valuable lives, as have *countless* others in human history, including innumerable numbers of ordinary folks like my parents and grandparents! Moreover, when one recalls the extraordinary suffering that some innocent people have had to bear as victims of rape or abuse, as slaves, in torture chambers, in concentration camps, and so on, claims to the effect that *nothing* matters *at all*—for good *or* bad—stretch well beyond the bounds of credulity.

Or consider the following two possible worlds. In one, billions of innocent people each live in heaven for a billion years. In the other, billions of innocent people each live in hell for a billion years. Before and after the billion year periods there is nothing but emptiness, and there are *no* other relevant facts about either world. I have no doubt whatsoever, *none*, that (if properly qualified) the first world would be *better* than the second. *If* there were a god contemplating which of the two worlds to bring about, she ought *not* to be indifferent between them. She *ought* to bring about the first, rather than the second. These are value judgments that I cannot believe might be mistaken.

Or take a simple, small-scale example. I have three children, whom I love greatly, Daniel, Andrea, and Rebecca. I don't doubt for a second that I *do* have reason to care about their well-being. It simply *cannot* be true that it doesn't matter *at all* whether they have lengthy lives in which they flourish, or horrible lives filled with unending torture, grief, and depression.

These are, of course, mere assertions. I don't deny that. But I assume that most readers of this essay, who are not themselves psychopaths, severely psychologically damaged, or skeptics of the most extreme sort, will accept some judgments of the sort I have just made. This is important, because as attracted as I am to the sort of meta-ethical position Parfit espouses, I think it is a serious and open question as to whether his meta-ethical view is correct! This makes me think that whether or not anything matters *cannot* depend, in the way Parfit suggests, on the truth of Parfit's particular meta-ethical view.

It may help to think about how we should respond to Parfit's claim, if we imagined someone making a similar claim about the existence of trees rather than value. Over the centuries, there has been virtually universal agreement that trees exist (by all but the most extreme skeptics, people severely out of touch with reality, or those who have never come in contact with any evidence of trees!), but there has been considerable philosophical and scientific disagreement as to the exact nature of trees.[33] Suppose that at some point an exceptionally brilliant philosopher/scientist had come along, and advocated a particular view about the nature of trees, and then claimed that *unless* his particular view of the nature of trees is correct, there *are* no trees, and he, and everyone else who has tried to discover and account for the nature of trees, has *completely* wasted their

---

[33] I won't detail the full extent of this, but in different times and places trees have been thought to have souls, to have spirits, to be material substances, to be immaterial substances, to be reincarnated beings, to be ideas in the minds of the perceiver, to be ideas in god's mind, to be solid, to be guardians of people, to be composed of atoms which are mostly filled with space, etc.

lives in doing so. (Indeed, to flesh out the analogy fully, the brilliant scientist/philosopher might add that *unless* his account of the nature of trees is correct, there are no physical objects of *any* kind, and anyone who has tried to determine the nature of any kind of physical object has wasted his or her life in doing so.) I believe that regardless of the merits of the particular view advocated by our hypothetical philosopher/scientist, and regardless of how attractive his further claim might seem in light of his view, *no one* would actually take seriously his further claim about the devastating skeptical implications that would follow *if* his view were false.

More accurately, while I suspect that some people might *initially* come to believe both his view about the nature of trees and his further claim about what would follow if his view were false, *if*, in fact, people later discovered that his view *was* false, I think they would revise their judgment about the supposed connection between the truth of his view and the existence of objects. That is, people would continue to believe, rightly I think, that while the exact nature of trees, and other objects, may be in doubt, there is *no* doubt that there *are* trees, and other objects, and that such objects have always played, and continue to play, a significant role in our lives.

I think the same is true about normativity. It is, I think, a serious and open question what the nature of normativity is, but whatever the particular answer is to that question, normativity does, and must, play a significant role in our understanding of ourselves and our relations with others. However attractive Parfit's meta-ethical view may be—and I find it very attractive—and however tempted one might be by the claim that *if* his meta-ethical view were *not* true, then nothing would matter, nevertheless, at the end of the day, whether or not some lives are more valuable than others, or whether or not we have reason to make some choices rather than others, *cannot* depend on whether Parfit's particular meta-ethical account is correct.[34]

---

[34] My claim here is not about what is or is not *logically* possible, but rather about what is or is not even remotely likely to be the case.

My third set of observations is related to the second set. When I teach my large introductory ethics course, I tell my students that, for many of them, it will be the most *important* class that they ever take in college. I base my claim on many factors, including the fact that many former students of mine have written me long after their class ended, telling me just that. I also add that *whatever* one's view about the ultimate objective basis of morality, the fundamentally important issues raised in the class have to be faced. So, for example, even if one believes, as Mackie and Harman do, that ethics is *invented* rather than discovered, we still have to decide, both as individuals and as societies, what kind of ethics to invent.[35]

We need to answer the questions of what kind of people we want to be, how we want to raise our children, and what kind of societies we want to live in. Do we want to be the sort of person who is honest, kind, and generous, or not? Do we think we "should" care for our children, and look out for their well-being? Or do we think it is perfectly okay to abandon them, or worse, to rape or torture them? Do we want to help construct a society whose principles and institutions provide for the general welfare of its citizens, or that looks out for its weakest and most vulnerable members, or not? Similarly, do we want our society to promote such ideals as freedom, autonomy, utility, justice, or equality, and if so, why; if not, why not, and how "should" we choose between different ideals that we may find attractive? Even if it is, in some sense, "up to us to decide," we still need to decide whether we want our society to permit or prohibit different forms of abortion, or euthanasia, or capital punishment. And we need to decide whether or not we want to be part of a society that ignores the plight of the needy in other countries, or the plight of future generations who will have to live with whatever decisions we make about the consumption of natural resources, global warming, population growth, and so on.

The point is that all these issues are *pressing*—one way or the other they have to be made, and *will* be made, and it is natural, in asking such

[35] See nn. 12 and 21, for citations to works where Mackie and Harman defend a social convention view of ethics, according to which ethics is a human construction. On their views, people have to decide whether to create and participate in a convention of ethics at all, and if so, what they want its contours to be.

questions, to put our questions in normative terms. What *ought* we to do? Which choice, or principle, or institution would it be *better* to adopt or create? And the vast literature that philosophers and others have offered on these topics has a bearing on such questions. They offer arguments and considerations that make it more "appropriate" or "reasonable" to answer our questions one way rather than another. I, and others, make such claims to our students, and I am confident that we are correct in doing so.[36]

To paraphrase Parfit, we are the animals *for whom things matter*. It *matters* to us whether we realize our life plans. It *matters* to us whether we are in relationships with others that are genuinely loving and mutually respectful. It *matters* to us whether our loved ones flourish. It *matters* to us whether we are free, and whether we live in a society or world that is just. It *matters* to us whether or not the world ends on our watch, or soon afterwards, because of global warming, or some chemical, biological, or nuclear disaster that *we* are responsible for. The fact that such issues matter *to* us is not up for debate. They do. This is enough, seemingly, to ground the claim that some things do, indeed, matter, even if, as many internalists claim, they only matter in the sense that, and because of the fact that, they matter to creatures like us.[37]

This brings me to my final set of observations. Parfit may be correct that if his externalist non-natural view of normativity is mistaken, then *nothing matters* in *his* sense. And I, for one, would very much like it to be true, and would be very disappointed if Parfit's view was false, so that nothing mattered in his sense. But Parfit's sense is *not* the only possible sense of "not mattering" that is meaningful and significant; so, even *if* nothing mattered in *Parfit's* sense, it wouldn't follow that nihilism was true, and that nothing mattered *simpliciter*.

---

[36] I mentioned to Shelly Kagan that I make such claims to my classes, and he immediately asserted that he does as well. I am sure that we two are not alone in taking such a stance.
[37] Mind you, we would like to be able to substantially develop the claims I have just presented, to avoid the implication that atrocities and genocide have value, simply in virtue of the fact that they are valued by racists. Unfortunately, I cannot do that here. Still, my point is simply that we are confident that many things *do* matter, and *will* matter, for creatures like us, regardless of whether or not Parfit's particular meta-ethical view is correct.

Let me offer a visual analogy to help illustrate my view of this issue. Consider diagram one.

A. # VALUES

H. VALUES

NIHILISM (NO VALUES)

View I

A. # VALUES

B. # VALUES

C. ## VALUES

D. VALUES

E. VALUES

F. VALUES

G. VALUES

H. VALUES

NIHILISM (NO VALUES)

View II

DIAGRAM ONE

View I seems to represent Parfit's position regarding our meta-ethical options. If his meta-ethical view is correct, then there are values in a very strong, robust, sense; we might, for exposition, refer to such values as *A-values*, and we can say that on this view things can matter in an analogous strong, robust sense, which we can call *A-mattering*. On the other hand, for Parfit, if his meta-ethical view *isn't* correct, then we are left with nihilism, or at best there are only values in a very weak, pale sense, which is akin to nihilism; in that case, Parfit thinks, nothing matters *at all*, or if it does matter, it does so only in a very weak, pale sense, which we can call *H-mattering*, where if something only H-matters, it *hardly* matters at all, which is to say that it basically doesn't matter! So, Parfit believes that we face a very stark, either/or, all-or-nothing situation regarding the nature and existence of values (and its many correlate notions of *reasons*, "genuine" *normativity, mattering*, and the like).

My own view is different from Parfit's. Between very strong, robust A-values, and very weak, pale, H-values (that are basically akin to the nihilistic view that there are *no* values), many other types of values are possible ranging in their degree of strength and robustness. Indeed, there are an indefinitely large number of such intervening possibilities, some of whose members are represented in View II of diagram one. So, for example, there might be B-values which are not quite as strong and robust as A-values, but which are still very strong and robust, or C-values which are a bit less strong and robust than B-values, but which are still quite strong and robust, down to G-values, which are stronger and more robust than H-values, but which are still quite weak and "pale."

Here are some examples of the sort of intervening positions I have in mind.[38] Parfit believes that normative truths hold in *all* possible worlds, and would provide reasons for *all* fully (including substantively as well as procedurally) rational beings. I agree. We might say that the values corresponding to such truths would be very strong and robust, presumably A-values in View II of diagram one. But suppose that there were no such truths. There *might* still be normative truths that held in all worlds that were sufficiently like ours, or in all worlds for creatures that were

---

[38] I am grateful to Jeff McMahan for urging that I provide a few such examples, so as to make my view a little less abstract, and hence clearer and more attractive to the reader.

sufficiently like us (here, I leave open the criteria for being "sufficiently" like our world, or like us). In that case I think it would make perfect sense to say that there were, indeed, *values* in such worlds, and for such creatures, namely those values corresponding to the normative truths in question. Such values would not be quite as strong and robust as A-values, but they would still be quite strong and robust. Perhaps they would be good candidates for B- or C-values in View II. Next, suppose there were no normative truths that held for all worlds sufficiently like ours, or all creatures sufficiently like us, but that there were nonetheless normative truths that held for *our* world, and for all of *us*. That would be enough, I think, for us to say that there were meaningful and significant values. Such values would not be *as* strong and robust as A-, B-, or C-values, but they would still be fairly strong and robust; perhaps we might think they correspond to D-values in View II. And similarly, we can see how certain normative truths might only hold for certain periods of time, but not others, or for countries at certain stages of development, but not others, or for all members of certain groups, with certain characteristic features, but not others, and so on.

So, to put some of these points slightly differently, there might be rival meta-ethical views that might explain and predict intersubjective agreement about certain value judgments arrived at independently across all rational beings, places, and times; or across all animals of sufficient cognitive development at most places and times; or across all humans in many places and time periods; or amongst certain well-defined groups of humans who share a common culture, history, and genetic makeup; or perhaps there is only intersubjective agreement amongst participants in common social arrangements, and the judgments agreed upon are not arrived at independently, but only as the result of some kind of social convention or some process of democratic deliberation; or perhaps there is very little agreement at all, or what agreements there are reflect a mere *modus vivendi*, or tend to be transitory, or are widely recognized as the sort that one can opt in or out of at will, as one's interests or circumstances change, and so on. And there may be lots of variations of such possibilities, and entirely different ones as well. The point is that most of these different kinds of agreements might reasonably count as reflecting *values*, but we might agree that they vary in their strength and robustness, with some being more like View II's A-values, some being more like View II's nihilism, or H-values, and the rest lying somewhere between the two ends of the spectrum.[39]

As indicated, Parfit contends that if the views of his meta-ethical opponents are correct, we are left with nihilism, or a bleak view about values that is akin to nihilism, so that nothing matters, or at best things can only H-matter, which is akin to not mattering at all. I believe that Parfit's contention may be defensible for *some* of his meta-ethical opponents, but probably not most, and certainly not all of them. That is, without taking on the difficult task of arguing where, precisely, on the model depicted by View II different meta-ethical views lie, I think many of

---

[39] Though the analogy is not perfect, in some ways my view about this matter is similar to the kind of view that Nagel advocates regarding subjectivity and objectivity in *The View from Nowhere* (Oxford University Press, 1986) and in his article "Subjective and Objective" (in *Mortal Questions*, Cambridge University Press, 1979, pp. 196–213). Nagel denies that there is a stark either/or, all-or-nothing choice between looking at the world subjectively and looking at the world objectively. Instead, he suggests that subjectivity and objectivity run along a spectrum, so that there are varying degrees of subjectivity and objectivity, with multiple positions lying between the extremes of the "purely" subjective and the "purely" objective, and with the latter corresponding to what Nagel calls "the view from nowhere." Accordingly, for Nagel, any point lying between the two extremes will be subjective to some degree, and objective to some degree, and as such it will count as "objective" relative to a still more subjective perspective, but "subjective" relative to a still more objective perspective.

As I say, the analogy is not perfect, but the point is that, for Nagel, if one believed that the purely "objective" perspective was not, in fact, a realizable perspective (as Nagel thinks is actually the case for us, it is only an "idealized" perspective we can hope to approach), that would not give one reason to think that the only alternative is to approach the world from a purely "subjective" perspective. To the contrary, as indicated, Nagel insists that there would be a whole range of more and less objective perspectives, many of which would be quite objective indeed (relative to all of the other possible perspectives), even if none of them would be *as* "strong and robust," in terms of their degree of objectivity, as the view from nowhere *would* be if such a view were, contrary to fact, possible.

If one thought that the more objective one's viewpoint, the stronger and more robust would be the values one recognized from that perspective, then there would be a nice correlation between Nagel's picture of the subjective/objective spectrum and my picture of the value spectrum from nihilism through the kind of values Parfit defends, and which are represented by A-values in View II of diagram one. The position in question is a fairly natural one to take, up to a point, though Nagel's own view is that as one approaches the most objective perspective along the subjective/objective continuum, the so-called "view from nowhere," all values disappear.

Parfit's opponents could plausibly argue that their view does not commit them to nihilism, or at best, H-values. Instead, I think some will be able to plausibly contend that their view is compatible with E-values, or D-values, or perhaps even C- or B-values. Of course, I haven't *argued* for this position, I have just *claimed* it. But I believe my claim is more plausible than Parfit's, notwithstanding his many claims and arguments to the contrary.

Parfit does not, I think, have to worry about whether his life has been wasted. It has not! And I think all parties to the debate about meta-ethics can and would agree to this. Similarly, the same can be said for the lives of Beethoven, Einstein, Curie, and countless others, including, as implied above, most ordinary folks for that matter! Parfit may be right that if his meta-ethical view isn't correct, then his life can't matter in the strongest, and most robust sense in which both he and I believe that it does, in fact, matter. But that only means that Parfit's life wouldn't A-matter! It could still, and no doubt does, B-matter, or C-matter, or D-matter, and to matter in such ways *is* a way of *mattering* that is a far cry from the bleak alternatives that Parfit thinks we face if his meta-ethical view is wrong: either nihilism or, its close cousin, H-mattering!

5. Conclusion

Let me end by briefly summarizing my main claims. In Section 2, I argued against Parfit's claim that non-natural normative facts have no causal impact on the natural world. If it is true, as Parfit believes, that "We are the animals that can both understand and respond to reasons," then it is also true that in countless cases our beliefs, desires, or actions would have been different but for the normative facts that we understood and responded to. This is, I suggested, enough reason to believe that normative facts *can* have a causal impact on the world, through the cognitive capacities we have (often referred to as our "faculty of reason") which enable us, sometimes at least, to recognize and appropriately respond to reasons. I put my discussion in terms of a counterfactual account of causation, but suggested that it might also have been put in terms of a deductive-nomological account of causation. I also considered, and rejected, various views that might be thought to support the position that non-natural normative facts can have no causal impact on the natural world.

In Section 3, I tried to suggest that the gulf between Parfit's externalist view, and that of his internalist opponents, may not be quite as large as Parfit's discussion seems to imply. In particular, I argued that externalists can, and should, accept two of the most important internalist insights. The first is that, in a very important sense, *reasons* are always reasons *for* creatures like us. That is, normative facts only serve as *practical* reasons for beings whose cognitive capacities (faculty of reason) enable them to understand and appropriately respond to whatever reasons there are. Since our cognitive capacities are features about *us*, and depend on something which is *in* us, namely our brain, this makes it true, as internalists have claimed, that in an important sense practical reasons depend on something about us and on something which is in us. The second is that there *is* a close connection between reasons and motivation, as internalists have long insisted, though the connection may not be what internalists have taken it to be. The connection obtains in virtue of our cognitive capacities which enable us to understand and respond to reasons. Given those capacities, as Parfit recognizes, a *fully* rational person *would* be motivated to believe, desire, or do what she had most reason to, assuming that she had perfect information, was clear thinking, and had no other "distorting" factors influencing her. So, the gap between the *normative* question, concerning what we are *justified* in believing, desiring, or doing, and the *empirical* question, concerning what we will be *psychologically motivated* to believe, desire, or do, is mediated, in ideal circumstances, by our cognitive capacities; the very capacities in virtue of which we are "the animals that understand and respond to reasons."

Finally, in Section 4, I suggested that Parfit was mistaken in claiming that we face an either/or, all-or-nothing choice between his version of externalism and the many distinct meta-ethical views of his opponents, according to which unless Parfit's view is true, *nothing matters* and Parfit's life will have been wasted. I contended that we can be confident that Parfit's life, and the lives of countless others, have *not* been wasted, even if we cannot be confident that Parfit's meta-ethical view is true. In addition, I suggested that there may be a spectrum of ways of "mattering," such that even if nothing matters in *Parfit's* sense, many things may still matter in other senses that have varying degrees of significance. Parfit's sense may be the strongest and most robust sense of "mattering," but I do not believe that it is the *only* strong and robust sense of "mattering." Parfit presents us with a stark, and false, dichotomy. Surely, rejecting Parfit's version of externalism does not commit one to nihilism, or to a view of "mattering" which is so weak and pale as to be akin to nihilism. Between such extreme positions a host of other positions are, I believe, possible.

I end by reminding the reader that my own meta-ethical views closely dovetail with Parfit's. Hence, I see my points as mere quibbles with an ally. Parfit could, I think, accept everything I have claimed here, without significantly revising his views. Part Six is not the last word on meta-ethics but, to my mind, it is the most important work to date on the fundamentally important question of what matters. Given the importance of Part Six, together with that of the rest of the book, and given the extraordinary significance of his previous masterpiece, *Reasons and Persons*, we can be confident that Parfit's life has *not* been wasted!

2

TWO SIDES OF THE META-ETHICAL MOUNTAIN?

Peter Railton

1. Introduction

Derek Parfit's *On What Matters*[1] is a book that matters. It is a contribution to systematic ethics of such sweep and cumulative argumentative force that it will have a central role in debates in moral philosophy for years to come. There is a great deal in *On What Matters* that I find compelling. In an age marked by rather stark oppositions between "Kantian" and "Humean" approaches to ethics, or "Deontologist" and "Consequentialist" normative theories, *On What Matters* achieves a remarkable synthesis. For it suggests that these approaches, properly understood—and therefore liberated to some extent from a number of their contemporary advocates—might be seen as climbing different sides of the same mountain, to find themselves united at the summit.

In meta-ethics, however, Parfit sees things differently. Naturalists never get beyond the foothills of normativity. When they try to scale the heights, the bottomless crevice of Nihilism awaits them, not re-union

---

[1] In two volumes. Oxford: Oxford University Press, 2011. Parenthetic page references in the text, unless otherwise indicated, are to Volume Two.

with the Parfitian Non-Naturalist: "Normativity is either an illusion, or involves irreducibly normative facts" (267). Were Naturalism to be our only option, Parfit writes, much of his philosophical life, as well as much of the lives of such great modern moral philosophers as Sidgwick and Ross, would have been "wasted" (303–4). Worse, "we would have learnt that nothing matters" (367).

This sad thought is made all the more poignant by the fact that Parfit sees the situation as asymmetric. Even if they prove wrong on matters meta-ethical—as it seems we must hope they are—the great Naturalists of the past such as Hobbes, Hume, Bentham, and Mill will not have wasted *their* philosophical lives: they will have taught us something about the natural *reason-giving* features of the world. That is, the Naturalists might have described everything that is of genuine *normative importance*—pleasures and pains, well-being, Mill's "permanent interests of man as a progressive being," and so on—even though the nature of normativity itself altogether eluded them. The non-natural *normative properties and facts* Parfit insists upon, he explains, themselves have no such importance. They serve to formulate reasons-relations, but do not give "any *further* reason" for acting in their own right (279–80).

2. The "Decisive Battlefield"

Thus, we might be aware of pleasure and pain, weal and woe, hope and despair, helping and harming, truth and falsehood—everything that is of normative importance—and yet, absent recognition of independent reasons-relations, "that importance would be unknown to us—as it is unknown, for example, to some active, intelligent cat" (288). Were I to say, "You would enjoy this book" or "Your wine is poisoned," this would "tell you facts that would give you reasons for acting," which you might take to heart and be glad you did, but this could not constitute genuine *advice*—for that we need the irreducibly normative concept of *reasons for acting* (281).

Of course, many Naturalists would accept the existence—and useful-ness—of irreducibly normative concepts, precisely for such purposes as reflecting individually or together on what matters, and deliberating, deciding, and advising about what to think or feel or do. They also accept the existence of substantive truths involving these concepts. Parfit thus calls such views "Soft" Non-Analytic Naturalism, and Parfit himself has sometimes seen the initial plausibility in such a position, despite his long years of adamant resistance to Naturalism (349). Moreover he allows that Naturalists of various kinds might be able to give a plausible account of such forms of normativity as the normativity of correctness (including truth or falsity for belief or correctness for assertion, 266), rules, customs, laws, meaning, well-being, and even beauty, rationality (in the procedural sense), and moral rightness (in the attitude- or practice-based sense)—as these notions are often understood (267–9).

But explaining these forms of normativity is not the "decisive battle-field" in meta-ethics (269). Nor is the battle over what we ordinarily have in mind when making normative judgments. Rather, it concerns what we *should* have in mind, at least, when thinking at the most fundamental level of normative reflection (272). And that is the idea of unqualified reasons—reasons *full stop*. It is "reasons" in this sense that enable us intelligibly to ask, of any of these other normative categories, *Do we, in the end, have sufficient reason to take them seriously—to guide our lives by these rules, procedures, attitudes, or practices, or to hold ourselves to these standards of correctness?* This is the *"reason-involving"* or *"reason-implying"* sense of normativity, the sense in which it implies the existence of "some reason or apparent reason" (268). And this is where the buck stops when we are asking what really matters—or seeking decisive guidance as to what we ought to think and do.

Thus, a Naturalist might be able to give an account of morality in something like the sense in which Hume understood it (310)—the sense in which it is embodied in a constellation of human attitudes, traits of character, norms, practices, and concerns as grounded in relationships of cooperation, discussion, and mutual restraint, which promote the "general interest" and earn our reflective approval and motivated commitment by making our lives go better on the whole. But accepting that something is moral in this sense does not logically imply that I have sufficient reason to take its values or injunctions as action-guiding. I might decide that I should do so, even that it would be a terrible mistake not to, but then in giving this answer I am to be understood as answering a normative question neither posed nor precluded by the original standards themselves. Fortunately, Parfit believes that there are *objective*, *external* reasons, independent of what we happen to care about or find motivating, and that these reasons can speak on behalf of morality. And because they are reasons *full stop*, I cannot in a similar way ask a meaningful normative question about whether I ought to heed them. For to ask such a question is simply to ask whether I have sufficient reason for so doing.

Now it might seem that we *could* ask such a question, precisely because these reasons are external. We might see that an act is supported by external reasons, yet find that these reasons simply do not speak to us and our deepest concerns. But regarding what actually or reflectively moves us, or is endorsed by us, Parfit writes:

> There is, I believe, no normativity here. An irresistible impulse is not a normative reason. Nor is an impulse made rational by its ability to survive reflection on the facts. Even after carefully considering the facts, we might find ourselves irresistibly impelled to act in crazy ways. [291]

After all, someone might find that bloody revenge is what speaks to him—even after full reflection, and even at the acknowledged cost of any hope of future happiness for all concerned. If so, and if he exacts vengeance as a result, he is acting with no reason and making a "*terrible mistake*" (437, 292).

"There is something else, and something better, for normativity to be" (285). Indeed, even the hard-core "Internalist" who disagrees with Parfit is in fact making a contrary "external" or objective claim of her own—a claim about what reasons there are, *full stop*. Parfit concludes, "To avoid confusion, we should use the phrase 'a reason' only in its external, irreducibly normative sense" (290).

3. Concepts and Properties: The Soft Naturalist's Dilemma

Parfit argues at length that, at the core of the dispute between the Non-Naturalism about reasons he favors and Non-Analytic, Soft Naturalism—hereinafter what I will mean by "Naturalism" when the term is used without qualification—lies a seemingly rather subtle question. Namely, whether statements like:

(A) What we have most reason to do is to maximize happiness

admit a reading in which they can coherently be understood as something like synthetic property identities, in which two concepts, one normative (<most reason to do>) and one natural (<maximizing happiness>), pick out one and the same natural property, *maximizing happiness*, without any intermediation by a non-natural property.[2] Such a reading would permit the Naturalist to accept that normative concepts cannot be reduced to natural concepts, while at the same time having no need to enlarge her metaphysics beyond natural properties. The property *maximizing happiness* would do double duty, descriptive/explanatory and normative. In consequence, the Naturalist's ontology would not need to admit irreducibly non-natural properties. On such a reading, a Naturalist who adhered to (A) could be saying that an act's rightness "consists in" its maximization of happiness, or that, to maximize happiness "is what it is for" an act to be right. (A), if true, would be a synthetic, substantive truth, discovered a posteriori.

An analogy would be with a "Soft" Materialism according to which, for example, the property of *having C-fibers firing* can do double duty, figuring in physiological explanations of neurological and behavioral phenomena, on the one hand, and as the referent for the mental concept <experiencing pain> and truth-maker for pain ascriptions, on the other.[3] This would allow the Materialist to recognize the distinctive inferential and conceptual roles of mental ascriptions—situating talk of "pain" within the common-sensical mentalistic conceptual framework. It would also account for the a posteriori nature of the discovery that pain consists in C-fiber firing, while at the same time positing no irreducibly mental properties or substances.

Another analogy would be with a "Soft" Physicalism according to which the microphysical property of a system *having a certain mean*

---

[2] I will use the convention of italicizing *properties* and placing <concepts> in corner brackets. (A) is unrealistically simple, but it will serve for illustrative purposes.
[3] This example, too, is unrealistically over-simple.

molecular kinetic energy can do double duty, figuring in thermodynamical explanations of the system's behavior, on the one hand, and as the referent for (what physicists call) the phenomenological concept <having a certain heat> and the truth-maker for heat-attributions, on the other.[4] This would allow the Soft Physicalist to recognize the distinctive conceptual and inferential roles of heat attributions—situating talk of "heat" within a macroscopic, observational conceptual framework. It would also account for the a posteriori nature of the discovery that phenomenological heat consists in microscopic kinetic energy, while at the same time positing no irreducibly non-physical properties or substances.

Parfit believes that all these "Soft" views are incoherent. They face a kind of dilemma, in which the only form in which claims like (A), or

(B) To be in pain is to have one's C-fibers firing,

or

(C) To have a certain degree of heat is to have a certain mean molecular kinetic energy,

could be true and informative—as they are intended to be—is a reading according to which they involve a relation between *two* distinct properties. That is:

(A+) Whatever act has the normative property of being what we have most reason to do has the different, natural property of maximizing happiness.

(B+) To have the mental property of being in pain is to have a different, physical property of having C-fibers firing.

(C+) To have the phenomenological property of possessing a certain degree of heat is to have a different, microscopic property of possessing a certain mean molecular kinetic energy.

Here is how the argument goes:

On one horn of the dilemma, the Soft Naturalist (or Materialist, or Physicalist) sees herself as advancing a substantive, informative, and

---

[4] Again, an unrealistically over-simple example.

positive claim in asserting (A) (or (B) or (C)). Let us take (A), and suppose this claim to be right. What sort of claim is (A) and what would it take for such a claim to be substantive, informative, and positive?

Could (A) be a purely non-normative claim? No, since putting this claim forward has implications about a whole range of questions about what we have most reason to do, and that is, at least on one influential view, what normativity is all about. Someone dissenting from (A) on the ground that following the Golden Rule is what we have most reason to do, would have a normative disagreement with (A). So (A) has non-trivial normative content.

Can we say more precisely when a normative claim is *substantive*? Parfit offers us this definition:

[def. 1] Some normative claim is *substantive* when this claim both (a) states that something has a normative property, and (b) is *significant*, by being a claim with which we might disagree, or which might be informative, by telling us something we didn't already know. [275]

And when would such a claim be *significant* or *informative*? Parfit gives these quasi-definitions or explications:

[qdef. 2] Any such information must be statable, however, as the claim that such acts would have one or more other, different properties. [344]

[qdef. 3] As I use the concept of a *property*, any information about such acts could be stated as the claim that these acts would have some property. [348]

And finally, when would a normative claim be *positive*?

[qdef. 4] normative claims are *positive* when they state or imply that, when something has certain natural properties, this thing has some other, different normative property. This property might be linguistic. [343]

But now it is clear that, given these definitions, (A) can be substantive, informative, and positive only when it is interpreted as:

(A+) Whatever act has the normative property of being what we have most reason to do has the different, natural property of maximizing happiness.

And yet (A+) is plainly incompatible with the Soft Naturalist's claim that only one irreducible property, the natural property *maximizing happiness*, need be in play in (A).

Thus, the effort to make the Soft Naturalist's position something worth asserting—a substantive, informative, positive claim—makes it false. A similar argumentative strategy works, *mutatis mutandis*, to show that (B) and (C), if they are to be substantive, informative, positive claims, must be interpreted as (B+) and (C+), making Soft Materialism and Soft Physicalism false.

On the other horn of the dilemma, the Soft Naturalist insists upon something like a "referential" reading of (A), so that it reaches directly to the underlying natural property, with no recourse to an intermediating normative property. Let us grant this reading. But then stating (A) in effect equates the reference of <having most reason to do> with the reference of <maximizing happiness>. Yet this is to say nothing more than:

(A*) Whatever act has the property of maximizing happiness has the property of maximizing happiness.

And that is trivially true. *Mutatis mutandis*, (B) and (C) would say nothing more than:

(B*) To have the property of having C-fibers firing is to have the property of having C-fibers firing.

(C*) To have the property of having a certain mean molecular kinetic energy is to have the property of having a certain mean molecular kinetic energy.

So, on the "referential" reading, (A)–(C) would all come out true, but as thinly disguised tautologies, not substantive, informative, positive philosophical positions.

Thus, the effort to make Soft Naturalism (or any of its Soft mates) true makes it trivial, not substantive. Since we have already seen that the effort to make it non-trivial makes it false, the dilemma appears to be complete.

If Soft Naturalism is thus incoherent, and normative concepts must be seen as referring to normative properties—even though normative concepts may *also* refer to natural features *via* referring implicitly to normative properties (331)—then to adhere to a Naturalistic metaphysics that *excludes* unreduced normative properties would force the would-be Naturalist to be a "Hard" Naturalist, holding an Error Theory about normative claims. Thus Naturalism is "close to" Nihilism (368)—where normativity is seen as an illusion and "nothing would really matter" (cf. 367). Similarly, Hard Materialism would lead to an Error Theory about the mental (e.g. in reality, there are no pain experiences, just physical states) and Hard Physicalism to an Error Theory about the phenomenological (e.g. in reality, nothing is hot or cold, or red or blue, there are just microphysical differences in energy level, or colorless light-reflectance properties).

These are surprisingly powerful results. If the Naturalist were attempting to scale the same meta-ethical mountain as Non-Naturalists like Sidgwick, Ross, and Parfit, she would just have tumbled off a ledge into normative oblivion.

4. Types of Naturalism

There are many steps in the arguments rehearsed above against Soft doctrines.[5] How are we to assess them?

First, how did we get to the conclusion that (A+)–(C+) were the mandatory interpretations of (A)–(C) when these are substantive, informative, and positive? Via the definitions or quasi-definitions [def. 1]–[qdef. 4], repeated below:

> [def. 1] Some normative claim is *substantive* when this claim both (a) states that something has a normative property, and (b) is *significant*, by being a claim with which we might disagree, or which might be informative, by telling us something we didn't already know. [275]

> [qdef. 2] Any such information must be statable, however, as the claim that such acts would have one or more other, different properties. [344]

> [qdef. 3] As I use the concept of a *property*, any information about such acts could be stated as the claim that these acts would have some property. This property might be linguistic. [348]

---

[5] We will come to an argument peculiar to the Soft doctrine in the normative case, the "Normativity Argument" in Section 7.

[qdef. 4] normative claims are *positive* when they state or imply that, when something has certain natural properties, this thing has some other, different normative property. [343]

A philosopher should perhaps be allowed whatever definitions or quasi-definitions he wants; the chief interest lies in what they enable him to establish, so long as they don't beg relevant questions and we keep in mind that the terms thus defined are quasi-technical terms. But [def. 1]– [qdef. 4] have the interesting feature that they all introduce "property" or "normative property" or "different property" into the definiendum or quasi-definiendum. Unsurprisingly, then, they together have the result that (A)–(C) won't be substantive, informative, and positive *in Parfit's senses of the terms* unless the predications they contain are interpreted in terms of the attribution of different properties, that is, as (A+)–(C+).

To block this, we need only find coherent, alternate ways of explicating how (A)–(C) could be *in some other, philosophically interesting sense* substantive, informative, and positive, even if Soft Naturalism, Materialism, or Physicalism were true.

Why bother? Perhaps Soft Naturalism, Materialism, and Physicalism are radically implausible doctrines, the brain-children of metaphysically obsessive-compulsive philosophers who dogmatically insist at the outset that:

(G) All irreducible properties or facts are natural.

(H) All irreducible properties or facts are material.

(I) All irreducible properties or facts are physical.

Parfit writes of "*Normative* Naturalists" that:

most are also *Metaphysical* Naturalists, who believe that all properties and facts are natural, so that there could not be any irreducibly normative facts. [267]

But it seems to me that Hobbes, Hume, Mill, and a great many historical and contemporary naturalists, myself included, are motivated primarily by *methodological* as opposed to a priori *metaphysical* considerations. If they resist non-natural entities, properties, or forces, it is because they see them as problematic in the effort to conduct fruitful, empirically-disciplined inquiry that leads to the development of genuinely explanatory theories.

Methodological Naturalism is the view that, in inquiry, we should try to proceed by following the ways of observing, hypothesis-forming, testing, formal modeling, axiomatizing, and explaining that have been so successful in the natural, biological, social, and mathematical sciences (Railton, 1997a). Hobbes and Hume, for example, saw themselves as applying emerging methods of scientific inquiry to develop an empirically-based "science of man," not trying to duplicate the dogmatic metaphysics of their predecessors, only with a Naturalistic flavor.

Methodological Naturalists do not begin with bald metaphysical assertions like (G)–(I), since their approach to metaphysical questions has to be: "Let's see." That is, "Let's see how far we can go with the hypothesis that all facts or properties are of a kind that figure in the forms of inquiry and explanation found in the sciences—or can be understood in terms of conceptually clear constructions from such facts and properties." It could turn out that there is a great deal that science cannot account for, even granting that every mode of inquiry is allowed to let explanations stop somewhere.

Prior to Darwin, for example, religious and irreligious Methodological Naturalists worried how to explain the extensive evidence of "design" and "pre-established harmony" to be found in nature. Were there no evidence for evolution or other possible mechanism of natural selection, then a methodological preference for non-coincidental explanation would leave us today in the situation described by Hume: "Those, who delight in the discovery and contemplation of *final causes*, have here ample subject to employ their wonder and admiration" (Hume, [1888], IV.ii.44). More recently, methodological considerations led to a metaphysical shift within the Naturalist camp. Many Naturalists who had been drawn to Central-State Materialism shifted to some form of Functionalism once the development of programmable computers and evolutionary psychology convinced them of the greater generality and explanatory power of Functionalism.

What has tended to drive Methodological Naturalism is the thought that philosophy has frequently been led into ineffectual speculation, dead ends, unnoticed incoherencies, non-explanatory theories, and ad hoc hypotheses by dogmatic metaphysics, theological commitments, or uncritical reification of common sense. The empirical and exact sciences, by contrast, have developed methods that have been enormously productive of new, surprising, predictively powerful, formally insightful, and explanatory theories.

On such an approach, a preference for what David Lewis called "sparse"—as opposed to "abundant"—views of properties is not arbitrary (Lewis, 1983). The introduction of *any* irreducible properties, entities, or facts raises fresh questions about intelligibility, epistemic and semantic access, coherence with existing theory, explanatory gain, and appropriate forms of discipline in attribution. Such worries become acute if these properties figure in synthetic claims involving putative metaphysical features outside the causal order. Parfit frankly allows that "when I say that we have some reason,…what I mean cannot helpfully be explained in other terms" (272), and that, in contrast to prosaic natural language, it is more difficult to explain "how we come to understand [normative] words and the concepts they express, and how we can recognize any irreducibly normative truths" (293).

He correctly notes that this is not decisive, and later in the book deals extensively with the problem of how we gain epistemic access to non-natural properties and facts (488–542). But it is hardly arbitrary to think that these explanatory problems might speak in favor of a sparser account of the properties and facts involved in normative discourse. If we already countenance both naturalistic *reason-making* properties and facts and the irreducibly normative *concepts* needed to discuss and deliberate upon them, one might well ask, isn't this sufficient for understanding normativity? Moreover, supervenience guarantees that natural facts will suffice to draw whatever genuine normative distinctions might exist among acts or outcomes. For there can be no genuine normative differences without genuine natural differences.

5. *Concepts and Properties, Second Pass*

Let us now return to the problem of showing whether (A)–(C) could be given a coherent interpretation that preserves the "Soft" idea that normative, mental, and phenomenological concepts might be irreducible, even if normative, mental, and phenomenological properties, states, or facts are not. Are there credible alternatives to (A+)–(C+)?

Historically, few topics have led to the spilling of more philosophical ink than whether properties are needed to explain predication, and if so, when and in what sense? Nominalists, Conceptualists, Tropists, Fictionalists, Minimalists, and other deflationary theorists hold that statements like (A)–(C) can be understood without recourse to properties as irreducible, abstract elements of reality. Some treat properties in a nominal or linguistic sense (e.g. as "the shadow of a predicate"). Others analyze properties in terms of classes or sets of individuals, actual or possible, worldly or trans-worldly or centered-worldly, and see predication in terms of membership in such classes or sets. And so on.[6] It would be surprising if all of these views were incoherent, so that interpretation of (A)–(C) in terms of irreducible abstract properties were mandatory.

Moreover many philosophers, some moved by methodological concerns about semantic or epistemic access, have pursued *selective* forms of Nominalism, Fictionalism, or other forms of deflation. For instance, some recently have sought to show that metaphysical commitment to abstract mathematical entities and properties lying outside of the causal order can be avoided without giving up elements of the formal or conceptual apparatus of mathematics needed in science (Field, 1993; Yablo, 2001). Others have pursued Fictionalism about the normative as an alternative to Expressivism (Kalderon, 2005).

Parfit can argue that Nominalism, Fictionalism, and the like face problems sufficiently grave to warrant rejecting them (464–87). But the question is, can Parfit show they are *incoherent* without making potentially question-begging assumptions like [def. 1]–[qdef. 4]? As Parfit points out in his discussion of "speech act" arguments that purport to derive *ought* from *is*, the mere *intelligibility* of Act Consequentialism as a normative view, regardless of whether we are warranted in rejecting it, shows that these inferences cannot go through without adding some substantive normative claim (310–14). Similarly, the mere coherence of even one form of Nominalism, Fictionalism, Tropism, etc., shows that

---

[6] Similar remarks apply to deflationary views about *facts*.

Parfit's attempt to show that (A)–(C) must be read as (A+)–(C+) requires some further assumptions involving properties. Indeed, [def. 1]–[qdef. 4] could be seen as reflecting just such assumptions. For example, on a natural reading [qdef. 3] corresponds to an "abundant" view of properties; moreover, it appears to take sides on the controversial question whether all information—including, say, the essentially indexical and practically vital information that an act is *one's own*—is "statable" as a property.

Defenders of Nominalism, etc., about non-natural, immaterial, or non-physical properties—whether as part of a general deflationism about properties or as a "sparse" view of properties that accepts only causal/explanatory kinds as *bona fide* properties—give philosophical reasons for preferring an account of statements like (A)–(C) that does not invoke irreducible non-natural, immaterial, or non-physical properties. Whether to accept any such interpretation seems to me more a matter for philosophical cost/benefit calculation, as Lewis would say (Lewis, 1986), than a situation in which one side refutes the other.

To get a feel for costs and benefits, consider how Parfit's preferred account analyzes statements akin to (A)–(C). On his account, macroscopic "heat" means:

> [i] the property, whichever it is, that has the *different*, second-order property of *being the property that can have certain effects*, such as those of melting solids, turning liquids into gases, etc. [330]

Therefore,

When scientists discovered that

> [ii] heat is molecular kinetic energy,

what they discovered was that

> [iii] molecular kinetic energy is the property that has this different, second-order property. [330]

But it seems odd to ascribe "*hav[ing] certain effects*, such as those of melting solids, turning liquids into gases, etc." to an abstract second-order property that is, moreover, distinct from the first-order physical property of possessing a certain molecular kinetic energy. Is such meta-physical ascent or reification really needed to understand (C)?

Here is an alternative, de-reifying approach. Think of *causal effi-cacy* as residing in actual or potential spatio-temporal individuals or systems. *Causal explanations* then can be given in terms of properties that carve the world into classes of individuals or systems along the lines of similarities and differences in such causal efficacy—"natural kinds." Since such properties are not something over and above these classes of individuals or systems with similar causal powers, invoking them explanatorily does not suggest that they make any *independent* contribution to causal effects. They therefore raise no naturalistic objections.

A phenomenological concept like <possessing a certain degree of heat> has a distinctive place in our conceptual framework, and we can explicate this in terms of a complex role or "job description" to be satis-fied by whatever would satisfy this concept—involving a capacity to melt solids, turn liquids into gases, etc., but also to do work, to produce certain characteristic sensations ("hot" or "cold") in observers under standard conditions, to correspond to temperature differences and changes ("heat flow"), etc. Such a "job description" need not be a *concep-tual analysis* properly so called, since it involves a great deal of substan-tive empirical content and since any of its particular elements—detailing conceptual interrelations, causal or constitutive connections, paradigm cases, etc.—might in turn be revised or abandoned without leading us to abandon the phenomenological concept <heat> altogether. For exam-ple, some early modern theorists would have included substantiality in the job description, but this was given up when the kinetic theory emerged. Similarly, phenomena like sensations of hot and cold and heat transfer were discovered to be influenced by *density* and *conductivity* as well as *heat*. But neither of these theoretical developments led to drop-ping the concept <heat>. It is this complex job description that philoso-phers and historians of science tease out when they try to reconstruct the concept of <heat> as it has functioned and evolved in common-sense and scientific discourse and practice.

We now can say that (C) can be interpreted as saying, in effect,

(C•) Collections of molecules possessing a certain mean kinetic energy uniquely fulfill the job description associated with satisfying our phenomenological concept <possessing a certain degree of heat>.[7]

(C•) is plainly a substantive, informative, positive claim. Certainly it was non-trivial news as it emerged over the course of experimentation and the development of thermodynamics. It is quite distinct from the claim:

(C*) To have the property of having a certain mean molecular kinetic energy is to have the property of having a certain mean molecular kinetic energy.

(C•) thus is enough to enable a Soft Physicalist to explain the substantive, informative, positive character of (C), without positing irreducible phenomenological properties, and while allowing that phenomenological concepts cannot be reduced to physical concepts. Parallels in the case of mind, in which mental concepts are associated with psychic and "folk theoretic" roles, which then are realized by neurophysiological or functional systems, are well known. The Soft Materialist's interpretation of (B) might be:

(B•) C-fiber firings in the central nervous system uniquely fulfill the job description associated with satisfying the mentalistic concept <pain>.[8]

6. Normative Concepts and Normative Roles

Let's return to the normative case. Can we use the approach just discussed for (C) to explain the substantive, informative, positive character of (A)?

(A) What we have most reason to do is to maximize happiness.

---

[7] In a serious treatment, (C•) would be strengthened to a claim of necessity, and would be a matter of molecular kinetic energy *best* or *sufficiently* fulfilling this role. Once these qualifications are spelled out, the option becomes available of using such roles or job descriptions to provide a kind of "non-obvious" definition or analysis (Lewis, 1970; Railton, 1993). For reasons suggested previously, as well as independent reservations about what "Ramsification" in general can establish, it seems to me preferable not to see them this way.

[8] See the preceding qualifications for (C•).

As we saw, on Parfit's view, there is not a lot to say about the concept of a reason *full stop*. On the other hand, he certainly does think that <most reason to do> has a distinctive, all-important role in our conceptual scheme—it expresses "stops the buck" in deliberating and deciding what we ought to do, what ultimately matters. Moreover, he also thinks there are paradigm cases of what is relevant to <most reason to do>, or what it includes or excludes, which recur throughout the book: future pain and well-being count, while considerations of pure vengeance or acrophobia do not.

If we did not have at least this rather "thin" idea of the role of <most reason to do> in thought and deliberation, we would be hard put to learn it, teach it, or distinguish it inferentially from other primitive concepts that can be applied to acts, like <actual> or <possible>. Why would attaching <most reason to do> to an act have any relevance in deciding what to do different from attaching <possible>, if both were simply inexplicable simples with no articulable roles? How would you know I had mastered the concept <most reason to do> if there were no paradigm cases, and the only examples I could give you after careful reflection were *skipping rope* and *bragging*?

Parfit's view of the role of <most reason to do> may be "thin," but for those who think that some form of internalism is part of this concept— that reasons must be the sort of thing *for which* one can act, that could engage positive affective interest and motivation or gain considered endorsement without further incentive, and so on—the associated job description would be considerably "thicker" and richer.

Given some such relatively "thin" or "thick" role, how might (A) be interpreted by the Soft Naturalist as substantive, informative, and positive?

(A•) Acts that maximize happiness uniquely fulfill the job description associated with satisfying the normative concept <most reason for action>.[9]

---

[9] See the preceding qualifications for (C•). (A•) could be more fully paraphrased into role talk as the substantive claim:

(A••) Acts that fulfill the job description associated with satisfying the naturalistic concept <maximizing happiness> also uniquely fulfill the job description associated with satisfying the normative concept <most reason for action>.

(A•) is plainly more informative than:

(A*) Whatever act has the property of maximizing happiness has the property of maximizing happiness.

That (A•) is true would come as news to a great many normative inquirers, past and present, while (A*) would not. Moreover, (A•) is normatively substantive and positive, since one would learn something positive about what one ought to do in learning it, e.g. that *maximizing happiness* always stops the buck in deciding what one ought to do. Someone who thought that only the Golden Rule had this status would urge instead:

(J) Acts that conform to the Golden Rule uniquely fulfill the job description associated with satisfying the normative concept <most reason for action>.

And a Nihilist or Error Theorist would urge:

(K) No acts could possibly fulfill the job description associated with satisfying the concept <most reason to do>.[10]

(A•) takes substantive issue with (J) or (K). Moreover, if true, it would have the status Parfit thinks normative truths must have, for, fully spelled out, it would formulate a necessary but non-analytic claim, as would (J)

For the Naturalist, the next question is whether the class of acts that best satisfy these two job descriptions constitutes a sufficiently unified group to count as a "psycho-social kind" of a sort that could enter into *bona fide* causal-explanatory claims. Such claims could support, e.g., appropriate forms of individual and social learning, and shared semantic access. And the fact that the role associated with a normative concept like <most reason to do> is best fulfilled by a "psycho-social kind" permits *bona fide* "normative explanations" that need not presuppose a metaphysics of irreducible normative properties (cf. "mentalistic explanations" of acts, abilities, or practices for functionalists; Railton, 1997b). There is an interesting affinity here with Parfit's "Non-Metaphysical Cognitivist" argument that explanations couched solely in terms of non-normative properties (a Soft Naturalist would say, couched solely in terms of non-normative *roles* or *concepts*) will fall short of providing a full understanding of why our mathematical calculations, abilities, and practices have the character they do (488–503).

[10] Again, see the qualifications on (C•). Since Mackie suggests that perhaps the existence of God would make "objective prescriptivity" possible (1977, 48), his Error Theory would take the form of asserting that "No acts fulfill the role specified by the concept <most reason to do> in any Godless world," along with "Our world is Godless."

or (K). Since the role specified by <most reason to do> will essentially involve other normative concepts—e.g. <ought to do> in the "thin" role, additionally, <ideal conditions> in the "thicker" role, etc.—this role cannot be reduced to a naturalistically-characterizable role, and so would not afford a naturalistic reduction of the concept.[11]

As far as I can see, (A•) is as coherent as (B•) or (C•). Parfit will of course prefer a translation of (A•)–(C•) into a language of properties and higher-order properties, e.g. "the property *being such as to fulfill the role*..., is had by whatever has the property...," but as far as I can see this is a philosophical choice, not mandated by the need to distinguish (A) from (A*), since (A•) does that. Moreover, (A•) does this without imputing causal features to second-order *abstracta* and it is metaphysically less profligate, since conceptual roles come along with concepts, but for "sparse" thinkers, (A•), like (B•) and (C•), can be accepted without invoking basic properties that go beyond the natural kinds delineated by fundamental causal/explanatory similarities.

In a less contentious spirit, however, I wonder whether there might in fact be less difference than it seems between Parfit's view and the Soft theories discussed here. Parfit's definitions and quasi-definitions have the effect of generating a new property wherever there is new information. Normally, it is not *properties* but *properties under descriptions* that carry information, but since Parfit allows that the property might be linguistic [qdef. 3], this distinction is blurred. Now, even Nominalistically inclined Naturalists can tolerate *linguistic* or *nominal* properties. Moreover, they can tolerate as well the conveyance of certain kinds of information about individuals by citing such properties, so long as this does not involve adding anything to their *ontologies* beyond individuals— including linguistic entities—and classes, functions, or worlds thereof. And Parfit claims that non-natural properties exist only in a *non-ontological sense* (482). Moreover, as we saw at the outset, Parfit believes that normative properties and the normative facts involving them are, in themselves, of no independent *normative importance* (279–80), and so do not figure in any fundamental metaphysical explanation of what really matters.

---

[11] For an alternative view, see Jackson (1998).

Soft Naturalists, too, can accept *non-natural* properties in a nominal or linguistic—and to that extent *non-ontological*—sense. Soft Naturalists also allow us to talk meaningfully and truthfully in terms of normative concepts—making reasons claims in which *normative predicates* figure. True reasons claims can be called *normative facts* by the Soft Naturalist in one familiar sense of this term—a *fact* is a true statement or proposition. Of course, the Naturalist of this kind will say that such facts do not have a *sui generis* ontological status, and make no contribution in their own right to the fundamental explanation of what has normative importance—but Parfit isn't saying that they have such a status or provide such explanations. Neither does Parfit claim that we have some special, quasi-perceptual mode of access to normative properties or facts—ordinary perceiving, thinking, and acting in the world, involving capacities that could be the upshot of ordinary evolutionary processes, suffice (488–542).

Reflecting on all this, I'm not sure how strenuously a Soft Naturalist should object, if at all, to "non-ontological" non-natural properties or to the non-natural facts attributing them. Soft Naturalists surely object to Platonistic Non-Naturalism, complete with an ontic conception of non-natural properties, knowledge of which is secured through a distinctive, "quasi-causal" faculty of synthetic a priori intuition, but Parfit's Non-Naturalism is not of this kind (502).[12]

Of course, there is much more to be said. This is only an attempt to lob the ball back into Parfit's court in the wake of his arguments against Soft Naturalism, and to invite a return shot.

7. *"Undeniably in Different Categories"—The Normativity Objection*

But Parfit raises another objection that suggests the Soft Naturalists' lob must fly wildly out of court. In this case, the objection pertains specifically to *normative* properties and facts, not properties and facts in general. Parfit allows that Naturalists *could* be right about many normative matters, as we noticed earlier. Moreover, as we noted, he allows that the

---

[12] For a further form of rapprochement between Soft Naturalism and Parfit's "Non-Metaphysical Cognitivism," see my n. 9.

Naturalists' particular proposed candidates for the natural properties picked out by normative terms might be acceptable as accounts of what normatively matters—natural properties can *make* an act be wrong, or what we have most reason to do. Parfit's "Normativity Objection" (324–7) is that none of these natural facts or features could possibly be what *being wrong* or *being a reason* could consist in. They are "undeniably in different categories"—"Rivers could not be sonnets, experiences could not be stones," and "Natural facts could not be normative in the reason-implying sense" (324–5).

Given the differences between the concepts involved, he believes, it simply is not "left open" that rivers could turn out to be sonnets, or stones experiences, or natural facts normative facts. So we cannot even entertain such identities coherently—the attempt to accept them results in nonsense. This in itself would suffice to rule out Soft Naturalism, even setting aside all that has gone before.

However, there is a crucial difference between the case of sonnets and rivers or experience and rocks, on the one hand, and the case of natural and normative facts, on the other. Rivers do not supervene upon sonnets, nor experience upon rocks. All the sonnets in the world do not determine which rivers there are, nor do all the rocks determine which experiences. But all the natural facts of the world, taken together, *do* suffice to determine (metaphysically, not analytically) all the normative facts.[13] This is an important feature of normative facts. Some would say that it is part of our a priori understanding of value or the normative that it is supervenient upon the non-normative in this way.

And that makes sense. After all, as Parfit agrees, the things of normative importance include plainly natural things like pain, happiness, accurate belief, and so on. Fix these things, and you have fixed what the reasons-making facts are. Not so with sonnets and rivers, or stones and experiences. We can imagine a God-like being arranging all the features of all the stones in the world, then wondering whether to add to this world any consciousness—perhaps, to appreciate Her handiwork. But

---

[13] To the best of my knowledge, Parfit discusses supervenience only in an endnote (300n), where he comments simply that normative supervenience needs separate treatment from the supervenience of the mental.

we cannot imagine such a being fixing all the features of an act of inflict-ing prolonged agony upon another person for one's own amusement, then having a choice to make about whether to make this a good or bad thing, or something there is a reason to stop. Here, I think, we do encounter inconceivability. Normative judgments are relevant to the guidance of action because of supervenience—what we *can* affect is the very stuff that makes for goodness or badness, so acting for the good is within our power.

Whatever value is, and however it might be different from fact, this profound connection between the natural and the normative is central to it. That makes the fact/value relationship more intimate than sonnets to rivers, or even of complex neurological states and consciousness (the supervenience of the mental not being in the same way part of our men-tal concepts). More strongly, as Moore thought, value is "derivative" in relation to the natural—there is an *asymmetric dependence* (Moore, 1942, 588). This suggests there is something metaphysically *explanatory* going on, with the natural having primacy.

Mere supervenience commits us to the existence of *some* natural prop-erty—perhaps complex and disjunctive and uninteresting *qua* natural—that holds for all cases in which a given evaluative concept applies. But the distinctive asymmetric dependence of the normative upon the nat-ural suggests something stronger. For example, grasping the conceptual role associated with the concept <reason for action> involves some notion of "*ought* implies *can*," and someone would have a defective understanding of the concept <intrinsically valuable> if he found it mystifying why things that affect us in the way pleasures and pains do could have value, or why pleasures would be on the value side and pains on the disvalue side.

Of course, there are fundamental differences between presenting an act under a naturalistic guise of <maximizing happiness> vs. presenting it under a normative guise of <what there is most reason to do>. The one has a *directly* deliberative role and *analytic* entailments to claims about how one ought to act that the other lacks. But do we need a *metaphysical* difference in facts or properties to understand this? The question whether to describe these differences in terms of differences in "non-ontological" properties and facts, vs. differences in non-ontological con-ceptual roles, seems to me not the sort of thing that could make Parfit's philosophical life-efforts in vain. Or make Naturalists like Hume or Mill close kin with Nihilists. Or risk making nothing matter.

Parfit argues that, while natural kind concepts like <water> and <heat> have a "gap" in them, waiting to be filled by some underlying property, evaluative concepts do not (302). This would seem to count against the Soft Naturalist's job-description story. But it should be recalled that the concept <water> was taken as picking out a *fundamental substance* from Antiquity to the Early Modern period, leaving no "space" for underlying composition by more elementary substances. Similar remarks apply to mentalistic concepts and *mental substance*, or the concept of <vital force> or <life>, where there was no pre-conceived "space" for realization by purely physical systems (cf. 324). And what could be more "undeniably in different categories" than the mental vs. the physical (as Parfit's example of "Experiences are stones" suggests), or colors vs. colorless vibrations, or living beings vs. aggregates of lifeless matter?

It seems better, in a methodological spirit, not to restrict the possibility of finding an underlying explanation or reduction of common-sensical categories by limiting this only to those concepts "ready made" for such explanation or reduction, or to those cases that are intuitively "close." Certainly history should caution us on this score, and speak against using such considerations to dismiss a philosophical approach as inappropriate or incoherent.

In such an open-minded spirit, the concepts, distinctions, practices, etc. of everyday life and prior philosophizing *do* have a "gap to be filled." Philosophers extract from everyday, non-controversial "senses" of things roles or job descriptions or "truisms," asking: (1) What would it take for this role or job to be filled, or nearly so? And (2) Is there—or could there be—in humans and the world anything that would answer to this? Nor is this a Naturalistic obsession. Kant as much as Hume proceeded from the common-sense understanding of morality to frame questions about what it would take for morality in this sense to be vindicated, and then asked whether a rigorous account of the human mind and the world it inhabits could supply this—so that it not turn out that morality's "secret basis is merely some high-flown fantasticality" (Kant, 1785, 6:395), and so that our "sense of morals...when reflecting on itself,...approves of those principles, from whence it is deriv'd" (Hume, 1739, III.iii.6). In this sense, they were climbing the same meta-ethical mountain, too, using different gear—"transcendental" vs. "experimental" methods and ontologies—but aiming for the same summit.[14]

I think the same can fairly be said of Parfit and contemporary Soft Naturalists. Our moral concepts do not have a "gap" ready to be filled by "non-ontological" non-natural properties and facts, either. But Parfit thinks there must be some such properties and facts for normativity to be other than an illusion—and argues that we can indeed give the beginnings of a credible understanding of how there might exist such properties and facts, and how we might have semantic and epistemic access to them, compatibly with accepting the contemporary scientific view of mind, language, and the world. Is this so deeply different from the Soft Naturalist's approach and ambitions? Might we be scaling the same meta-ethical mountain after all? Meet you at the summit![15]

References

Field, Hartry. 1993. *Science without Numbers: A Defense of Nominalism.* Princeton: Princeton University Press.

Hume, David. 1739 [1888]. *Treatise of Human Nature.* Ed. L. A. Selby-Bigge. Oxford: Clarendon Press.

Jackson, Frank. 1998. *From Metaphysics to Ethics: A Defence of Conceptual Analysis.* Oxford: Clarendon Press.

Kalderon, Mark. 2005. *Moral Fictionalism.* Oxford: Oxford University Press.

Kant, Immanuel. 1785. *Groundwork of the Metaphysics of Morals.* Trans. H. J. Paton. New York: Harper, 1956.

Lewis, David. 1970. "How to Define Theoretical Terms." *Journal of Philosophy,* 67: 427–46.

---

[14] And with some rather surprising similarities in how they conceived the *subjective* conditions for normativity (Railton, 1999).

[15] Parfit does suggest that some Analytic Naturalists might end up sharing a mountain with him, were they to "give up [their] Analytic Naturalism" (363)—a rather one-sided reconciliation. Here I am not imagining that Parfit give up his commitment to "non-ontological," informationally (or perhaps even linguistically) individuated, non-natural properties and facts.

As always, I am grateful to colleagues for discussion, and especially to Allan Gibbard and my former colleague Stephen Darwall. Like everyone in the field, I also owe a great deal to Derek Parfit. The errors are of course mine alone.

Lewis, David. 1983. "New Work for a Theory of Universals." *Australasian Journal of Philosophy*, 61: 343–77.

Lewis, David. 1986. *On the Plurality of Worlds*. Oxford: Blackwell.

Mackie, J. L. 1977. *Ethics: Inventing Right and Wrong*. Harmondsworth: Penguin.

Moore, G. E. 1942. "Replies to My Critics," in *The Philosophy of G. E. Moore*, ed. P. A. Schilpp. Volume Two. La Salle, IL: Open Court.

Railton, Peter. 1993. "Noncognitivism about Rationality: Benefits, Costs, and an Alternative." *Philosophical Issues*, 4: 36–51.

Railton, Peter. 1997a. "Made in the Shade: Moral Compatibilism and the Aims of Moral Theory." *Canadian Journal of Philosophy*, suppl. vol. 21: 79–106.

Railton, Peter. 1997b. "Explanations Involving Rationality." In *The Cosmos of Science: Essays of Exploration*, ed. John Earman and J. D. Norton. Pittsburgh and Konstanz: University of Pittsburgh Press and Universitätsverlag Konstanz.

Railton, Peter. 1999. "Normative Force and Normative Freedom: Hume and Kant, but Not Hume *Versus* Kant." *Ratio*, 12: 320–53.

Yablo, Stephen. 2001. "Go Figure: A Path through Fictionalism." *Midwest Studies in Philosophy*, 25: 72–102.

3

PARFIT ON NORMATIVE CONCEPTS AND DISAGREEMENT

Allan Gibbard

Does anything really matter? Of course! Among other things, it matters whether people suffer. It matters whether we lead lives engaged in our pursuits and tied in fulfilling ways to other people. Where Derek Parfit and I differ is on how to understand truisms like these.

1. Parfit's Non-Naturalism

Parfit maintains that normative claims ascribe properties that are non-natural and non-ontological (*OWM*, 475–87).[1] With our normative intuitions we respond to these properties, but non-causally (*OWM*, 498–502). I don't myself know what non-natural, non-ontological properties are or what a non-causal "response" is, though Parfit says some things on this and perhaps intelligible explanations can be given. As I read Parfit, he doesn't claim to know either, but does think that in invoking these notions, he is on the right track toward an explanation of normative thinking. It is of course fair enough to place one's bets on an approach that we don't much understand; these matters are immensely difficult. But do his dicta go in the right direction?

[1] All references are to Volume Two of *On What Matters*.

If, as I'll be arguing, Parfit's kind of non-naturalism fails to provide a basis for explaining normative judgments, an alternative might have to start with materials different from Parfit's. My own analysis begins with something like "plans" for what to do, what to prefer, what to believe, and how to feel about things. It also begins with "disagreement" in a wide sense in which we can disagree with preferences and plans.[2] Both Parfit's approach and mine thus have starting points that are not fully explained: ascriptions of non-natural, non-ontological properties in his case, or plans and disagreement in expanded senses in mine. Each of us, lacking a straight elucidation of these starting points in terms more basic, is called upon to elucidate them in some other way. We can apply canons of interpretation, saying what a thinker must be like to be, say, ascribing a non-natural, non-ontological property, or to be "planning" in the sense that I invoke. Or we can just point to basic concepts the audience has mastered, like that of a reason to do a thing. This last is in effect what non-naturalists do, and it is legitimate as far as it goes—but Parfit and I each think there is more to be said. I will argue that my starting points for this further explanation are more satisfactory than Parfit's.

1.1. Reasons and Mathematics

Parfit, like many non-naturalists, envisions basic normative knowledge as parallel to knowledge of mathematical first principles. Mathematical properties are his prime examples of "non-ontological properties," and mathematical knowledge, he thinks, is best understood as a non-causal response to mathematical facts. Normative knowledge, he proposes, works in a parallel way. Now I find it difficult and puzzling what to say about mathematics, but this, I maintain, is the wrong way to go about explaining it. An illuminating explanation of how we can know mathematical necessities won't treat "non-causal responses" as primary to the explanation, and it won't carry over to normative knowledge in general. The notion of a response is primarily causal: responses are caused, at

---

[2] I proceed starting from disagreement in my *Thinking How to Live* (2003). My *Meaning and Normativity* (2012) tries to explain the concept of disagreement and other concepts involved in logic and meaning, though in a way that starts out with some understanding of disagreement.

least in part, by what they are responses to. Parfit removes this causal link, and we have to think what might be left.

Computers, he tells us, get right answers to questions of arithmetic. Their doing so involves causality, but the causal responses are to things like voltages, not to non-natural facts about numbers. When we ourselves get arithmetic right, we are "responding" to arithmetic reasons, albeit non-causally. Now with computers, of course, what happens depends on the programming. We can explain why certain sorts of electronics yield sums and the like. A computer can also be programmed with correct moral views or with diabolical moral views; which it is depends on the programming. Which kind of computer are we ourselves like, then, who causally are products of natural selection and social dynamics? Parfit thinks, if I understand him, that the story of why we tend to get arithmetic right will carry over, in crucial ways, to why we tend to get reasons right in general. He thinks that there is a unity in stories of why we tend to be right on reasons of diverse kinds: epistemic reasons, including those in mathematics, self-regarding practical reasons, and moral reasons. What might this unity be, if it doesn't stem from analogies with literal seeing that Parfit explicitly rejects? Talk of "non-causal responses" isn't an explanation but an expression of hope for an explanation.

Our powers of arithmetical and geometrical knowledge seem to me to be far from utterly mysterious. We "respond non-causally" to abstract structural features by being affected causally, over evolutionary and developmental time, by situations that roughly have these features. Mathematics, though, Parfit challenges us, tells us not only how numbers are but how they *must* be (*OWM*, 518). Natural selection might explain why we have genetic potentialities to get sums right, but not how we could be capable of knowing that sums are necessary. I don't have a quick answer, but I have a rough idea why we attribute necessity to sums. Although with pebble counts, following the laws of arithmetic isn't a metaphysical necessity, whether pebbles will violate our expectations needn't enter our thinking about them. Any surprise is most likely to stem from miscounting or from a lapse in our a priori thinking. So we learn to think about numbers and sums without reasoning from evidence about pebbles. Doing so amounts to treating mathematics as a priori and necessary. A priori mathematical beliefs pay off in empirical expectations, and do so more simply than would treating arithmetic as contingent on something else.

Can't Parfit say the same kind of thing about our potentialities to respond non-causally to moral reasons? No one has a satisfactory story of the kind I seem to be demanding, and so why should Parfit? Though the causal history of our moral judgments is uncertain, I respond, we have some idea of how selection pressures for cooperation would give rise to selection pressures that would give us the potentialities for the sorts of moral judgments and motivations that we observe. Parfit's picture of moral judgments and motivations, though, leaves us with no idea why these selection pressures would give rise to a tendency to get them right. Why would the upshot be that we tend to get it right, say, whether suffering can be deserved?

1.2. *Evolutionary Forces and Rational Judgments*

Parfit sometimes talks as if certain stories of refined common sense compete with evolutionary accounts. Now to be sure, genetic evolution doesn't by itself give rise to adult phenotypes capable of judging reasons. Causal accounts of what we are like must include not only the evolution of our genotypes, but consequent social dynamics and an individual's development from newborn to adult with complex abilities and judgments. The writers Parfit responds to often speak just of "evolution," but what evolution yields on its own is just a newborn's potentialities to develop in complex ways in interaction with its environment.

Perhaps this is all that Parfit means to say when he delimits the causal role of "evolution," but some things he says suggest a picture that we must be careful to reject: that correct deliverances of common sense compete with evolution and the rest as explanations of our rational abilities. Other things he says get matters right on this score, but here are a few passages that worry me. The ability to reason, he says, "is sometimes claimed to be mysterious. But when it seems to us clear that some belief must be true, there is nothing in our cognitive experience that is more transparent and intelligible, or less mysterious" (*OWM*, 520). "If we ask *why* we believe that we have these epistemic and practical reasons, the answer, I suggest, is that these beliefs are obviously true" (*OWM*, 530). We respond "to the intrinsic credibility of these beliefs, or to our reasons to have them" (*OWM*, 531). Some necessary truths we know simply "by thinking about them" (*OWM*, 490). These sayings characterize the psychic mechanisms involved in making judgments, and none of these, if correct, would be competitors to a correct causal evolutionary, social, and developmental account of how we come to make the sorts of normative judgments we do.

Our cognitive abilities, he says, "were partly produced by evolutionary forces. But these abilities later ceased to be governed by these forces, and had their own effects" (*OWM*, 520). This could just mean that social dynamics matter too, but again we should be careful not to think that rational forces compete with evolutionary forces. Evolutionary forces shaped our genetic potentialities to reason correctly or incorrectly just as much as they shaped our potentialities to want food or sex. They shape propensities of newborns that will be actuated in interactions with the environment over a lifetime of development. The path from selection pressures on genes to adult theorizing will of course be vastly complex, and any tractable story of all this will be oversimplified. Still, our potentialities for whatever aspects of rationality we embody will have a causal background that is evolutionary, social, and developmental. Anything purposeful-seeming in our makeup, if it is refined and complex, has behind it a story of selection pressures shaping our genetic "recipe"—though not necessarily to do what it does now. What humans accomplish and chimps raised as humans don't is the work of psychic mechanisms whose development stems, among other things, from a background of intricate genetic selection peculiar to humans. Somehow, that must go for judgments of reasons.

Parfit is right when he says that rational and causal necessity can be aligned (*OWM*, 500). We need to understand, though, how this might happen for each kind of rational necessity. Parfit proposes how we might come to have a general tendency to get reasons right, but his proposal can't be on the right track. "Just as cheetahs were selected for their speed, and giraffes were selected for their long necks, human beings were selected for their rationality, which chiefly consists in their ability to respond to reasons. By responding to epistemic reasons, our ancestors were able to form many true beliefs which helped them to survive and reproduce." For this to be the right story, there would have to be some uniformity in psychic mechanisms whose workings constitute judging reasons, so that a recipe selected to eventuate in a tendency to get reasons of one kind right will now yield psychic mechanisms that tend to get reasons right in general. We can see why psychic mechanisms might evolve to be "non-causally responsive" to reasons of certain sorts—for example, reasons to believe that the prey one was tracking had gone one way or the other. But why would that mechanism, or any evolved psychic mechanism, evolve to be non-causally responsive to basic truths about reasons for action, such as whether in truth there is reason to want revenge for its own sake? Reasons are diverse, and evolutionary shaping to get one kind right needn't handle reasons of quite different kinds. There's no one general mechanism of "rationality." Rationality, inasmuch as we have it, is realized by a collection of psychic mechanisms for its various aspects.

I don't have a glimmering of how we come to "respond non-causally" and correctly to the non-natural properties that figure in Parfit's moral thought experiments. I therefore look for another account of what is going on with our powers of normative judgment and why to place some trust in them. If we can make somewhat reliable judgments of basic reasons, the story of what this consists in must be quite different from Parfit's.

2. If We Don't Take Responding Non-Causally as Basic to Explanation

My own hope has been to explain normative thinking less mysteriously—though I too find these issues immensely difficult, and I don't think I have got nearly to the bottom of them. Besides just appealing to the audience's command of normative concepts—for example, to responses that indicate what's synonymous with what—there is, I maintain, a further illuminating way to elucidate their nature, an expressivist way. Expressivists explain meanings by explaining the states of mind in which they figure. Normative concepts I try to explain by saying how they figure in reasoning to decisions and the like. Such a further explanation doesn't appeal to extraordinary non-natural properties and our non-causal responses to them—unless talk of these things merely amounts to what I am saying.

I can't address all of Parfit's critiques, but my views have two main aspects to which he objects. One is the expressivism, and the other is the way I put matters in terms of properties and concepts. I'll start with expressivism, which is central to what I am saying. Whether concepts of properties work as I claim for them isn't so important for me, since I could have formulated my expressivism treating our thoughts of properties as Parfit does, but I'll engage this issue too.

Parfit takes the basic normative notion to be that of a reason to do or believe, along with a separate basic notion of "ought" in a decisive-reason-implying sense—a sense that isn't definable in terms of being a reason. In rendering Parfit's claims and critiques, I'll sometimes speak canonically of being "warranted" or "rational" vs. "unwarranted," but understand that calling something unwarranted is just saying, in Parfit's terms, that there is decisive reason against it. This, I take it, is chiefly a matter of convenient terminology, though my way is more economical: we can render the concept of a reason to do something in terms of warrant, whereas Parfit has two primitive concepts: being a (*pro tanto*) reason to and being a decisive reason to.

2.1. *Non-Minimal Truth*

When Parfit turns specifically to expressivism, his chief worries concern truth and facthood and "what it is" to be rational. Non-cognitivists, Parfit says, hold that normative claims are not intended to state facts except in some minimal sense (*OWM*, 327). They are not beliefs, and "should not be regarded as intended to be true" (*OWM*, 380). In my 1990 book *Wise Choice*, I did claim that minimal truth contrasts with some robust sense in which normative statements are neither true nor false. Subsequently, Paul Horwich convinced me that I didn't know what non-minimal facthood and truth were. Once we have states of mind that are subject to agreement or disagreement, I then argued, an expressivist can explain the concepts of truth and falsity.

Parfit complains that since, on my theory "there isn't any property of being rational, there can't be anything *that it is* for some act or feeling to be rational" (*OWM*, 404). If, though, we have an account of what it means to call something rational, what is missing? We'll still need an account of what being rational consists in—whether or not, for instance, rationality in action consists in maximizing one's expected net pleasure—but that isn't what Parfit finds lacking. What, then, does Parfit himself have to say about "what it is" for an act or a feeling to be rational? Parfit has a vast amount to say about what makes an act rational in light of such things as the agent's beliefs, rational or irrational,[3] but to a very rough approximation, when I speak of an act or a feeling as "rational," I mean, in Parfit's vocabulary, that there is sufficient reason to do that thing or feel that way. Is there, then, according to Parfit, "anything that it is" for a consideration to be a sufficient reason? It is, he tells us, for the consideration to have a certain non-natural, non-ontological property, namely that of being a sufficient reason. That's not really informative, except in telling us that reasoning about reasons resembles, in certain respects, reasoning about manifest, paradigm properties like size and shape. Our next question is why this is. The similarities of normative to naturalistic reasoning, I argue, stem from the possibility of disagreement. Apart from the finding that certain kinds of reasoning apply to normative claims—which Parfit and I explain differently—neither of us thinks there's anything informative that's directly to be said as to "what it is" to be a sufficient reason. I think we can explain the meaning of "a sufficient reason" obliquely, in terms of what it is to believe something to be a sufficient reason. But apart from that, I have to join Parfit in saying, in an empty way, that to be a sufficient reason is just that: to be a sufficient reason.

2.2. *Disagreeing with Preferences and Acts*

I explain normative concepts and reasoning in terms of such things as coming to a decision and agreeing or disagreeing with a decision. Parfit insists that we can disagree with beliefs but not with acts, decisions, or preferences—except in a sense for which talk of disagreeing misleading (*OWM*, 385). I think that we can come to understand such "disagree-

---

[3] See extensive discussion in Parfit's secs. 1, 7, 16–18.

ment" in a way that makes it a suitable starting point for explaining normative thinking, and that the materials I start out with in my explanations are more intelligible than non-natural properties we learn of simply by thinking.

Can one, then, disagree with an act or a preference? The maiden prefers death to dishonor; can an advisor disagree? Disagreeing, as I mean it, isn't having an opposing preference, wanting the maiden to live, as with Stevenson's "disagreement in attitude." It is rejecting the maiden's preference for the case of being the maiden oneself, having all the maiden's characteristics. One way to do this is to prefer being the maiden alive and dishonored to being the maiden dead. Another way is to be indifferent between the two states.[4]

What we can disagree with must be a belief, insists Parfit, such as the belief that the maiden's preference is warranted (*OWM*, 385). Now Parfit and I agree that "disagreeing with the preference" amounts to the same thing as "believing that the preference is not warranted." At issue between us is which of these explains the other. Each of us helps himself to something that won't be explained by further conceptual equivalences. Parfit helps himself to a non-natural property of being warranted and to believing that a preference has that non-natural property. My talk of "disagreeing with the preference" he explains as believing that the preference is not warranted. I myself think that the notion of being warranted itself needs explaining. I start with the phenomenon of rejecting a preference. I reject a preference when I imagine having the preference and think "No!". I might then come to have the opposing preference or to be indifferent. This state of rejecting a preference is, I think, a familiar mental attitude.

An explanation of either kind owes us an elucidation of its starting point. What is it to be correctly interpretable as being either in the state of mind I start with or in the state of mind Parfit starts with? I envision explaining disagreement by saying what it is to be correctly interpretable as disagreeing. Parfit might instead try explaining what it is to be correctly interpretable as believing that a preference has a certain non-natural property. I don't see that my debt is more onerous than his.

[4] Cf. Parfit, *OWM*, 387–8.

2.3. *What to Do*

In my 2003 book *Thinking How to Live*, I adopted the slogan, "Thinking what I ought to do is thinking what to do." To this Parfit objects. I would not now put everything the way I did in that book, and I now think that the issues require something more nuanced than this slogan. Thus I accept aspects of Parfit's critique. Still, I'll argue, a place to start in explaining the basic normative concept of warrant is its place in reasoning coherently to a decision. Buridan's ass, if coherent, would conclude that eating from either bale is warranted and that tarrying between them isn't, and would then straightaway pick a bale and eat from it. (Such reasoning, of course, wouldn't ordinarily be explicit and conscious.) Cogent reasoning to a decision, I still say, may terminate in action, or in picking from indifference. The role that normative concepts play in this explains their nature: to believe an alternative warranted is to include it in the set among which one picks from indifference.

In such cases, Parfit says, "Rather than concluding what to do, we would reach conclusions about what we should do" (*OWM*, 386).[5] Two questions must be distinguished, he says: "What ought I to do?" and "What shall I do?" (He means "shall" in a sense such that "What shall I do?" is answered with a decision, not a prediction. When I wonder what to do and come to an answer, I call this deciding "what to do" and Parfit calls it deciding "what I shall do.") Even for consistent beings, Parfit says, we must distinguish belief from action, or we misunderstand practical reasoning (*OWM*, 387). Now, in *Thinking How* I had trouble settling on what to say about all this, and I might now agree to distinguish these two questions. There are cases of *akrasia*, I might agree, where we can correctly attribute an answer to my question "What ought I do?" that conflicts with my decision. Again, though, at issue between Parfit and me is order of explanation. We can characterize a concept, I say, by explaining its role in thinking that is conceptually coherent—or "structurally rational" in Scanlon's terminology.[6] If I am coherent, then what I decide

---

[5] Parfit calls my talk of "Why to care" about something "unusual." But the question "Why care about etiquette?" wouldn't be strange—and what should a correct answer to this be said to explain if not why to care about etiquette?

[6] T. M. Scanlon, "Structural Irrationality" (2007).

I ought to do is what I decide to do, and I don't decide to do a thing that I decide I ought not to do. The chief point of distinguishing "ought" beliefs from restrictions on decisions thus seems to be to allow us a way of being incoherent or structurally irrational, so that, among other things, we can congratulate ourselves when we avoid this kind of incoherence. Conceptual entailments are a matter of coherence: for *P* to entail *Q* is for it to be incoherent to believe *P* and disbelieve *Q*. Meanings are a matter of the conceptual entailments that obtain. I want to explain the meanings of normative terms in parallel ways, by the conceptual ties of normative beliefs to decisions.[7] Just as believing that snow is white rules out disbelieving that something is white, so believing that I must surrender rules out deciding not to surrender.

Still, as Parfit says, "We may decide *not* to do what we believe we ought to do," (*OWM*, 387). How do I characterize such cases? In *Wise Choices,* I tried to explain *akrasia* by distinguishing the "normative control system." When I decide not to do what I believe I ought to do, my normative control system tells me to do it but contrary motivations prevail. By 2003 in *Thinking How to Live*, I worried about depending on a dubious psychology. More recent psychological findings on self-control seem to fit the speculative psychology of *Wise Choices*, and so I should probably go back to my earlier view.[8] The kind of disagreement with a decision that constitutes believing the decision to be irrational is the work of a faculty of self-control which may be overwhelmed by other motivations.

Although in *Thinking How* I started with the slogan "Thinking what I ought to do is thinking what to do" I then had to retreat from the slogan for cases of ties. I agree that thinking what I ought to do is not all of coming to a decision, even for an ass who is fully coherent. A more accurate slogan would have been, "Thinking what I ought to do is explained by its role in coherent thinking what to do." If I'm allowed to use disagreement as my primitive and apply it to a wide range of states of mind for which such talk makes sense, I can say this: To believe I

---

[7] I elaborate this in Ch. 10 of my *Meaning and Normativity* (2012).
[8] I have in mind work on "dual process theory" and "decision fatigue." See, for instance, Kahneman, "A Perspective on Judgment and Choice: Mapping Bounded Rationality" (2003).

ought to go left is to disagree with not going left, and to believe it okay to go left is to disagree with disagreeing with going left. All this is a matter of conceptual equivalences, pairs of states of mind such that it is incoherent to be in one and disagree with being in the other.

Change of preference, I said, involves coming to disagree with one's earlier preference. Parfit, though, speaks of a different kind of change from what I had in mind. In his example, I change my mind and buy sea land rather than mountain land because I come to enjoy sailing more than climbing (*OWM*, 388). This example calls for care about time. Suppose that all along, I expected to enjoy climbing more than sailing before retirement and sailing more afterwards. Then, there's no change of mind, just a matter of scheduling and trade-offs over time. If, though, I had expected to enjoy climbing most after retirement and I then come to believe that I'll enjoy sailing more, then I change my mind about what I'll enjoy most when, and so genuinely change my resultant preferences for after retirement. I don't reject my more basic aim of securing enjoyment, but I do change my mind on whether to go for mountain land or seashore land upon retirement. Contemplating my intention to buy mountain land just prior to retirement, I think "No!" and come to prefer sea land. I start, then, with this phenomenon, and take it that my trajectory amounts to a change of belief as to which policy is warranted.

2.4. *The Point of Tracking Disagreement*

Why take disagreement as the basic notion with which explanations of truth and logic begin? The negative part of the answer is, of course, that otherwise we find ourselves forced to something like Parfit's starting point of non-natural, non-ontological properties, which I find mysterious. A positive part, I have been arguing, is that talk of disagreeing with a preference or a decision is something we can be brought to understand without appeal to non-natural properties. I also, though, try to explain the basic role of disagreement, and here I turn pragmatic. In our own thinking, we need to track agreement and disagreement. We need to track what agrees with what and what disagrees with what. As for agreeing or disagreeing one with another, interpersonally, that, I say, is a matter of "putting our heads together" to think with each other about the questions we can address individually. I may be helped in my own thinking by having you join me, so that I can regard myself as agreeing or disagreeing with your thoughts on the matters that puzzle me. This included sharing or rejecting your agreement or disagreement with preferences. We understand a way of thinking most deeply when we understand its point and understand its characteristics as stemming from that point.

Parfit objects, "We cannot believe that such people *are* disagreeing merely because, if we had this belief, that would be better for us. We could at most *pretend* that such people are disagreeing" (*OWM*, 389). Now of course I embrace a distinction between what it would be good to believe and what's true. Still, I don't think the cogency of a way of thinking is utterly divorced from whether the way of thinking is fit to do its job. What we should aim for, I think, is a pragmatism that goes more to the root of matters.

The best example of deep pragmatic rationale that I know is epistemological, with the concept of warranted degrees of credence given one's evidence. Warranted credences are of course not always the ones it is best to have. Comfort, for instance, may in some instances matter more than facing what the evidence indicates. Still, there is a job that rational belief invariably does best: it serves to guide decisions. More precisely, if a person has rational aims and a rational policy of pursuing her aims in light of whatever her credences might be, then the prospective value of a credence measure in guiding her in pursuit of her aims is maximized by credences that are rational. Warranted degrees of credence aren't always best all told, but they provide prospectively best guidance in pursuit of warranted aims.[9] Rational belief, then, is belief with this special kind of value. I'm suggesting that, in a parallel way, disagreement is what there's a special kind of value in regarding in a certain way.

Parfit takes beliefs in non-natural properties and disagreement with beliefs as unproblematic starting points for explanation. I think that we can see disagreement with the most prosaic kinds of beliefs—manifest descriptions of objects in our surroundings, for instance—as instances of a broader phenomenon that applies to acts and preferences as well. If

[9] I argue this in my "Rational Credence and the Value of Truth" (2008).

Parfit's starting points for explanation can't just be taken as unproblematic, we may need to rethink such things as belief, negation, agreement, and disagreement, and not just adduce these notions unquestioningly in our analyses.

3. Concepts and Properties

I claim that the phenomena to which Moore and Parfit appeal can be explained without recourse to non-natural properties. What Moore-like arguments establish is that normative concepts are non-naturalistic. I mean this as something that both expressivists and anti-expressivist "normative realists" could accept. Since, as I see it, this is the best schematization regardless of whether or not expressivism is right, I couch my expressivism in these terms, as a theory of normative concepts. The normative-naturalistic distinction, I say, applies to concepts, not to properties. Parfit, though, rejects this help I offer non-naturalists as no help but a hindrance.

Note at the outset that if my view is right, then many of the things Parfit says can have at least two quite different interpretations. Parfit speaks of "facts," "claims," and "information." These might be read as structures of concepts, or they might be read as structures of properties. To elucidate these two readings, I set up some terminology. Words can *voice* concepts and *signify* properties or structures consisting of properties, individuals, and the like. Take, for example, Frege's famous story of the Evening Star and the Morning Star. The most ancient Greeks saw the planet Venus in the evening at some times of year and called it Hesperus and saw it in the morning at other times of year, when they called it Phosphorus. It was a great astronomical discovery that they were the same planet. They had, then, two concepts of the same planet and two concepts of the property of being that planet. The phrase "is Hesperus," then, I'll say, *voices* the concept of being Hesperus, and it signifies the property of being Hesperus (that is, of being Venus). I'll write the concept of being Hesperus in small caps as IS HESPERUS, and I'll write the property of being Hesperus in bold italics as *is hesperus*. A *thought* is a concept voiced by a complete sentence. The thought HESPERUS = PHOS-

PHORUS is not the thought HESPERUS = HESPERUS, and the more ancient ancients coherently believed the second without believing the first. A *state of affairs* is what is often called a "Russellian proposition," a structure of properties, individuals, quantification, and the like. The state of affairs of Hesperus being Phosphorus, which I'll write **hesperus = phosphorus**, is just the state of affairs **venus = venus**. In conclusion, then: there is no such thing as plain believing this state of affairs to obtain; one can disbelieve one thought of it and believe another.

Parfit, as I say, rejects the use I make of this framework. If I am right, though, then when Parfit argues in terms of "facts," "claims," and "information," we have to ask whether these are meant to consist in thoughts or in states of affairs, in concepts or in properties. Is the "fact" that Hesperus is Phosphorus different from the fact that Venus is Venus? Are the "claims" different? Do they convey different "information"? Parfit writes in a summary, "According to Non-Analytical Naturalists, any true normative claim states some fact that is both normative and natural. If this fact were natural, it could also be stated by some non-normative claim. If these claims stated the same fact, they would give us the same information." He goes on to speak of being the same fact "in the informational sense" (*OWM*, 337). Suppose, though, the property **good** is the property **pleasurable**. Then with "fact" read as state of affairs, the fact **good = pleasurable** is natural and trivial, but if "information" is read as consisting of thoughts, then different thoughts of this state of affairs capture different information.

I take it that we don't think properties or states of affairs in a direct and unmediated way, so that there is no such privileged thing as *the* thought of a state of affairs. Take the property of being a meter long. As Kripke argued, we can fix the reference of a word or an item in our thinking in various ways to signify this property. "The standard meter bar is one meter long," though contingent, is analytic if the reference of "meter" is fixed rigidly as the length of the standard meter bar, but not if it is fixed in terms of a krypton-86 wavelength. We have two distinct thoughts, then, of the same state of affairs, and one can coherently believe one and disbelieve the other. There's no such thing as plain believing a state of affairs to obtain, and no thought that is *the* thought of the state of affairs **the standard meter bar is one meter long**. Likewise, there is no such thing as plain believing the state of affairs **good** = **pleasurable** to obtain.

"True claims about the *identity* of some property," says Parfit, "use two words or phrases that refer to the same property, and tell us that this property is the same as itself. When that is *all* that such claims tell us, these claims are trivial" (*OWM*, 334). What the statement "Hesperus = Phosphorus" tells us, though, is best understood as the thought it conveys, which is non-trivial and distinct from the thought that Venus is the same as itself. The state of affairs that it signifies, though, involves a single planet. Likewise, if ethical hedonists are right, the statement "good = pleasurable" conveys a non-trivial thought, signifying a state of affairs involving a single property.

Still as Parfit in effect notes (*OWM*, 335–6), with the references of "Hesperus" and "Phosphorus" suitably fixed, the thought we put as "Hesperus = Phosphorus" is a priori equivalent to the thought we put this way: "The brightest heavenly body ever to appear in the evening = the brightest heavenly body ever to appear in the morning." The first is a thought of a necessary state of affairs and the second of a contingent state of affairs, but the two thoughts are a priori equivalent. Indeed any true thought whatever, we can show, will be a priori equivalent to a thought of the state of affairs $1 = 1$. Fix the reference of the name "Charlie" as follows: let it rigidly designate the number 1 if the stock market will rise on the first day of trading in year 2100, and let it rigidly designate 0 otherwise. Then the thought that Charlie = 1 is a thought of the necessary state of affairs $1 = 1$. It is a priori equivalent, though, to the thought that the stock market will rise on the first day of trading in year 2100. What this shows is that the objects to which we give credence are not plain states of affairs, but rather thoughts of states of affairs, where quite different thoughts can be of a single state of affairs and a priori equivalent thoughts can be of vastly different states of affairs.[10]

So is there a framework that is satisfactory and that will fit the things that Parfit says? Russell himself believed that we can think states of

---

[10] Soames reports discussing this with Kripke, though he thinks that the argument can be blocked from reaching this conclusion (*The Age of Meaning* [2003], 410–13). I argue that it can't. See Appendix 1, "The Objects of Thought," in my *Meaning and Normativity* (2012).

affairs in a way unmediated by Fregean senses. In his system, concepts play no role distinct from properties. We can't, though, think the state of affairs **venus = venus**. The things and properties that compose propositions that we can think must be ones with which we are directly acquainted. Seeing Venus in the sky is not a case of direct acquaintance. Indeed, the only elements of propositions with which we can be directly acquainted are our sense data and universals—so thought Russell. Direct reference theorists for Venus and the like also sometimes speak of "acquaintance," but Russell placed a requirement on acquaintance that won't work with Venus: that if we are directly acquainted with a and directly acquainted with b, then we will know whether $a = b$. Ordinary acquaintance with Venus doesn't satisfy this condition. There is a proposition **venus = venus**, on this way of thinking, but we can't think this proposition; we can only describe it.

If Parfit adopts Russell's own views and not the views that these days are called "Russellian," then he can coherently say the things he does. He needs to deny that we can directly think Venus self-identical, since how can we think the identity of Venus with itself in a way that says nothing more? "Hesperus = Venus" says something more, and so names like "Hesperus" and "Venus" contribute more to what is said than just the planet, which is one and the same in the case of both names. The *echt* Russellian view isn't popular these days, but its correctness would make the things Parfit says true and relevant. Since the property **warranted** and the relation **is a reason to** are universals, we can be directly acquainted with them on this view, and they can figure in propositions we can directly think.

If I had adopted this *echt* Russellian framework, I would have had to couch my theory differently from the way I did. My claim would then be that we don't need a "queer" non-natural universal **warranted** with which we are directly acquainted to account for our normative thinking. Once we have attitudes toward non-queer properties like that of packing one's bags and we can agree or disagree with such attitudes and structures of disagreement and the like that involve them, we have a way of thinking that acts the same as our alleged communion with non-natural universals would. So if this is right, we can ask why we should attribute to ourselves this mysterious communion with non-natural universals.

Attitude complexes that are subject to agreement and disagreement would act the same in our lives. I wouldn't then be making my claims in terms of the identity of **good** and the property that makes things good, but I would be explaining how, though there are no non-natural properties, our thinking is as if we thought there were and thought ourselves directly acquainted with them. This legitimates our thinking, even if belief in non-natural properties can't be legitimated. (And when I say that our thinking is legitimate, I am saying something like "Think that way!")

Holding this would not be any form of skepticism with regard to ordinary normative convictions. It would be skeptical of a philosophical theory of what is going on in our normative thinking—the theory that we are directly acquainted with non-natural universals.

4. *Mattering*

According to Parfit, if my view were true, things could only mimic mattering (*OWM*, 408), and there would be nothing to get right as to what matters. On my view, though, since suffering matters, if you say that it does, you get it right, and if you say that it doesn't, you get it wrong. What you've got right or wrong is whether suffering matters. To this I add that in saying that suffering matters, I am saying to care whether there is suffering, and if you believe what I say, you tell yourself to care whether there is suffering. Parfit, to be sure, rejects these additions, but on my view just as much as on his, there is something to get right as to whether suffering matters—namely whether suffering matters.

Parfit says of my 1990 theory in *Wise Choices*, "If there could not be facts or truths about what it is rational to believe, as Gibbard's view implies, it could not be rational to believe anything, including Gibbard's views. This bleak view is close to nihilism" (*OWM*, 409–10). I later gave up my claim that there is some robust sense in which there are no facts or truths as to what is rational. But in *Wise Choices*, too, I maintained that some claims are rational and some are not. It was just that these aren't truths in the robust sense of "true."

Then and now, I hold that many things matter greatly, but their mattering doesn't fit Parfit's account of what mattering amounts to. If Parfit considers me a nihilist or close, I could say the same of him. He fails to agree with what I contend "thinking things to matter" consists in. Thus—so long as I am right in my views—his view isn't consistent with anything's mattering. His view, then, along with a correct view of what it means for something to matter, yields the conclusion that nothing matters, even if some things have the most amazing non-natural properties. In short, on Parfit's view, things matter in Parfit's sense, which he explains, and on my view they don't matter in his sense, whereas on my view, things matter in my sense, which I explain, and on his view they don't matter in my sense. Nihilism is the view that nothing matters in the ordinary sense. Parfit and I both insist that in the ordinary sense, some things matter greatly—though we don't agree on how to explain the ordinary sense.

References

Gibbard, Allan. 1990. *Wise Choices, Apt Feelings: A Theory of Normative Judgment*. Oxford: Oxford University Press.

Gibbard, Allan. 2003. *Thinking How to Live*. Cambridge, MA: Harvard University Press.

Gibbard, Allan. 2008. "Rational Credence and the Value of Truth," in *Oxford Studies in Epistemology*, ed. Tamar Gendler and John Hawthorne. Volume 2. Oxford: Oxford University Press.

Gibbard, Allan. 2012. *Meaning and Normativity*. Oxford: Oxford University Press.

Kahneman, Daniel. 2003. "A Perspective on Judgment and Choice: Mapping Bounded Rationality." *American Psychologist*, 58/9: 697–720.

Scanlon, T. M. 2007. "Structural Irrationality," in *Common Minds: Themes from the Philosophy of Philip Pettit*, ed. G. Brennan, R. Goodin, and M. Smith. Oxford: Oxford University Press.

Soames, Scott. 2003. *Philosophical Analysis in the Twentieth Century*. Volume 2: *The Age of Meaning*. Princeton: Princeton University Press.

4

ALL SOULS' NIGHT

Simon Blackburn

1. *An Analogy*

Although it is Parfit's views about motivation, reasons, and ethics that concern me, I am going to start with a comparison at a little distance from his discussion, and indeed from moral philosophy altogether, in the theory of probability. We return to moral philosophy soon enough.

Single-case probabilities are those of particular events, such as Eclipse winning the 2.30 p.m. race this afternoon, or my dying within the next twelve months. The contrast is with probabilities whose topic is general, and more naturally introduced with the indefinite article: 'the probability of a child being autistic' or 'the probability of a philosophy book weighing over two kilos', for example. Here frequencies provide natural truth-conditions, or truth-makers, but in the single case it is not so easy, and this motivates the pessimistic but plausible view that no satisfactory theory of such probabilities is to be had. Frequencies require sets of events, and putting singular events into sets does not help unless we have a principle for selecting the right sets. Any such principle is in danger of leaving all single-case probabilities at either 0 or 1, although we will usually not know which, or, if the world is indeterministic, leaving them equally unknowable. Hence, probabilists such as Richard von Mises had banned them altogether, and scepticism about the notion—either counselling elimination, or at best an error theory—seemed to be the only scientific course.

And yet outside the philosophy classroom the notion refused to die. Horse races still took place, and bookmakers thrived as before. Discussions about a particular horse's chances filled sporting columns and bars. Insurance companies and actuaries still worked. People made up their minds, or changed them, oblivious to the pained cries of philosophers. So Ramsey, more charitable than von Mises, offered an explanation and vindication of the practices connected with voicing and discussing single-case probabilities. The manifestation, he said, of a sincere judgment of this kind is a distribution of confidence, and that in turn can most easily be regarded as a disposition to buy or sell bets at appropriate prices, under certain idealized conditions.[1] Such dispositions, of course, are not true or false in themselves. But they have what I called a propositional reflection, in the single-case judgment. Thus, if I am inclined to risk \$1 on Eclipse winning the 2.30, in the hope of getting \$2 back if he does, I can voice this disposition by saying that Eclipse's chances are at least 50–50. The disposition is discussable, for it may be that this is a very foolish bet. If you know that Eclipse is off form, or entirely outclassed by the field, or has shown symptoms of equine flu, you may helpfully seek to dissuade me. It is these discussions that fill racecourse bars and the sporting columns and the single-case probability proposition is the focus for them. This is only a sketch of Ramsey's story, but it represented, in my view, a considerable improvement on the error theory of von Mises, or indeed any other proposal on the table.[2] It is naturalistic, explanatory, and justificatory, all in one shot.

Consider now a bookmaker Bill who is worth listening to on his subject. He offers odds more shrewdly than his competitors—that is, while

---

[1] More generally, to incur costs or benefits in acting on the supposition that an event will occur. Thus confidence that a large asteroid will hit the earth shortly would not be manifested in betting on it, since there will never be a chance of collecting on the bet, but it could be manifested in what would otherwise be behaviour to be avoided as too costly, such as spending all one's retirement savings on sex, drugs, and rock 'n' roll.

[2] Of course in 'Truth and Probability' Ramsey does much more. (A) He imposes a logic, showing how the need to avoid being in a state in which you could lose whatever happens implies conforming to the classical probability calculus. (B) He develops a joint theory of value and probability: a way of solving both for a scale of values and a scale of probabilities jointly. (C) He frees up the dispositions in question from even idealized betting, to more general measures of value and belief jointly.

offering better prices than they do, thereby attracting punters, he still makes a nice profit. Bill listens to gossip, looks at gallops, studies form more carefully than, say, a worse bookmaker, Kevin. Bill can offer 100 to 1 against horses like Eclipse, say, and still rake in a profit, although Kevin only dares offer 10 to 1 against it: a worse price, with fewer buyers, netting less profit.

Nevertheless, Bill will not regard himself as infallible. There may be occasions when he kicks himself, not because an outsider won, since the improbable sometimes happens, but because he should have known better. He neglected a possible source of evidence, relied on a stable boy of whose plausibility he should have been more wary, and so on. 'I was wrong', he might say, 'Eclipse's chances were nothing like as bad as I made out'. In other words, Bill has, in thought or talk, a discursive practice of improving and refining his sensitivity to evidence, and thence his dispositions to buy and sell bets, and to make the judgments that are the propositional reflection of those dispositions. Kevin does the same, but is not as good at it as Bill.

In all such thought and discourse, the single-case probability is quite naturally, and quite faultlessly, treated as a topic. But now the single-minded philosopher comes along, and says that this is all very well, but what on Ramsey's theory does the *truth* that Eclipse's chances have one value or another *consist in*? This is not a particularly useful question, for as I discuss below, it is shoehorning a distinctively pragmatic theory about the nature of a practice into one working in terms of truth-conditions, and although pragmatists should not be frightened of talk of truth, it is not the first item on the agenda. If the question is insisted upon, it can get either of two answers. One is the unhelpful homophonic answer: it is true that Eclipse's chances are high if and only if Eclipse's chances are high. Nothing wrong with that. Alternatively, the response might be to point to the evidence—the standards in virtue of which Eclipse is to be regarded as a good bet, or the grounds for his being a good bet: such things as him being fit, trained, healthy, ridden by a champion jockey, and having a better record than the rest of the field. These are not the things that identify the *semantics* of the term—'being ridden by a champion jockey' is no part of the meaning of 'likely to win'. The semantic anchor of the judgment lies in the dispositions that make up the degree of confidence in the event. But these grounds are the kinds of things to which Bill is exquisitely sensitive. Kevin is not.[3]

2. *Applying the Analogy*

We now turn to ethics, where, over many years, I have tried to articulate and defend a parallel position, standing, for instance, to error theorists exactly as Ramsey stood to von Mises.[4] Moral and evaluative propositions are foci for the arguments and thoughts with which men and women discuss, reject, accept, ways of conducting their lives. We urge them on each other in order to change people's practical inclinations: their motivations and concerns, their sense of honour, guilt, and shame, or of what will do and what will not. So now I turn to examples of the things Parfit says, and see how they might sound if we applied them to Ramsey's theory. Since I do not want to put words into Ramsey's mouth, I shall invent a persona, Bramsey, to act as his spokesman.

> Blackburn suggests that such attitudes (moral and conative attitudes) might be mistaken in the sense that we would not have these attitudes if our standpoint were improved in certain ways. But to explain the sense in which this standpoint would be improved, Blackburn would have to claim that, if we had this standpoint, our attitudes would be less likely to be mistaken. This explanation would fail because it would have to use the word 'mistaken' in the sense that Blackburn is trying to explain. (*OWM*, II, 16)

The parallel will be:

---

[3] I am indebted to Jamin Asay for pointing out that it is quite consistent for the expressivist to describe these grounds as 'truthmakers' for the normative or probabilistic judgment, but with a distinctive non-metaphysical account of the truthmaking relation. See Jamin Asay, 'Truthmaking, Metaethics and Creeping Minimalism' in *Philosophical Studies*, 163 (2013): 213–32.

[4] We could expand the discussion to cover not only practical but theoretical reason, and the norms in play governing our conduct of it. But for brevity I shall talk only of practical reason.

Bramsey suggests that betting dispositions might be mistaken in the sense that we would not have these dispositions if our standpoint were improved in certain ways. But to explain the sense in which this standpoint would be improved, Bramsey would have to claim that, if we had this standpoint, our betting dispositions would be less likely to be mistaken. This explanation would fail because it would have to use the word 'mistaken' in the sense that Bramsey is trying to explain.

But Bramsey already explained why Bill is a better bookmaker than Kevin, and why Bill might wish to be better still, and avoid the mistakes he regrets and that trouble his midnight hours. Similarly with ethics. The only asymmetry is that in actual betting the desirability of a particular upshot, winning the bet, is a given, whereas in ethics what counts as desirable is often itself contestable. But just as some people pretty much know what to look for in horses, so too in ethics we have our standards, and scramble about for grounds as best we can. Often enough one fairly uncontroversial improvement for most of us would be becoming better informed. Others might include becoming more sympathetic or imaginative or coherent, or better able to prioritize or select information. So say I, and I hope you do as well.

Parfit, however, believes that expressivists are not entitled to a conception of improvement.[5] They are not to be allowed to use the words 'better than'. When I say that some evaluative opinion is defective, he asks rhetorically 'in what sense are these opinions *bad* rather than merely different from Blackburn's opinions?' (*OWM*, II, 394). Parfit does admit that we have to 'give priority' to our own present point of view (*OWM*, II, 395). But he thinks that he alone can explain 'what it would be' for our present beliefs to be mistaken: 'they would be mistaken if they were false'. Since he also admits that expressivists can say that evaluations are

---

[5] It is not only expressivists, however, whom he might be fighting. Moral sense theorists presumably stand in the dock as well; most of his objections apply as much to writers such as John McDowell and David Wiggins as they do to me. Hume interpreted as a moral sense theorist would not escape Parfit's wrath. In fact expressivism as such might not be itself a sensible target for him, given his relationship to Kant, whose morality of imperatives and law is naturally interpreted as expressivist but who thought that obedience to some imperatives or laws is demanded by pure reason.

false (see below), brandishing this explanation scarcely helps. But in any case anyone should be able to distinguish between saying 'X is bad' and 'X diverges from my view': in my midnight hours I can fear that there are divergences from my view that are not bad, and vice versa, since I have no doubt that I am imperfect, like everyone else.

We all have standards and we all have views about to whom it is worth listening, and the kinds of deployment of information that makes them so. Anyone can be worried that he might be falling short *by those standards* or even *by standards of which he is as yet unaware but which he should be grateful to learn*, but that is not the same as worrying that he might be falling short *in his opinion*. One of his worries might be that his opinion of himself is unduly complacent. But let us push on:

> In defending quasi-realism Blackburn also claims that some apparently external meta-ethical questions are really internal moral questions. That may be so. If we ask expressivists whether it is really true that acts of a certain kind are wrong, they can consistently answer Yes. But we are asking what it would be for conative attitudes and moral judgments to be true or false, correct or mistaken. This is not an internal moral question. Though Blackburn suggests he need not answer this question, that is not so. (*OWM*, II, 16)

> *In defending quasi-realism Bramsey also claims that some apparently external, meta-probabilistic questions are really internal probability questions. That may be so. If we ask expressivists whether it is really true that certain probabilities obtain, they can consistently answer Yes. But we are asking what it would be for betting dispositions and probability judgments to be true or false, correct or mistaken. This is not an internal probabilistic question. Though Bramsey suggests he need not answer this question, that is not so.*

First of all Bramsey never says that betting dispositions are true or false (nor have I ever said that desires or other conative states are true or false).[6] Betting dispositions are not true or false, or in that sense correct

---

[6] Other expressivists may say this. Michael Smith, for instance, favours the idea that moral commitments may belong to the subset of beliefs that are also desires. I prefer to

or mistaken, but in choosing one a person can certainly be foolish and in need of advice. Their propositional reflections, in the judgments that express them, are what may be said to be true or false, correct or mistaken. As with probability judgments Bramsey has the two kinds of account of what this means: he can give the homophonic answer, which ought to be enough by itself, and he can go on to say in virtue of what evidence he makes any particular judgment. I don't believe I have ever 'suggested' that I need not answer the question: I have only suggested that the answer that can easily be given is unlikely to be found interesting.[7]

Parfit is himself in no position to insist that the question 'what would it be' for our judgments to be true or false needs a rich robust answer. When he is not just repeating that they are true or false, the answers he himself gives are no richer or more robust than mine. His own best explanations of 'what it would be' for moral judgments to be true or false consist in restating them in closely equivalent terms. 'What it would be' for something to be wrong, for instance, is that there are decisive reasons against doing it, and so forth. Like talk of things 'meriting disapproval' or 'deserving censure' these are moral claims, voiced from within a particular sensibility. It takes a moral vocabulary to voice them. Hence, as contributions to meta-ethics, they are of no value by themselves.

say that they are practical commitments that are voiced in sentences that naturally take on the clothing of expressions of belief. But nobody says that they are both capable of truth or falsity, and not so capable. Perhaps the combination of seeing a commitment in terms of mental states with a practical direction of fit, and seeing it in terms of a propositional reflection or expression of such a state, is not easy to comprehend at first glance. The parallel problem preoccupied Kant, as he discussed the antinomy of taste in *The Critique of Judgment*. But it would not be an adequate commentary on that great work to write that silly old Kant thought that disinterested pleasure in an object is both incapable of truth (falls under no rule, etc.) and capable of truth (the resolution of the antinomy of taste).

[7] Parfit may have been misled by my allowing that if asked what it is for a value judgment to be true, I am 'not very forthcoming'. But he had, after all, read the entire passage for he later quotes it (*OWM*, II, 398). It says: 'Just as the quasi-realist avoids naturalistic reductions, so he avoids saying *what it is* for a moral claim to be true, except in boring homophonic or deflationary terms. The only answer we should recognize to the question "what is it for happiness to be good?" is happiness being good'. This, far from suggesting that I need not answer the question, answers it.

Similar charges are repeated throughout *OWM*. Rather than go through them one by one, which, although there are further things to correct, would involve a good deal of repetition, I shall stand back a little and offer four mutually supporting diagnoses of what has gone wrong.

3. What Went Wrong

(1) The first is Parfit's bizarre, bipolar, division of the realm of reasons into those that are 'object-given' and those that are 'subject-given' or 'state-given'. This immediately blinds him to the actual structure of Humean theories. The Humean holds, in St. Augustine's lovely phrase, that 'in the pull of the will and of love appears the worth of everything to be sought or avoided, to be thought of greater or less value'. In other words our reaction to what our reason determines to be the facts of the case is also a function of our concerns (passions, desires, inclinations). It is not that we typically attend to our passions or desires, for our beliefs about what we are like do not serve as premises in any kind of inferential process. But the passions themselves are nevertheless determinants of what we prioritize and adopt as reasons for choice or action. They have to be, if reasons are to engage the will. Kantians differ from Hume on this, certainly, but that is no reason for denying Hume his theory, nor is there any serious reason for thinking that Hume is wrong about it. Mill, for example, thought that Kant's attempt to disengage our submission to the categorical imperative from our dislike of how things might go in the worlds where some maxims are made universal was a 'grotesque' failure.

To the Humean, 'object-given' reasons exist, of course. That there is a bull in a field gives me a reason to detour around it. That is because I am rather afraid of bulls. It might only give some young Spanish blood an opportunity to go and pirouette at it. The difference lies in our feelings about bulls, or about danger, or the sources of pride or shame in each of us, or in other words, our different characters and temperaments. There is the same given, but two different ways of receiving the gift. Perhaps Parfit means that there are some things that are reasons for everyone, regardless of their motivational structures. Below, I argue that as a piece of edifying moralizing, this might be true; but as a description of how much we share, simply qua beings who can perceive, infer, and calculate, then in spite of Kant it is false. Aristotle, incidentally is at one with Hume on this, holding both that a person's character determines how the ends of action appear to him, and that the understanding does nothing without desire (*De anima* III 10 433^{a}22–9).[8]

(2) Second, Parfit is ungenerous, to say the least, in the resources he allows to the Humean tradition.[9] He supposes that Hume can only talk, as he constantly does, of policies, precautions, demands, rules, and other elements of practical life being reasonable or not, by forgetting his own views. But that mistakes the entire point of *Treatise* Book II, part III, sec. 3, and equally of Book III, part I, sec. 1. Hume is not concerned there to circumscribe the use of the terms 'reasonable' and 'unreasonable' as terms of approbation or the reverse, but to discover the influencing motives of the will and to locate them partly in our passionate natures.[10] A Humean can perfectly well say that if I become scarlet with rage because someone overtakes me on the motorway, I am unreasonably angry. But he will go on to add that it is my passionate nature that is at fault, not my perception of the road nor my causal inferences, nor my perception of the 'relations of ideas', or in other words my capacity for such things as logic or mathematics, or even my ability to put my maxim through the formula of universal law. This last is especially likely to be impotent, because

[8] Theoretical understanding 'never contemplates what is done in action and says nothing about what is to be avoided or pursued' (*De anima* III 9 432^{b}27–9). I am indebted here to David Reeve's book *Action, Contemplation, and Happiness: An Essay on Aristotle* (Cambridge, MA: Harvard University Press, 2012). Aristotle is at least as sensitive as Hume to the contingent influences of culture and upbringing on any basic human nature.

[9] I give a more detailed analysis of Hume's actual account in 'Hume, Morality and Scepticism', forthcoming in *The Oxford Handbook of David Hume* (ed. Paul Russell).

[10] I believe there is but one sentence in the entire discussion that Hume needed to have amended: 'actions may be laudable or blamable; but they cannot be reasonable or unreasonable...' from the beginning of Book III (*Treatise*, p. 458). But in the context it is clear that he is still talking as an anatomist, not as a moralist. In other words he is still talking of which faculties are in play when we make moral distinctions (more than those of cognition), not about which words we can select to abuse people who do silly things, or commend those who avoid them. For similar reasons a Humean need not be afraid of calling some of Parfit's queer (but under-described) specimens 'irrational', signalling an inability to understand or get on all fours with them, and a conviction that this is not due to them having a superior understanding of anything. I certainly couldn't get on all fours with people who don't care about agony to come on Tuesdays, and so forth. Hume himself never uses 'rational' or 'irrational' in his writings on morals, except in the first sense that the OED gives, to designate creatures capable of using reason, or not.

such a person probably thinks that other people are already just like himself, when they have been provoked as he has just been.

(3) Thirdly, I find it curious that, in a work so concerned, rightly, to distinguish normative from descriptive issues, Parfit disallows Hume or myself, to do the same. Thus, talking of Williams's wife-beater, a character on whom no improving considerations can get a purchase, he imagines me saying 'you have decisive reason to treat your wife better, whether you want to or not', and believes that I can only say this if I withdraw some other claims (*OWM*, II, 458). I cannot imagine what he has in mind. I would prefer to put my distaste at this character by saying '*there is* decisive reason to treat your wife better, whether you want to or not', which makes it slightly clearer that I am moralizing rather than just describing this person's profile of concerns. The decisive reason—the one that should motivate any decent person to desist—is his wife's distress, but this evidently fails to move him. I do not particularly commend the other locution, according to which 'he has decisive reason' since it runs more risk of being taken simply as a false description of this vile agent's psychology, instead of a true evaluation of the matter. The unfortunate locution 'his wife's distress is a reason for him to desist' admits of each reading, one true and one false, and far too much noise in debates about reasons depends upon confusing them.

Parfit then describes my distinction, in *Ruling Passions*, between reasons as described by Humeans and Reasons, with an upper-case 'R', as described by Platonists, Kantians, and intuitionists. He says that I ought to revise my view to claiming that 'there are object-given Reasons. There are some reasons that everyone must acknowledge, whatever their sympathies and inclinations' (*OWM*, II, 459). This, allegedly, would put me 'closer to Hume's real view'. It's particularly hard to follow the train of thought here, since it seems to suggest that really Hume endorsed something approximating to Parfit, or perhaps Plato or Iris Murdoch, celebrating goodness or norms or reasons as primitive realities that 'would give us reasons in the way the sun gives light, "because it is out there, shining down"' (*OWM*, I, 46).[11] I do not think this interpretation will gain many adherents among Hume scholars.

[11] Citing Christine Korsgaard, *Creating the Kingdom of Ends* (Cambridge: Cambridge University Press, 1996), 278.

My own immediate response is that the statement that 'there are some reasons that everyone must acknowledge, whatever their sympathies and inclinations' is not normally taken as a remark about transcendental sunshine. It is usually taken as a moral remark, and one that I naturally applaud, just as I might say, for example, that you must pay your debts if you can, whether you want to or not. I do not advocate letting you off the hook because you don't want to pay. But if it were a descriptive remark, entailing that people must of physical or metaphysical necessity acknowledge some particular things as reasons for some particular behaviours or concerns, from which it follows that they *do* so acknowledge them—whatever their sympathies and inclinations—then it is on the face of it false, and saying so puts me entirely at one with Aristotle and Hume. (If 'acknowledging' a reason includes motivation by it, then my view is also at one with Kant, for not everybody has the dignity that, according to Kant, is manifested when duty triumphs over inclination.)

The ambiguity or slide I am describing is not particularly difficult to spot: 'you cannot be a sensible knave' might be an injunction or plea to someone tempted in that direction, or, much less likely, a crashingly false assertion entailing that a particular option is one that human beings never take. Once more, then, we have a simple confusion between moral assessment of someone's situation, and a description of the psychological elements that actually play a role in motivating them.

(4) The fourth point cuts more deeply philosophically. The pragmatist tradition, of which Ramsey is one example, and expressivism another, takes as its starting point not the 'truth condition' or the 'analysis' of a proposition, but the activities in which it occurs. It is the activity of giving and accepting odds that is Ramsey's focus, and those of voicing admiration and other attitudes that are Hume's focus. If we think, as perhaps 'analytical' philosophers have occasionally thought, that providing analyses and 'accounts' of facts and truths exhausts the business of philosophy, then we shall be blind to the merits of many philosophers, from Berkeley to Wittgenstein. Hume is especially made invisible by this prejudice, both in his writings on moral philosophy, and those on causation. Hume is very little concerned with 'analysis' in the twentieth-century sense, but centrally concerned with the mechanisms of the mind that eventually issue in our making the kinds of judgment we do. He is

often much more nearly a naturalized epistemologist than anything else, and of course his pyromaniac attitude to metaphysics, and that would include 'analytic metaphysics', is always in the background.

A salient example of insensitivity to this tradition comes when Parfit endorses Andy Egan's attempt to land me with *a priori* certainty that my own stable moral beliefs are true.[12] He writes:

> Blackburn might instead reply that, on his view, each of us could still claim to know that our own judgments were true. We can talk of 'knowledge', Blackburn writes, 'if we rule out any possibility that an improvement might occur'. But we cannot turn our judgments into *knowledge* merely by claiming that we could not possibly be mistaken. And people with conflicting judgments might all make such claims. Blackburn's claim would then mistakenly imply that contradictory beliefs could be true, and count as knowledge. (*OWM*, II, 396)

But of course I never dreamed of saying that whenever we talk of knowledge it follows that we are right to do so. For pragmatists and expressivists it is the human *practice* that is the explanandum, and our practice with epistemic vocabulary is, I hold, insightfully described by seeing a claim to knowledge, or the allowing of such a claim, as an evaluation of the remoteness of the possibility that improved positions should undermine confidence—with the consequent removal of motivation to further investigation and inquiry. I think this approach, seeing a claim to knowledge as a kind of stop-valve, is much better than that of post-Gettier 'analyses' of 'truth conditions' for knowledge claims which have spectacularly led nowhere over nearly fifty years.[13] Obviously claims to know things can be false. Inquiries can be closed too early, when further investigation would indeed have reversed a judgment. Seeing someone claiming to know something when in my view it's a very open question

---

[12] Andy Egan, 'Quasi-Realism and Fundamental Moral Error' in *Australasian Journal of Philosophy*, 85/2, 2007: 205–19. My rebuttal is 'Truth and *A Priori* Possibility: Egan's Charge Against Quasi-Realism' in *Australasian Journal of Philosophy*, 87/2, 2009: 201–13, also on the web at <http://www2.phil.cam.ac.uk/~swb24/PAPERS/Egan%20final.htm>.
[13] The work which best explains this is Edward Craig's neglected masterpiece, *Knowledge and the State of Nature* (Oxford: Oxford University Press, 1990).

whether what they claim to know is true, I refuse to allow their claim, precisely because in my view the issue is not closed and further thought or investigation might reverse their verdict. Seeing someone claiming to know that *p* while someone else claims to know that ~*p* then (like anybody else) I can allow that at most one of them is right, or, very often, if they are each sensible enough fellows, that the confidence of each of them is unwarranted, and they are both premature.

4. For Their Own Sake

I have offered these four suggestions in a friendly spirit, as perhaps explaining things that might otherwise remain bewildering in *OWM*. For I confess that on first reading in it my understanding was quite baffled. I could not construe much of Parfit's discussion unless he genuinely believes that 'these people' cannot appeal to reasons at all.[14] Reasons, he appears to think, are his own private property. The rest of us flounder in darkness, cut off from the sunshine beaming down on Parfit. But he himself has written that 'reasons for acting are facts that count in favour of some act'[15]—so does he really believe that Humeans are somehow debarred from looking for, finding, selecting, and prioritizing such facts and features? Can Augustine not take the fact that it is raining as a reason for carrying an umbrella? Or take the fact that its food is inedible as a reason for avoiding a restaurant, or take the fact that it's not a bull but a cow as a reason for relaxing? And so on and so on? Does Parfit really think that Hume and Hare, Williams, Gibbard, and myself, are debarred from the most elementary forms of practical life?[16]

[14] Perhaps he has been lulled into this view by works such as Christine Korsgaard's 'Skepticism about Practical Reason' in *The Journal of Philosophy*, 83/1, 1986: 5–25, or Elijah Millgram's 'Was Hume a Humean' in *Hume Studies*, 21, 1995: 75–94. But neither Hume nor Humeans are sceptical about practical reason; they give highly plausible accounts of it. They are at most sceptical about *pure* practical reason, which is a different thing altogether. Even in Korsgaard's view what she calls 'content skepticism' about pure practical reason is a formidably plausible position.

[15] D. Parfit, 'Reason and Motivation', in *Proceedings of the Aristotelian Society, Supplementary Volume* 71, 1997: 121.

[16] One of the commentators in *OWM*, Allen Wood, evidently does, holding that Humeans are 'either radically defective specimens of humanity who are incapable of feeling respect for anyone or anything, or else every time they do feel it they commit themselves to

Perhaps he does. He repeats many things along these lines: Blackburn (or Gibbard) cannot appeal to value-based, object-given facts about the objects of desire since 'we have no reason' to want certain things for their own sake. The phrase is a bit off-key, since if I want something for its own sake, I typically need not have some other reason for wanting it. Waiving that for a moment, I am certainly happy wanting some things for their own sake. I want the welfare of my children for its own sake, not for the sake of anything else, such as their ability to support me in old age or annually to put flowers on my grave. And the question of whether my children are happy or flourishing is 'object-given' in any sense I can imagine to matter—it is a question of how things stand with my children—while the fact that it matters to me as much as it does is a fact about my values, sentiments, and concerns. The fact that the welfare of my children matters little to Parfit is a fact about his. Playing along with Parfit's terminology I suppose I might say that my reason for cherishing them is object-given sure enough—but only given to a certain kind of subject, of which I am one and he is not.

Do I have a reason for wanting the welfare of my children for its own sake? As I say, the question is more than a bit off colour—if I want it for its own sake why should I need to scramble around for a reason? Wouldn't another reason mistake the phenomenon, distracting my thoughts from where they paternally and kindly rest, which is on my children's welfare? But I certainly think I am reasonable in wanting it. I am unlikely to admit criticism of any movement of mind that has led me to wanting it.[17] It is not as if I feel ashamed of my care and concern. I wouldn't want to lose it, or to allow an unusually mad Kantian or Stoic or Buddhist therapist to try to take it away.[18]

contradicting their own metaethical theories' (*OWM*, II, 62). I find it sad that this radically defective specimen of writing should have been passed to appear in a book with a reputable publisher. If we descend to this, what sermon might I not preach on those who think their own attitudes but reflect the instructions of the universe, and what circle of hell should be reserved for philosophers who weave fantasies encouraging them to think that this may indeed be so?

[17] The importance of this concept is developed in my paper 'The Majesty of Reason' first published in *Philosophy*, 85, 2010: 5–27 and reprinted in *Practical Tortoise Raising* (Oxford: Oxford University Press, 2010), 283–307.
[18] I am aware that many current defences of Kant ignore the bits about inclinations, including sympathy and warm-hearted fellow feeling, being burdensome, and things it

5. A Misreading and a Log-Jam

I shall end by drawing attention to two other issues. The first is quite short, and the second more interesting. The short one is that Parfit quotes me as saying that inconsistent desires (that is, desires that cannot both be realized) 'can be faultlessly inconsistent' (*OWM*, II, 391) and says that this stands in conflict with the use I make of 'desire or other conative states' when I develop quasi-realism, which, of course, requires me to see people as disagreeing with each other in moral judgments. Alas, I am impenitent. I only said that desires *can* be faultlessly inconsistent. And I had in mind only impractical desires—ones at the same end of the spectrum as idle wishes. Here is the footnote from which Parfit extracts the saying:

> One reason why I do not think 'desire' is a good response to work with is that evaluation is an activity that imposes norms of consistency whereas, in their less practical manifestations, desires can be faultlessly inconsistent. It is only when we come to do something about them that we have to tidy them up.[19]

I find it almost incomprehensible that Parfit could miss the clear point of this footnote, much expanded throughout the book.[20] The point was that the attitudes that gain expression in moral and evaluative discussion are typically more than 'mere' desires, although of course sharing their practical direction of fit. This is why I preferred the word 'concern' and emphasized that expressing a concern or attitude is putting something into public space for acceptance or rejection. Morality is centrally focused on the social world. It is about what *we* are to choose, condemn,

would be blissful to shed. However see *Critique of Practical Reason*, trans. L. W. Beck (New York: Macmillan, 1956), 122–3.

[19] *Ruling Passions* (Oxford: Oxford University Press, 1998), 118, footnote.

[20] In the Introduction to *Spreading the Word* I wrote that in my opinion too few philosophers framed the golden words of Quintilian, the Roman rhetorician, above their desks: 'Do not write so that you can be understood, but so that you cannot be misunderstood'. On a subsequent occasion Bernard Williams protested to me that this was an unrealistic aim: one can always be misunderstood, and there may often be deep psychological forces making it almost impossible for some people to understand you. This is indeed so, and this particular part of *OWM* sensitized me, not to the impropriety of Quintilian's ideal, but to the just pessimism of Williams's reservation.

encourage, avoid, forbid, and insist upon. Hume, of course, realized that this need to coordinate on a 'common point of view' was the essential core of morality, explaining why we had impersonal terms of approbation or disapproval in the first place.[21] And secondly, the whole point of having the moral proposition, the reflection of our practical stances, as a focus for discussion, is to enable us to make public these things. Its function is to further coordination. And then disagreement comes in.

Suppose, to take a simple example, that my wife prefers hill-walking to sailing, and I prefer sailing to hill-walking. Our desires are different but there is no disagreement. However, if we are both to take a holiday together, then plans reflecting those preferences are inconsistent; we have to do something about it, and we may well disagree what it is. Gibbard's gerundive judgments 'hill-walking is the thing to do' or 'sailing is the thing to do' are the focus for the attempt to coordinate and reconcile our preferences. That is what the propositional judgment is *for*. When it is a moral issue rather than one of whim or taste, we enter the territory of shame and guilt, anger and resentment. We are further up the scale of importance where coordination matters more. One of our concerns might be never to do one thing or another, and then we conceive of ourselves as being under a necessity. But it is we who put on the yoke of necessity, as the Chorus so perceptively said of Agamemnon.[22] Ajax, having slaughtered only sheep, felt he had no alternative but to kill himself, whereas anyone of lesser mettle might have put up with the other heroes' sniggering, and a sufficiently barefaced anti-hero might have gone on insisting that they weren't sheep but men.

Parfit is fond of saying that headaches cannot conflict, or be mistaken or unsoundly based (*OWM*, II, 393ff.). But neither are they subject to discursive pressure, from our own thoughts or those of others, and nor are they matters on which coordination is an issue. Plans often are. Parfit pillories Gibbard for allegedly implying that they all are, which he can then refute with Buridan's ass cases, in which planning to go for one bale of straw does not imply disagreeing with, or rejecting as bad, a previous plan to go to the other. But all Gibbard needs to do is section those off,

[21] David Hume, *Enquiry Concerning the Principles of Morals*, 9.1.
[22] Aeschylus, *Agamemnon*, l. 217.

and talk of the same kinds of publicly expressed, gerundively girded plans that require coordination, perhaps unanimity, and resolution in standing by them. When we start to reach for normative vocabulary, we signal that this is what we are about.

The last thing on which I want to comment is one where I am in the dock with unusually large and distinguished company, including Hare, Williams, Korsgaard, Nowell-Smith, and Gibbard.[23] These writers have each charged, as Hume did in the sections I mentioned above, that rational intuitionism fails to engage with the practical nature of ethics. But Parfit cannot see that there is a problem. Suppose there is a moral judgment which we accept, to the effect that we ought to do something. These writers fear that on a purely rationalist or cognitivist account a gap opens up: we might accept the judgment, but what then? Parfit construes us as asking whether we *should* take account of the judgment. But, he complains, this is asking whether we should do what we should do—and that is hardly an open question. Hence rationalism's critics cannot frame a question that is not answered by the same cognitive judgment that is already premised.

This is not the way to understand the dialectic. If it were, we would indeed have an odd kind of standoff. The critics fear a gap between cognition and practice. Parfit replies with another cognition. He sees this as answering any question they intend to ask; they see it as just more of the same, leaving as big a gap as before.

To undo this log-jam we should interpret the critics differently. They intend to ask how, on the cognitivist view, motivation and cognition are related. And to make the question pointed, let us phrase it more carefully in this form: could there be a society with impeccable cognitions, ones that pick out just the right 'normative reasons' or 'object-given reasons', but whose awareness of these (including their awareness that they are reasons) do *not* engage with any motivations: any concerns, desires, attitudes, endorsements, or feelings? The answer, such critics feel, ought to be that there could not. In the absence of at least some incipient motivations the 'cognitions' could not be construed as making the morality of the society. They require other interpretation. But Parfit's iterated

---

[23] The discussion of 'the normative argument' occupies *OWM*, II, 413–25.

'should's do not get him so far. Their direction of fit remains, in his eyes, representational, and he can provide no necessary connection with *any* states of mind with the motivational direction. All he will be able to say, in tackling this question, remains in the sphere of cognitions. Our thoughts, so pure and elevated, turn to the sun, revolve in the light of the sun, bask in goodness which, like mathematics, lies far above our contingent concerns and desires, passions and motivations. Affect has not been invited in. Of course, Parfit and other realists of his stamp may plead and cajole that we *make* these transcendental celestial cognitions practical. But on the rational intuitionist account it remains logically possible (and on the face of it, quite likely since it is the natural world of people and pleasures and pains that fills our attention) that nobody listens, in spite of their having the most perfect repertoire of moral judgments that they sincerely accept. And if nobody listens, then their motivations may be totally and blithely orthogonal to their cognitions. They have moral understandings, but across the board these are completely inert. It is the fact that his intuitionism opens *this* possibility that the critics with whom I am numbered rightly condemn.[24]

I have, perhaps selfishly, concentrated upon elements in *OWM* which particularly grated on my ears. If this means that I have sounded too self-centred, I apologize. My excuse is only that I think I speak for a significant number of scholars, philosophers, and psychologists, who look with some bemusement at the direction of contemporary meta-ethics. Why it has taken this turn must be a question for sociologists rather than philosophers, for we deal only with the arguments, and these, unfortunately, seem to offer no explanation.[25]

[24] Similar remarks apply to Scanlon's discussion of the issue of practicality, in Chapter 3 of *Being Realistic about Reasons*. Like Parfit Scanlon reinterprets the critics as bothered about the 'authority' of reasons. But it is the explanatory question, of why apprehension of a primitive non-natural property or relation is ever motivating for ordinary, natural, flesh-and-blood animals like ourselves, that is the issue. Why do we care about primitive transcendental (but not ontological, apparently) sunshine? It is no good answering this question by saying 'well we *should* care about it', if the *should* simply describes more sunshine.

[25] I owe thanks to Jonathan Bennett, Kate Manne, Peter Godfrey-Smith, Michael Smith, Valerie Tiberius, and David Wiggins for initial encouragement, and to Jamie Dreier, Rae Langton, Michael Gill, Robert Johnson, and other participants at a Reasons roundtable in Chapel Hill in December 2011 for valuable discussion.

5

PARFIT'S MISTAKEN META-ETHICS

Michael Smith

In the first volume of *On What Matters*, Derek Parfit defends a distinctive meta-ethical view, a view that specifies the relationships he sees between reasons, facts, beliefs, desires, aims, actions, and values. Parfit's meta-ethical view is a version of what he calls 'Objectivism', and he explicitly argues not just for his preferred version of Objectivism, but against all versions of Subjectivism, the meta-ethical view with which Objectivism is contrasted. Parfit's arguments for Objectivism, and his criticisms of Subjectivism, seem to me to be mistaken, so my aim is to identify where the mistakes lie. Though I do not expect Parfit to agree with me that the mistakes I identify are mistakes, I proceed on the assumption that this does not matter. The best we can do when we engage with philosophers like Parfit, whose detailed meta-ethical views are part and parcel of a comprehensive worldview with mutually supporting parts, is to state very carefully where our fundamental disagreements with them lie.

1. Reasons Fundamentalism and Reasons for Belief

At the very beginning of *On What Matters*, Parfit tells us:

> We can have reasons to believe something, to do something, to have some desire or aim, and to have many other attitudes and emotions,

such as fear, regret, and hope. Reasons are given by facts, such as the fact that someone's finger-prints are on some gun, or that calling an ambulance would save someone's life.

It is hard to explain the *concept* of a reason, or what the phrase 'a reason' means. Facts give us reasons, we might say, when they count in favour of our having some attitude, or our acting in some way. But 'counts in favour of' means roughly 'gives a reason for'. Like some other fundamental concepts, such as those involved in our thoughts about time, consciousness, and possibility, the concept of a reason is indefinable in the sense that it cannot be helpfully explained merely by using words. We must explain such concepts in a different way, by getting people to think thoughts that use these concepts. One example is the thought that we always have a reason to want to avoid being in agony. (Parfit, 2011: 31)

This is Parfit's first introduction of the underlying idea he defends and relies on throughout his discussion of meta-ethics in *On What Matters*, an idea that we might call 'Reasons Fundamentalism'.

According to Reasons Fundamentalism, there is a fundamental metaphysical relation that holds between facts, on the one hand, and beliefs, desires, aims, and actions, on the other. This relation holds when the fact in question gives a reason for the belief, desire, aim, or action. The relation is metaphysically fundamental, or so the suggestion goes, because we cannot define what it is for a fact to give a reason for some belief, desire, aim, or action, in terms of other facts; we cannot analyze the concept of a fact's giving a reason for some belief, desire, aim, or action, in terms of other concepts; we cannot reduce the property of giving a reason for some belief, desire, aim, or action, to some other property; and so on. (In what follows I will not fuss about the differences between real definition, conceptual analysis, and metaphysical reduction.) In particular, we cannot analyze the reasons relation in terms of subjective psychological concepts. Reasons Fundamentalism is thus Parfit's preferred version of Objectivism.

Reasons Fundamentalism provides the foundation for all of Parfit's meta-ethical views. But how plausible is the idea that the relation of 'being a reason for' is unanalyzable? Focus on reasons for belief. Parfit tells us that the reasons relation that holds between a fact that provides a reason for believing and belief is unanalyzable. But I doubt very much that that is so. Though the idiom isn't Hume's, we can understand Hume's famous endorsement of *deductive* reasoning, and attack on *inductive* reasoning, as tantamount to the suggestion that we can analyze the reasons relation in the case of belief, and hence the concept of reasoning as well, insofar as reasoning is a matter of updating our beliefs. The analysis, according to Hume, is to be given in terms of, *inter alia*, the concept of *entailment* (Hume, 1740). 'The fact that *p*' provides a reason for believing a proposition *q*, Hume seems to have thought, if and only if and because *p entails q*. Correspondingly, someone engages in reasoning to the extent that he treats propositions as though they stand in entailment relations to each other.

Hume's view is, of course, much maligned, but what's maligned isn't the background assumption that we can analyze the concept of a fact's being a reason for belief in other terms. What's maligned is rather his restrictive tying of the concept of a reason for belief to the concept of entailment—his elevation of deductive reasoning over inductive reasoning. If we reject this Humean idea, and extend our concept of a reason to include cases where certain facts provide evidence for the truth of other propositions, without entailing them, then we might suppose instead that the analysis of a reason is to be given in terms of some more liberal theory about the nature of belief that specifies the conditions under which even inductively formed beliefs count as knowledge. Reasons for beliefs would then be the considerations that provide the justifications for our beliefs in such cases.

What would such a theory look like? It would be a theory in which our concept of a reason for belief is our concept of evidence for the truth of what we believe when our beliefs count as knowledge. Such a theory would presumably draw on the theory of perception, on the one hand, and the theory of epistemic rationality, on the other, and drawing on the latter might in turn require us to draw on confirmation theory, the theory of statistical reasoning, the probability calculus, and so on. Here is not the place to go into details, and, to be perfectly honest, I am not sure how the details should be given. But the very fact that we have Hume's own reductive theory of reasons for belief in terms of entailment as a model, together with the fact that we can specify the materials in terms of which an alternative to Hume's theory might be given, makes the idea that we should embrace Reasons Fundamentalism, at least in the case of reasons for belief, premature to say the least. We should proceed on the assumption that the concept of a reason for belief can be analyzed.

This conclusion has far-reaching consequences. Parfit gives us no reason at all to think that the concept of a reason, in the case of reasons for belief, is unanalyzable, and since we have good reason to proceed on the assumption that the concept can be analyzed, this provides us with excellent reasons to reject Reasons Fundamentalism more generally. For how could the concept of a reason for a desire, or an aim, or an action, be metaphysically fundamental, if the concept of a reason for belief is not? That could be so only if the concept of a reason were itself a disjunction of something fundamental and something non-fundamental, where the disjuncts have nothing whatsoever in common with each other. The concept of a reason would be a ragbag, like the concept of a-number-or-a-dog. On the plausible assumption that our concept of a reason isn't such a ragbag, the only conclusion to draw, at least *pro tem*, is that Reasons Fundamentalism is quite generally false. The concept of a reason is the concept of a reason for belief, a concept that we can analyze. The only questions left to ask are how many reason concepts we can define in terms of the concept of a reason for belief, and what exactly those analyses are.

This is how Hume saw things. Armed with a reductive conception of reasons for belief in terms of entailment, he thought that we can give a straightforward analysis of the concept of a reason for having certain of our desires. The concept of a reason for an instrumental desire, Hume thought, reduces to the concept of a reason for belief because instrumental desires are complex psychological states that have means-end beliefs and non-instrumental desires as parts. The concept of a reason for an instrumental desire is therefore just the concept of a reason for the means-end belief part. But since non-instrumental desires do not have beliefs as parts—Hume thought that belief and non-instrumental desires were distinct existences (more on this in §4)—it follows that there is no concept of a reason for having non-instrumental desires. Of course, we might have qualms about Hume's line of reasoning. In particular, we might wonder whether we should follow him in supposing that having a reason to have the belief part of an instrumental desire suffices for having a reason for the instrumental desire itself, given that it has another part, a non-instrumental desire, for which there is no reason at all. But his basic philosophical instincts seem to be right. Either we can reduce the concept of a reason for desire to a reason for belief or the concept of a reason has no application to desires.

For his part, Parfit thinks that Hume's view is plainly wrong. It is wrong, Parfit thinks, because it is inconsistent with the obvious truth that 'we always have a reason to want to avoid being in agony'. But while it may well be true that we always have a reason to want to avoid being in agony, if the concept of a reason in play isn't a ragbag, then that concept must somehow reduce to the concept of a reason for belief. The question to ask is how that reduction might go.

2. *Reasons for Action*

The question on the table is whether we can reduce the concept of a reason for desire—both instrumental desire and non-instrumental desire— and the concept of a reason for aims, and actions as well, to the concept of a reason for belief. This question will prove much more tractable if we start by asking a more modest question. Can we reduce any of these reason concepts to other concepts?

Though in the passage quoted earlier, Parfit seems to suggest that the concept of a reason for action is just like the concept of a reason for belief, desire, or attitude, and so fundamental, a little further in *On What Matters*, we seem to be told that this is not so.

> According to Objectivists, though many reasons for acting can be claimed to be given by the fact that some act would achieve one of our aims, these reasons *derive their force* from the facts that give us reasons to *have* these aims. (Parfit, 2011: 45, emphasis in original)

Thus, for example, though my reason for typing these words is the fact that typing them will achieve my aim of writing a paper about *On What*

Matters, Parfit thinks that this reason derives its force from my reason to have the aim of writing a paper about *On What Matters*. If there were no reason for me to have this aim, I would have no reason to type these words. But since every action is performed with some aim, and since in every such case the force of the reason provided by the fact that the action would achieve the aim derives from the reason to have the aim, it follows that, at least on the assumption that no other reasons for action are in the offing—more on this presently—reasons for action are not fundamental. The concept of a reason for action is just the concept of a reason for having the aim of performing that action. Parfit has 'helpfully explained merely by using words' what the concept of a reason for action is after all.

Nor should we be surprised by this result. Parfit's Reasons Fundamentalism shares much in common with Scanlon's Reasons Fundamentalism, and Scanlon says quite explicitly in *What We Owe To Each Other* that the class of things 'for which reasons can sensibly be asked or offered' is a sub-class of mental states that he calls the 'judgment-sensitive attitudes', and that there are therefore reasons for action only because reasons for action are analyzable in terms of reasons for judgment-sensitive attitudes (Scanlon, 1998: 20). Here are the relevant passages.

Scanlon tells us that judgment-sensitive attitudes are those

> ... that an ideally rational person would come to have whenever that person judged there to be sufficient reasons for them, and that would, in an ideally rational person, 'extinguish' when that person judged them not to be supported by reasons of the appropriate kind. (Scanlon, 1998: 20)

These include intention, hope, fear, admiration, respect, contempt, indignation, and desire (Scanlon, 1998: 20–1). Since actions are not a kind of attitude, he wonders whether this casts doubt on the idea that the class of judgment-sensitive attitudes is the class of things for which reasons can sensibly be asked and offered, and he answers as follows:

> A reason for doing something is almost always a reason for doing it intentionally, so 'reason for action' is not to be contrasted with 'reason for intending'. The connection to action, which is essential to

intentions, determines the kinds of reasons that are appropriate for them, but it is the connection with judgment-sensitive attitudes that makes events actions, and hence the kind of things for which reasons can sensibly be asked for and offered at all. (Scanlon, 1998: 21)

In other words, though there are reasons for actions, that is only because the concept of a reason for action reduces to the concept of a reason for having an intention. Assuming that the states Scanlon calls 'intentions' are just what Parfit calls 'aims', it therefore follows that Scanlon and Parfit think alike. They both think that reasons for actions reduce to, or are analyzable in terms of, reasons for aims. Reasons for action are not fundamental for either Parfit or Scanlon.

It is worth pausing to say something about the exceptions Scanlon hints at in saying that a reason for doing something is 'almost always' a reason for doing it intentionally. What are the cases in which a reason for doing something isn't a reason for doing it intentionally, and hence isn't a reason for having some aim? I take it that the cases he has in mind are those in which we have reasons for (say) spontaneously squawking like a chicken. The fact that it would be amusing to spontaneously squawk like a chicken in certain circumstances is, let's suppose, a reason for spontaneously squawking like a chicken in those circumstances. But what's important about this reason is that, contrary to what's just been said, it cannot be reduced to a reason to intend to spontaneously squawk like a chicken, for the simple reason that it is impossible to intend to do something spontaneously. Intentions are states whose role is to lead us to do the thing that figures in their content. Since no one could spontaneously squawk like a chicken by acting on their intention to spontaneously squawk like a chicken, as the content of the intention would undermine the spontaneity of the act, it follows that when one spontaneously squawks like a chicken, though one must have some intention or other, the spontaneity has to appear in the acquisition or execution of the intention, not in its content.

These exceptions show something important about our concept of a reason for action. They show that we must distinguish very sharply between two cases in which one has reasons for action. In one case, reasons for action reduce to reasons to desire to act in certain ways, where you could come to act in those ways because you have the relevant desire. Most cases are like this, and cases in which reasons for action reduce to reasons for having intentions are, we might now suppose, a sub-class of these: intentions are just a sub-class of such desires. My reason for typing these words is a case in point, as my reason for typing these words reduces to my reason for desiring to write a paper about *On What Matters*, and what I desire to do, in this case, is something that I could do because I have this very desire. I could type these words, so writing a paper about *On What Matters*, because I desire to write a paper about *On What Matters*. The desire either is, or is a component of, the intention.

In the alternative kind of case, however, reasons for action reduce to reasons to desire to act in certain ways, but it isn't possible for you to come to act in those ways by acting on the relevant desire. The reason you have to spontaneously squawk like a chicken is of this kind. The fact it would be amusing is, let's agree, a reason for having a *desire* that one spontaneously squawks like a chicken—one can, after all, desire that one spontaneously squawks like a chicken, notwithstanding the fact that one cannot intend to do so—but, given that spontaneity figures in the content of this desire, it isn't the case that one could come to spontaneously squawk like a chicken by acting on this very desire. So though most reasons for action reduce to reasons for intending, which are just desires of a certain kind, some reasons for action reduce to reasons for desiring where the desires are not of that kind. We will return to this idea again shortly (§3), where it will emerge that reasons for action quite generally reduce to facts about the *desirability* of acting in the relevant ways.

Let me sum up. Though Parfit is right that we talk about 'reasons to believe something, to do something, to have some desire or aim, and to have many other attitudes and emotions', even he admits that only some of this talk is talk about the fundamental relation of being a reason for. Some of it is not. Our talk of reasons for action is a case in point, as Parfit thinks that the concept of a reason for action can be analyzed in terms of the concept of reasons for desires and aims. But once we have this conclusion firmly before our minds, a good question to ask is whether we can do for reasons for desires, aims, and other attitudes what we have just seen can be done for reasons for action. Just as reasons for action reduce to reasons for desires and aims, might reasons for desires and aims reduce to reasons for belief? If so, then on the assumption that we can fully reduce the concept of a reason for belief in the way suggested at the outset, the upshot would be that we can fully reduce the concept of a reason.

3. *Reasons for Desires, Aims, and Other Attitudes*

The question on the table this time is whether we can reduce the concept of a reason for desire, aims, and other attitudes to the concept of a reason for belief. Judith Jarvis Thomson offers what seems to me to be the most promising answer to this question in her *Normativity* (2008).

Thomson's answer starts with an observation about the correctness conditions of a variety of mental states. Many different mental states have *correctness* conditions, Thomson notes, where these conditions can be informally understood as those in which the mental states in question are *deserved* (Thomson, 2008: 116). Not all kinds of mental states can be deserved. There is, for example, no circumstance in which feeling dizzy can be deserved, so feeling dizzy has no correctness condition. But mental states of other kinds can be deserved, so they do have correctness conditions. Thomson illustrates this idea by focusing on the case of belief.

> A believing is a correct believing just in case its propositional content is true. Thus a believing is not marked as a correct believing by the fact that the believer's other beliefs lend weight to, or even entail, the propositional content of his believing. Smith's believing P is not marked as a correct believing by the fact that it is rational in him to believe P. Whether a believing is a correct believing is an objective, not a subjective, matter. (Thomson, 2008: 116)

Believing that *p* is thus supposed to be correct just in case *p*, as its being the case that *p* is the condition under which the belief that *p* is deserved. Moreover, according to Thomson, a similar line of thought reveals that other mental states have correctness conditions too. For example, *trustworthy people* are deserving of trust, so trustworthy people figure in the correctness condition of trust; *admirable objects and people* are deserving of admiration, so admirable objects and people figure in the correctness condition of admiration; *desirable objects and states of affairs* are deserving of desire, so desirable objects and states of affairs figure in the correctness condition of desire; and so on.

With the idea of the correctness conditions of various mental states in place, Thomson proceeds to ask what it is for there to be *reasons for* being in some mental state. Her answer to this question comes in two parts. In the first part, she insists that we can give an independent characterization of what it is for something to be a reason for believing. Reasons for believing are, she tells us, considerations that provide 'evidence for', or that 'make probable', or that 'lend weight to' the truth of the propositions believed (Thomson, 2008: 130). As I understand it, Thomson's suggestion here is in the same spirit as the earlier suggestion that we can analyze the concept of a reason for believing in terms drawn from the theory of perception and the theory of epistemic rationality. The crucial point, in other words, isn't her specific proposal about what these terms are, but rather her acknowledgement that we can analyze the concept of a reason for belief in other terms. Equipped with an analysis of what reasons for believing are, the second part of Thomson's answer comes in the form of a quite general analysis of reasons for being in a mental state that has a correctness condition. A consideration is a reason for being in a mental state that has a correctness condition, she tells us, just in case that consideration is evidence for, or makes probable, or lends weight to, the truth of the proposition that is that mental state's correctness condition (Thomson, 2008: 131).

How plausible is Thomson's quite general analysis of reasons for being in mental states with correctness conditions? Assuming, for the sake of argument, that she gets the specifics of the analysis of reasons for belief right, it certainly does seem to be plausible. For, on that assumption, reasons for belief are considerations that lend weight to the truth of the proposition believed, as the truth of the proposition believed is the correctness condition of belief; reasons for trust are considerations that lend weight to the truth of the proposition that the person trusted is trustworthy, as the truth of the proposition that the person trusted is trustworthy is the correctness condition of trust; reasons for admiration are considerations that lend weight to the truth of the proposition that the object of admiration is admirable, as the truth of the proposition that the admired object is admirable is the correctness condition of admiration; and reasons for desire are considerations that lend weight to the truth of the proposition that the desired object is desirable, as the truth of the proposition that the object of desire is desirable is the correctness condition of desire.

Note that we can now better understand what was going on in the case of reasons for action. We saw earlier that Scanlon thinks that reasons for action reduce to reasons for desire, where the desires in question might or might not be desires to act in ways that one could act by acting on those very desires: in other words, the desires might or might not be, or be components of, intentions. But now that we have the quite general analysis of reasons before us, it turns out that reasons for action can all be seen to reduce, at an even more fundamental level, to reasons for believing that acting in the relevant way is desirable. In most cases, we are able to act in the way that is desirable by acting on the desire that there is a reason for having, and in these cases, we can say that reasons for action reduce not just to reasons for believing that acting in the relevant way is desirable, but that they also reduce to corresponding reasons for intentions. The reason to write a paper about *On What Matters* is a case in point. But in other cases, though our reasons for action reduce to reasons for believing that acting in the relevant way is desirable, and though there are reasons to desire that we act in the relevant way, these reasons are not reasons for having corresponding intentions, because there are no corresponding intentions. The reason to spontaneously squawk like a chicken is a case in point.

Let's take stock. What's especially important about Thomson's quite general analysis of reasons for being in mental states with correctness conditions is that it tells us that and why:

> (General Thesis) All reasons-for are reasons for believing (Thomson, 2008: 130)

is true, and hence why reasons for belief, trust, admiration, desire, aims, actions, and so on are all of a kind. They are all of a kind because reasons for belief reduce in the way we suggested at the outset, and reasons for mental states with correctness conditions other than belief are reasons in virtue of satisfying the very same condition that reasons for belief satisfy:

that is, they are reasons in virtue of being considerations that support the truth of the proposition that is the relevant mental state's correctness condition. What's especially important about Thomson's quite general analysis of reasons for being in mental states with correctness conditions is thus that it tells us that and why the concept of a reason isn't a disjunction of something fundamental and something non-fundamental: it tells us that and why the concept isn't a ragbag. This is a major advance.

4. *The Analysis of Value*

So far I have been talking as though Thomson's suggestion that there are reasons not just for beliefs, but also for trust, admiration, and desire, is completely unproblematic. I have done this because I have been assuming both that she is right that these mental states have correctness conditions, and that her general analysis of what it is for there to be reasons for mental states with correctness conditions is along the right lines, as it provides us with the guarantee we need that the concept of a reason isn't a ragbag. There is, however, a residual puzzle.

Why do trust, admiration, and desire, have, as their correctness conditions, the trustworthiness of the person trusted, the admirability of the admired object, and the desirability of the desired object? Without an answer to these questions, we don't yet fully understand why there are reasons for trust, admiration, and desire. These questions become especially urgent when we realize that certain answers we might plausibly give, in at least some of these cases, don't readily extend to other cases. For example, the trustworthiness of the person trusted, and the admirability of the admired object, might be correctness conditions of trust and admiration because trusting someone and admiring something are, *inter alia*, a matter of believing that the person trusted is trustworthy, and believing that the admired object is admirable. But though this would certainly suffice to explain why trust and admiration have the correctness conditions that they do, the explanation proffered would not extend to the case of non-instrumental desire. It would not extend because it is manifestly implausible to suppose that non-instrumentally desiring something is, *inter alia*, a matter of believing that the desired object is non-instrumentally desirable. Quite in general, for reasons

Hume appreciated all too well (§1), non-instrumental desires do not have beliefs as parts. Beliefs and non-instrumental desires are distinct existences, as for any non-instrumental desire and belief pair, there is a possible world in which someone has the one, but lacks the other, and *vice versa* (Smith, 1987, 1988).

So let's confront what seems to me to be the core of the puzzle head-on. Why does desire have, as its correctness condition, the desirability of the desired object? Is there some Objectivist theory of desirability that provides us with the needed answer? Thomson herself thinks that goodness is an *attributive*: the kinds of thing that are judged to be good determine the standards for things of those kinds, and hence to judge things of a kind 'good', she thinks, is just to say that they meet those standards. A good toaster is one that evenly warms and browns bread without burning it; a good burglar is one who enters buildings from which he is prohibited entry and leaves again without getting caught; a good move in chess is one that efficiently contributes towards checkmating, or failing that, drawing with, one's opponent; and so on. Attributive goodness is thus an Objectivist conception. Might the concept of desirability just be the concept of attributive goodness? Would this explain why desire has the desirability of the desired object as it correctness condition?

The answer is that it would not. Consider the kind: *next move for a burglar to make in certain circumstances*. There might well be considerations that lend weight to the truth of the proposition that a good next move for a burglar to make in certain circumstances would be to (say) lie to the security guard. But this doesn't entail that there are reasons for the burglar to desire to do that, or reasons for us to desire that we do that if we find ourselves in the burglar's circumstances, or reasons for us to desire that the burglar does that, or indeed reasons for anyone else to desire anything either. There seems to be no connection at all between reasons for believing that something is attributively good and reasons to have desires concerning those things. The concept of desirability in play when we suppose that desire has the desirability of the desired object as its correctness condition thus isn't the concept of attributive goodness.

Is there some other version of Objectivism that provides the needed answer? In *On What Matters*, Parfit offers his own Objectivist theory of goodness. He tells us that when we call something

> good, in what we can call the *reason-implying* sense, we mean roughly
> that there are certain kinds of fact about this thing's nature, or prop-
> erties, that would in certain situations give us or others strong rea-
> sons to respond to this thing in some positive way, such as wanting,
> choosing, using, producing, or preserving this thing. (Parfit, 2011: 38)

Parfit's idea is that the property of something's being good, in the reason-
implying sense, is the second-order property of there being reasons in
the fundamental sense for having certain desires concerning that thing,
and for performing certain actions, actions like choosing, using, producing, or preserving the thing. Might the concept of desirability just be
the concept of goodness in the reason-implying sense? Would this
explain why desire has the desirability of the desired object as it correctness condition?

To begin, note that Parfit's analysis of goodness in the reason-implying sense is defective even by his lights, as there is built-in redundancy.
We have already seen that Parfit seems not to think that there are any
reasons in the fundamental sense for performing actions. He thinks that
reasons for action reduce to reasons for desires or aims. Having already
said that goodness is a matter of having fundamental reasons for having
certain desires, he therefore adds nothing to his analysis of goodness in
the reason-implying sense by mentioning reasons to act. Any reasons for
action are already implicit in the mention of reasons for desires. Worse
still, though, at least for present purposes, the analysis also gets things
the wrong way around. Following Thomson, we are now supposing that
reasons for desire reduce to reasons for believing desirable. But this
means that the concept desirability cannot in turn reduce to the concept
of what there is reason to desire, otherwise believing that something is
desirable would be a matter of believing that there is a reason to believe
that there is a reason to believe that... and so on and so forth ad infinitum.
The content of the belief would never get fixed. The concept of desirability in play is thus not the concept of goodness in the reason-implying
sense either.

Might we suppose that the concept of desirability is itself a primitive
property, not analyzable at all, not even in terms of the concept of a reason? This was, in effect, Moore's own preferred version of Objectivism

(Moore, 1903). But Moore's view famously makes it completely obscure why reasons to believe that something is good, in his sense, should be reasons to desire the things that have that property. After all, as we have already seen, there are certain goodness properties, namely, attributive goodness properties, for which there is clearly no such connection. So why should the primitive property that Moore posits have such a connection? Why isn't it, in this respect, just like attributive goodness, completely divorced from anything to do with what there are reasons to desire?

We could canvas other Objectivist possibilities, but the obvious alternative at this point is to revert to some sort of Subjectivism and see whether it fares any better. What we need is an analysis of desirability that at no point presupposes facts about what there is reason to desire, but an analysis that none the less makes it transparent why desire has as its correctness condition the desirability of the desired object. The version of Subjectivism that I have argued for elsewhere naturally suggests itself. According to that version of Subjectivism, when we believe that it is desirable that p, what we believe is (very roughly) that we would desire that p if we were fully informed and rational (Smith, 1994). Our desiring that p thus has the desirability of p as its correctness condition for the simple reason that this is what it would be for our desiring that p to match the desire of our fully informed and rational counterparts. In other words, incorrect desires are ill-informed or irrational.

To definitively spell out this version of Subjectivism, we must of course say what it is for someone to be fully rational, and, in so doing, we mustn't presuppose facts about what there is reason to desire. Again, though, as I have argued elsewhere, we might well be able to do this (Smith, 2011). So far we have in effect been assuming that being rational is a matter of having and exercising a pair of capacities: the capacity to believe for reasons and the capacity to realize desires. What's remarkable, though, is that these capacities don't fully cohere with each other. If one has certain sorts of desires, then the exercise of the capacity to realize desires can lead one to fail to exercise the capacity to believe for reasons—think of cases of wishful thinking—and *vice versa*. So if we suppose that our being *fully* rational is a matter of our having a *maximally* coherent psychology, then it seems that that might in turn be possible only if we have certain non-instrumental desires, non-instrumental desires whose realization ensures that, when we realize our desires, their realization never comes at the cost of our failing to exercise our capacity to believe for reasons. Such non-instrumental desires would themselves be, as it were, *coherence-makers*.

Here is not the place to rehearse all of the arguments required to make this suggestion fully convincing. Suffice it to say that considerations like those just adduced seem to me to tell in favor of our supposing that, in order to have a maximally coherent psychology, one has to have a dominant non-instrumental desire that one does not interfere with one's present or future exercise of one's capacities to believe for reasons or realize desires, or anyone else's for that matter. Moreover one also has to have a dominant non-instrumental desire that one does what one can to ensure that one has the capacities to believe for reasons and realize desires, both in the present and in the future, and to ensure that others have these capacities too. These non-instrumental desires are necessary because only so can the two capacities be brought into coherence with each other. If this line of argument, or something in the vicinity of it, is successful, and if, as seems plausible, the experience of agony, whether in the present or the future, is guaranteed to undermine one's exercise of the capacity to believe for reasons and realize desires—this, we might now suppose, is what the difference between mere pain and agony consists in—then it would follow that everyone who has a maximally informed and coherent psychology would have to have an instrumental desire to avoid agony.

The idea that Subjectivism supports some such argument amounts to the idea that certain desires, and in particular the desire to avoid agony, whether in the present or the future, can be derived from non-instrumental desires that are partially *constitutive* of what it is to be maximally rational, constitutive because their presence in a psychology makes for the coherence of that psychology. But if the desire to avoid present and future agony can be derived from non-instrumental desires that are partially constitutive of what it is to be maximally rational, then it follows that everyone would desire to avoid agony if they were fully rational, and it follows from that, together with the analysis of desirability already proposed, that everyone is such that, if they were to believe that it is desirable to avoid agony, then what they believe would be true. Reasons for believing that avoiding agony is desirable—reasons of the kind just spelled out—would therefore turn out to be reasons to desire to avoid agony. Subjectivism would in this way enable us to reduce reasons for desires to reasons for belief in just the way Thomson proposes. But what's key here, to repeat, is the fact that the analysis of desirability at no point presupposes facts about what there is reason to desire, while none the less making it transparent why desire has as its correctness condition the desirability of the desired object.

When Parfit objects to Subjectivism, he ignores the possibility that some version of the theory might support an argument of the kind just proposed. Here is his initial statement of the sort of Subjectivism about reasons for action that I myself might endorse.

> Some other Subjectivists appeal, not to what would best fulfil or achieve our desires or aims, but to the choices or decisions that we would make after carefully considering the facts. These people also make claims about how it would be rational for us to make such decisions. According to what we can call
>
> > (C) what we have most reason to do, or decisive reasons to do, is the same as what, if we were fully informed and rational, we would choose to do.
>
> But this claim is ambiguous. Subjectivists and Objectivists may both claim that, when we are trying to make some important decision, we ought to deliberate in certain ways. We ought to try to imagine fully the important effects of our different possible acts, to avoid wishful thinking, to assess probabilities correctly, and to follow certain other procedural rules. If we deliberate in these ways, we are *procedurally* rational.
>
> Objectivists make further claims about the desires and aims that we would have, and the choices that we would make, if we were also *substantively* rational. These claims are *substantive* in the sense that they [are] not about *how* we make our choices, but about *what* we choose. There are various telic desires and aims, Objectivists believe, that we all have strong and often decisive object-given reasons to have.

To be fully substantively rational, we must respond to these reasons by having these desires and aims, and trying to fulfil or achieve them if we can. Deliberative Subjectivists make no such claims. These people deny that we have such object-given reasons, and they appeal to claims that are only about procedural rationality. (Parfit, 2011: 62–3)

And here is his attempt to respond to an argument of the kind I've just outlined.

Deliberative Subjectivists appeal to what we would want and choose after some process of informed and *rational* deliberation. These people might argue:

(A) We all have reasons to have those desires that would be had by anyone who was fully rational.

(B) Anyone who was fully rational would want to avoid all future agony.

Therefore

We all have a reason to want to avoid all future agony.

As I have said, however, such claims are ambiguous. Objectivists could accept (B), because these people make claims about substantive rationality. According to objective theories, we all have decisive reasons to have certain desires, and to be substantively rational we must have these desires. These reasons are given by the intrinsic features of what we might want, or might want to avoid. We have such a decisive object-given reason to want to avoid all future agony. If we did not have this desire, we would not be fully substantively rational, because we would be failing to respond to this reason.

Subjectivists cannot, however, make such claims. On subjective theories, we have no such object-given reasons, not even reasons to want to avoid future agony. Deliberative Subjectivists appeal to what we would want after deliberation that was *merely procedurally* rational. On these theories, *if* we have certain telic desires or aims, we may be rationally required to want, and to do, what would best fulfil or achieve these desires or aims. But, except perhaps for the few desires without which we could not even be agents, there are no telic desires or aims that we are rationally required to have. We can be procedurally rational whatever else we care about, or want to achieve. (Parfit, 2011: 78)

What is remarkable about this passage is that Parfit doesn't distinguish, as he should, between the basic claims Subjectivists make in stating their theory, on the one hand, and the claims that they make because they think that they can be derived from their basic claims, on the other.

True enough, a Subjectivist might initially state his theory in largely procedural, or better perhaps *structural*, terms. The concept of coherence as applied to a psychology is, let's agree, a structural notion. The basic claims of the kind of Subjectivism I myself embrace, to repeat, are that a fully rational psychology is one in which the capacities to believe for reasons and realize desires are both possessed to the maximal degree, and are fully exercised, and are brought into coherence with each other. But having made these basic claims, the Subjectivist might argue in the way proposed that, for these capacities to be brought into coherence with each other, we would have to have a non-instrumental desire that we do certain things. I have suggested that we would have to have a non-instrumental desire that we do not interfere with our own, or anyone else's, exercise of the capacities to believe for reasons or realize desires, and that we would also have to have a non-instrumental desire that we do what we can to ensure that we and others have such capacities to exercise. Given that future agony would frustrate such non-instrumental desires, we would have to instrumentally desire that we avoid future agony.

The Subjectivist's argument for the conclusion that we all have a reason to desire to avoid agony would then proceed as follows. The fact that we would all desire that we avoid future agony if we were fully informed and rational entails that avoiding future agony is desirable; and it follows from this that there are reasons to believe that future agony is desirable, and that these reasons are reasons to desire that we avoid future agony; and it follows from this, via Parfit's own analysis of reasons for action in terms of reasons for desires or aims, that we have reasons to avoid future agony. Though Parfit is therefore right that the claim that we all have a reason for desiring that we avoid future agony is not one of the basic claims that the Subjectivist makes, he is wrong that the Subjectivist must deny this claim. On the contrary, the Subjectivist might end up making this claim precisely because he derives it from his basic claims. This kind of Subjectivism seems to me much more promising than Parfit's own Reasons Fundamentalism.

5. *Conclusion*

Let me summarize the conclusions argued for in this paper. Parfit thinks that the concept of a reason for belief is fundamental, but there is good reason to believe that this is a mistake, and that the concept of a reason for belief can be analyzed. Hume's reductive theory provides the model. Parfit also thinks that the concept of a reason for desire is fundamental, but if the concept of a reason for belief can be analyzed, then this too turns out to be a mistake. To suppose otherwise is to embrace an implausible conception of reasons as a ragbag, a disjunction of something fundamental and something non-fundamental. Parfit thinks that the concept of goodness can be analyzed in terms of the concept of reasons in the fundamental sense for desiring and acting, but this turns out to be a mistake even by his own lights, as he doesn't really think that reasons for acting are fundamental, and it is also a mistake for the reasons we have already given, namely, because there are no fundamental reasons for desiring. Parfit thinks that Subjectivists have to deny the claim that everyone has a reason to desire to avoid future agony, but this is a mistake, as all that Subjectivists have to deny is that this is one of the basic claims they make in stating their theory. They can quite happily agree that this claim is derivable from the basic claims they make, and some Subjectivists provide arguments for this conclusion. Finally and most importantly, Parfit dramatically underestimates the appeal and power of Subjectivism. The appeal and power of Subjectivism lies in the fact that it alone promises to explain something that desperately needs explaining, namely, why the correctness condition of desire is the desirability of the desired object.

References

Hume, David. 1740 [1968]. *A Treatise of Human Nature*. Oxford: Clarendon Press.

Moore, G. E. 1903. *Principia Ethica*. Cambridge: Cambridge University Press.

Parfit, Derek. 2011. *On What Matters*. Volume One. Oxford: Oxford University Press.

Scanlon, Thomas M. 1998. *What We Owe To Each Other*. Cambridge, MA: Harvard University Press.

Smith, Michael. 1987. "The Humean Theory of Motivation." *Mind*, 96: 36–61.

Smith, Michael. 1988. "On Humeans, Anti-Humeans, and Motivation: A Reply to Pettit." *Mind*, 97: 589–95.

Smith, Michael. 1994. *The Moral Problem*. Oxford: Wiley-Blackwell.

Smith, Michael. 2011. "Deontological Moral Obligations and Non-Welfarist Agent-Relative Values." *Ratio*, 24: 351–63.

Thomson, Judith Jarvis. 2008. *Normativity*. La Salle, IL: Open Court.

6

NOTHING "REALLY" MATTERS, BUT THAT'S NOT WHAT MATTERS

Sharon Street

1. *Introduction*

Does anything really matter? The answer depends on what one means by "really." If the question is whether anything "really" matters in Derek Parfit's robustly attitude-independent sense, then the answer is no, nothing really matters in that sense. Nothing matters, ultimately, independently of the attitudes of beings who take things to matter. To matter is to matter from the point of view of someone.

Should this antirealist answer to the question disturb us? Parfit thinks that it should. He believes that to conclude that nothing really matters in his sense is to conclude that nothing matters, full stop. He believes that the only genuine alternative to his position is nihilism, more or less well disguised. This is a false choice, however, and the aim of this essay is to explain why. Nothing "really" matters in Parfit's robustly attitude-independent sense, but plenty of things *matter*. Moreover, plenty of things "really" matter if we allow, as I think we should, that existing independently of a subject's point of view on the world is not the only way of being "real." Normativity depends on the attitudes of beings who take things to matter, but that doesn't mean it doesn't exist.

Parfit does not wish to call his meta-ethical position a brand of *realism* about normativity, but I believe that *non-naturalist realism* continues to be the least misleading term for it.[1] In this essay, I will argue that Parfit's defense of non-naturalist realism in *On What Matters* is undermined by a failure to distinguish clearly enough between the claim that

(1) There are reasons in the standard normative sense.

and the claim that

(1') There are *robustly attitude-independent* reasons in the standard normative sense.

To put it another way, Parfit's defense of non-naturalist realism is undermined by a failure to distinguish clearly enough between the claim that

(2) There are irreducibly normative truths.

and the claim that

(2') There are *robustly attitude-independent* irreducibly normative truths.

As I will try to show, at key moments in his defense of non-naturalism, Parfit sometimes assumes, without adequate examination or argument, that claims (1) and (1'), or claims (2) and (2'), are interchangeable. But they are not interchangeable. The upshot is that oftentimes when Parfit believes he is successfully defending (1') or (2')—*realism* about normative reasons—he is in fact successfully defending only (1) or (2)—*non-skepticism* about normative reasons. But the antirealist has no dispute with (1) or (2)—or anyway, shouldn't, I'll argue. The antirealist's

---

[1] In the index to Vol. 2 of *On What Matters* (Oxford: Oxford University Press, 2011), under "realism, normative," Parfit explains that realist views are "often assumed to make positive ontological claims," and that "the word 'realism' is not used by me for this reason" (p. 823). Parfit prefers to call his meta-ethical view "Non-naturalist, Non-metaphysical Cognitivism." As will emerge in this paper, I agree with Parfit (and other non-naturalists such as Ronald Dworkin, Thomas Nagel, and T. M. Scanlon) that merely asserting the existence of normative reasons is not, in and of itself, to say or commit oneself to anything metaphysically weighty or problematic. I will, however, continue to call Parfit's view a form of "realism" to mark the important point that Parfit (as well as Dworkin, Nagel, and Scanlon) asserts the existence not only of *normative reasons*, but also of *robustly attitude-independent* normative reasons. I believe it's fair to refer to such views as "realist" so long as we keep in mind that these theorists vigorously dispute the idea that their views involve any substantial metaphysical commitments.

dispute is with (1′) and (2′). *These* are the claims that give rise to meta-physical and epistemological problems, yet these are the claims that Parfit fails adequately to defend.

The essay is organized as follows. In Sections 2–4, I examine Parfit's treatment of Bernard Williams's views, arguing that Parfit does not distinguish clearly enough between the claim that there are reasons in the standard normative sense and the claim that there are *external* reasons in the standard normative sense. In Sections 5 and 6, I explain why all parties to the discussion—realists and antirealists alike—can agree *that there are reasons in the standard normative sense* without thereby taking on any commitments that are metaphysically or epistemologically problematic. I distinguish between *modest* and *robust* attitude-independence, and suggest that it's only when one supposes that there are *robustly* attitude-independent normative reasons that one gets into metaphysical and epistemological trouble. In Section 7, I examine Parfit's response, in Chapter 33 of *On What Matters*, to my "evolutionary debunking" arguments against non-naturalist realism. I argue that Parfit's response fails because Parfit does not distinguish adequately between skepticism about *normativity* (not my position) and skepticism about *realism* about normativity (my position).

In the final section, I turn briefly to some larger issues raised by the discussion. Locating the conceptual space for a position that is not either non-naturalist realism or nihilism is philosophically essential. But locating this space does not, of course, mean that life is easy. In particular, it does not mean that nothing remains to the deeper undercurrent of our worries about nihilism. On the view I suggest, the threat of nihilism never goes away, but the correct way to understand it is as a causal threat, not a rational one. We have good reason to fear the view that nothing matters, but we should fear it in just the same way that we fear illness, death, or a fall into depression.

2. We Can All Agree That the Concept of a Reason in the Standard Normative Sense Is Primitive and Irreducible

One of the most surprising claims in *On What Matters* is Parfit's claim that his friend and colleague Bernard Williams "did not understand the

distinctive concept of a non-psychological *purely normative* reason"
(*OWM*, II, 435). In one of the book's most autobiographically revealing
passages, Parfit quotes Hume on the "wretched condition" in which
Hume's philosophical thinking left him, then writes:

> My predicament is partly similar. Most philosophers seem to reject
> my meta-ethical and other meta-normative beliefs. In one way, my
> predicament is worse than Hume's. Many of these other people don't
> even understand what I believe. When I talk to these people, we
> can't even disagree. It took me some time to realize the state that I
> am in. Given the range, subtlety, and depth of Williams's writings
> about normative questions, I assumed for many years that Williams
> had some purely normative beliefs. I failed to see that Williams's
> claims about reasons, and about what we ought to do, are really psy-
> chological claims about how we might be motivated to act. I also
> failed to understand Mackie's similar claims. Since I knew both
> these people well, I am puzzled and disturbed by our failures to
> understand each other. (*OWM*, II, 452)

For reasons that will suggest themselves, I do not think this is the best
way for Parfit to read Williams. In what follows, however, I wish to set
aside all interpretive questions about Williams's writings. What matters
for my purposes is simply that, as I will argue in this and the following
two sections: (1) in discussing Williams's views, there is an important
distinction in the vicinity to which Parfit pays inadequate attention; (2)
the distinction is one that all of us who are party to the discussion here
and now can recognize and accept; (3) this distinction may be used to
locate more precisely the "thin" concept of a purely normative reason
that we all share and understand, and which may be used as our common conceptual currency in debating one another; and (4) this "thin,"
shared concept of a normative reason turns out to be nothing other than
the concept of a reason in the "standard normative sense" with which
Parfit himself is rightly so concerned, but which he sometimes supposes,
wrongly, to be interchangeable with the concept of an "external" reason.

Let us begin by looking at what Parfit says about the concept that he
thinks Williams did not understand—the concept of a "non-psychological,

purely normative reason." Parfit gives his first gloss of this concept on the opening page of *On What Matters*:

> It is hard to explain the *concept* of a reason, or what the phrase "a reason" means. Facts give us reasons, we might say, when they count in favour of our having some attitude, or our acting in some way. But "counts in favour of" means roughly "gives a reason for." Like some other fundamental concepts, such as those involved in our thoughts about time, consciousness, and possibility, the concept of a reason is indefinable in the sense that it cannot be helpfully explained merely by using words. We must explain such concepts in a different way, by getting people to think thoughts that use these concepts. (*OWM*, I, 31)

The concept Parfit has in mind is the same concept that T. M. Scanlon calls the concept of a reason in the "standard normative sense."[2] It is useful to quote Scanlon's language as well:

> I will take the idea of a reason as primitive. Any attempt to explain what it is to be a reason for something seems to me to lead back to the same idea: a consideration that counts in favor of it. "Counts in favor how" one might ask. "By providing a reason for it" seems to be the only answer. So I will presuppose the idea of a reason.[3]

I agree—and in my view, all parties to the discussion *should* agree—that Parfit and Scanlon are entirely correct to focus on, isolate, and distinguish from any psychological concept (such as the concept of a motivating reason), the distinctive concept of a normative reason. In other words, I agree that, just as Parfit and Scanlon claim, there exists a distinctive, non-psychological concept of one thing's *counting in favor of* or *calling for* another, and that this concept is primitive in the following sense. While we may point to the concept in various ways, locating it for one another and helping others to acquire it, there is no way to explain,

---

in other language, the sense of the expression "a normative reason" without in one way or another merely invoking other normative terms. Normative concepts are irreducible and indefinable in this sense.

While the next point is in one sense obvious, it is important for what comes later to pause here and take note: In agreeing with Parfit and Scanlon that there is—and that all of us understand and possess—the concept of a *non-psychological, purely normative reason*, we are not (certainly not yet, anyway) assenting to anything metaphysically or epistemologically problematic. Here's one way of explaining why this is so. As I see it, one way to point to the concept of a normative reason (and other normative concepts, such as the concept of something's being *required* or *demanded*) is to point to a certain type of conscious experience with which we're all intimately familiar. The intrinsic character of this experience cannot accurately be captured or described except by invoking normative language—just as, for example, the intrinsic character of the experience of redness cannot accurately be described except by invoking color language—but that doesn't mean we can't locate for one another the type of experience in question by pointing to the kinds of circumstances in which those of us who are party to the discussion tend to have it. In other words, just as we point to the experience of redness by pointing to the kinds of circumstances in which we typically have it—for example, when looking at ripened strawberries or a fire truck— so we may point to what we might call the experience of "to-be-done-ness" by pointing to the kinds of circumstances in which we typically have it—for example, when a car suddenly swerves toward us on the highway, or when we see a child in pain.

In such moments, we have a conscious experience of certain features of the world (the swerving car, the child's pain) as what we can only describe as *calling for, counting in favor of, demanding,* or *requiring* certain responses on our part (evasive action, a helping response, and so on). The intrinsic character of the type of conscious experience in question— the experience of something as *to be done*, or of one thing as *counting as a reason* for another—cannot accurately be described except by invoking normative concepts. But that doesn't mean that we don't all understand perfectly well the concept we're talking about here. And to be clear: I am of course not claiming that the concept of a normative reason is the same as the concept of the *experience* of something as a normative reason. These are obviously not the same concepts. The claim, rather, is that one way in which we get our handle on the simple, irreducible concept of a normative reason—the concept of one thing's counting in favor of, or calling for, another—is by having a certain kind of conscious experience.

Furthermore—as I take it to be clear—acknowledging all of the above doesn't (not yet, anyway) commit us to anything that should, from a meta-ethical perspective, raise metaphysical or epistemological worries. Roughly speaking, about the epistemology: There is no great mystery here about how we acquire normative concepts any more than there is a great mystery about how we acquire concepts such as **redness** or the **scent of roses**; we acquire normative concepts in virtue of having a certain kind of conscious experience and being part of a linguistic community whose practices help us learn to pick that kind of experience out. Roughly speaking, about the metaphysics: Merely acknowledging that we possess a certain concept, which we've come to understand in virtue of being the subject of a certain type of conscious experience, of course does not commit us to the view that there exists, "out there" in the world, some robustly mind-independent thing that "corresponds to" or is "tracked by" the concept in question. Maybe there is such a thing; maybe there isn't. We haven't said anything about this so far. In other words, acknowledging that we understand and possess the concept of a *purely normative reason* does not commit us to thinking that there is something (in particular, a normative reason) that exists in a way that is robustly independent of the type of conscious experience being talked about—any more so than acknowledging that one had a certain dream commits one to the view that the thing one dreamed about actually happened. Similarly—and this point is equally central in what follows—acknowledging that we understand and possess the concept of a purely normative reason of course also does not commit us to thinking that there *isn't* something (in particular, a normative reason) that exists in a way that is independent of the type of conscious experience being talked about.

Let all parties to the discussion agree, then, that the concept of a normative reason is the concept of one thing's *calling for*, or *counting in favor of,* something else, and that it is a primitive, irreducible concept in just the way that theorists such as Parfit and Scanlon claim. Let us furthermore take note that granting that much on all sides does not— certainly not without further argument, anyway—take us anywhere toward answering the question whether there do or do not exist any normative reasons in a way that is robustly independent of the states of conscious experience we have just been talking about. The concept we are pointing to is—on its face, anyway—entirely silent on the issue.[4]

3. The Concept of a Reason in the Standard Normative Sense Is Not the Concept of an External Reason

With these thoughts in mind, let us return to Parfit's discussion of Williams, and in particular, to Parfit's characterization of the internalism/externalism distinction. Trouble starts, in my view, when Parfit draws a distinction between what he calls *Analytical Internalism*, on the one hand, and *Externalism*, on the other. *Analytical Internalism*, as Parfit defines it, is the view that

> When we say that
>
> > (D) someone has *decisive reasons* to act in a certain way, or *should* or *ought* to act in this way,
>
> we often mean something like
>
> > (E) this act would best fulfil this person's present fully informed telic desires, or is what, after fully informed and procedurally rational deliberation, this person would be most robustly motivated to do, or would choose to do. (*OWM*, II, 270)

"This claim," Parfit says, "defines the *internal senses* of the words 'decisive reason', 'should', and 'ought'" (ibid.). Parfit then continues:

---

[4] As I discuss in Section 5, I do not think the concept is "silent" on the question whether it's possible to *make mistakes* about what counts in favor of what. It is obviously a presupposition of normative discourse that we can make mistakes about normative reasons. What I deny is that the concept has "built into it" an assumption of *robust* as opposed to *modest* attitude-independence.

According to some other people, whom Williams calls

> *Externalists*: We often use words like "reason," "should," and "ought" in other, simpler, irreducibly normative senses.

These we can call the *external* senses of these words. (ibid.)

One may define one's terms however one likes, of course, and this way of drawing the distinction finds some support in Williams's writings. None of that matters for my point here, though. The point I wish to make here is just that the moment Parfit decides to use the terms this way, he sets up a terminological situation in which important conceptual possibilities become far too easy to overlook. In particular, he sets up a situation in which it becomes far too easy to confuse the view that

(3) There are reasons in the standard normative sense.

with the view that

> (3′) Not only are there reasons in the standard normative sense, but among those reasons are ones with the following characteristic: agents have those reasons even if there is no sound deliberative route from their subjective motivational set to the conclusion that they have those reasons.

In other words, there is a position available here which: (1) agrees with Parfit's so-called "Externalist" that "we often use words like 'reason,' 'should,' and 'ought' in … [simple], irreducibly normative senses"; (2) furthermore agrees *that there are reasons* in this standard normative sense; but then (3) denies that *among those* normative reasons are "external" reasons in the *different* sense of normative reasons that agents have even in circumstances in which there is no sound deliberative route from the agent's subjective motivational set to the conclusion that he or she has those reasons.[5]

---

[5] Hereafter, I use the term *external reason* in this "different" sense just noted—i.e. the sense of a reason (in the standard normative sense) that an agent has even though there is no sound deliberative route from the agent's subjective motivational set to the conclusion that he or she has that reason. In my view, this is not only the more familiar sense of the term, but also, more importantly, the more philosophically helpful sense. I believe that it creates confusion to define the term *external reason* in such a way as to be indis-

It's not that Parfit doesn't see room for this position; he does. Indeed, Parfit explicitly considers the hypothesis that Williams held the above position. Parfit writes:

> When Williams makes claims about reasons for acting, he may seem to be using the phrase "a reason" in the indefinable normative sense that we can also express with the phrase "counts in favour." That is how Scanlon interprets Williams's view. This view, Scanlon writes,
>
> > does not reflect skepticism about reasons in the standard normative sense... Williams seems to be offering a substantive, normative thesis about what reasons we have.
>
> This interpretation is, I believe, mistaken. Williams did not understand this concept of a reason. (*OWM*, II, 433–4)

Here Parfit explicitly considers the possibility that when Williams denied the existence of "external reasons," he was not denying the existence of reasons in the "standard normative sense," but rather just the existence of a certain *kind* of reasons in the standard normative sense— namely ones that exist independently of our subjective motivational sets in a very robust sense. I agree with Scanlon that this is the best, most charitable interpretation of Williams's denial of the existence of external reasons. As before, however, the important point here has nothing to do with what Williams did or didn't think, or how most charitably to interpret his writings. It just has to do with a distinction that all of us here and now need, are capable of making, and which becomes extremely easy to miss when we draw the internalism/externalism distinction as Parfit does in these passages.

One way to put the point is this. As the above passage reveals, Parfit himself recognizes the possibility of reading the "internalism/externalism" debate as a *substantive normative debate* about what kinds of normative reasons there are, conducted in terms of the shared concept of a reason in the standard normative sense. On this way of understanding

tinguishable in meaning from the term *reason in the standard normative sense*, and that it would be unfortunate if this usage gained traction. For this reason, I don't follow Parfit's usage.

the debate, all parties to the debate agree at the outset that there are reasons in the standard normative sense—that is, in the primitive, irreducible sense of considerations that *count in favor of* or *call for* certain responses on our part—and then proceed to argue about what reasons in the standard normative sense there are, focusing on a specific set of cases. The specific set of cases they are arguing about are those in which it is stipulated that there is no sound deliberative route to a given normative conclusion from the agent's own subjective motivational set. According to *externalists*, there are some normative reasons that an agent has even if there is no sound deliberative route to that conclusion from his own subjective motivational set. *Internalists*, meanwhile, agree that there are reasons in the standard normative sense, but deny that there are any normative reasons of a certain sort—namely ones that exist independently of whether there is a sound deliberative route to the conclusion that they exist from the subjective motivational set of the agent whose normative reasons are in question.

Notice, moreover, that on this way of understanding the internalism/externalism debate, all parties to the debate grant at the outset that there is no *conceptually* necessary tie between normative reasons and motivation. For all either party to the debate is assuming, in other words, it is entirely possible, as a *conceptual* matter, for there to be normative reason for an agent to do something even though there is no sound deliberative route to that conclusion from the agent's subjective motivational set. Notice also, however: To agree that there is no *conceptually necessary* tie between normative reasons and motivation is of course not to agree that *there is no tie*. This is so in just the same way in which the following is so: To agree that it's not *conceptually true* that I have reason to brush my teeth regularly is of course not to agree that *I don't have reason to brush my teeth regularly*.

We may summarize the crucial point this way. Distinguish between the following three senses of the concept of a normative reason:

1. The concept ***normative reason***$_{INT}$, which has "built into it," as a presupposition involved in deploying the concept, that nothing can be a reason for agent A unless there is a "sound deliberative route" from A's subjective motivational set to the conclusion that it is such a reason.

2. The concept ***normative reason***$_{EXT}$, which has "built into it," as a presupposition involved in deploying the concept, that there *are* external reasons, in the sense of reasons for agents to do things even in cases where there is no sound deliberative route from their own subjective motivational set to the conclusion that it is a reason.
3. The concept ***normative reason***$_{NEUT}$, which has neither of the above presuppositions built into it; this concept of a reason is *neutral* on the issue of whether there are, or there aren't, any reasons that exist independently of whether there is a sound deliberative route to this conclusion from the subjective motivational set of the agent whose reasons are in question.

The problem that emerges in his discussion of Williams is that Parfit sometimes slips into assuming there are only two concepts of a normative reason in play (***normative reason***$_{INT}$ and ***normative reason***$_{EXT}$), when in fact there are three. Parfit rightly insists that the concept ***normative reason***$_{INT}$ is not the concept of a reason in the standard normative sense; this he sees and insists upon quite clearly. What he does not see so clearly is that the concept ***normative reason***$_{EXT}$ is *also* not the concept of a reason in the standard normative sense. It is not, as Parfit sometimes seems to assume, built into the concept of a reason in the standard normative sense that there *are* external reasons; rather, it is built into the concept of a reason in the standard normative sense that there *might* be external reasons. But as far as the concept itself is concerned, so to speak, there also might *not* be. My claim, then, is that Parfit sometimes fails to distinguish adequately between the concept ***normative reason***$_{EXT}$ and the concept ***normative reason***$_{NEUT}$. As a result, he sometimes ends up assuming that the concept of a reason in the standard normative sense is the concept ***normative reason***$_{EXT}$, when in fact it is not. The concept of a reason in the standard normative sense is the "thinner" concept ***normative reason***$_{NEUT}$.

We start to see here why Parfit doesn't really see room for a position that is not either his own or else a form of nihilism: Because of his failure to distinguish clearly enough between the concept ***normative reason***$_{EXT}$ and the concept ***normative reason***$_{NEUT}$, he hears any denial of the existence of *external reasons* as a denial of the existence of *reasons*. But these are not the same thing. One may be a skeptic about the former without being a skeptic about the latter.

4. Analytical Externalism?

One might object to what I've said so far as follows.[6] It's not that Parfit is in any way failing to distinguish between the concept of a reason in the standard normative sense and the concept of an external reason. Rather, the most charitable interpretation is that by this point in *On What Matters*, Parfit regards himself as having already established through argument that the two concepts are one and the same, such that he is now entitled to move fluidly between them without comment. On the proposed interpretation, we should read Parfit as holding (and having argued, albeit not explicitly in these terms) that it is *analytic* (presumably non-obviously so) that reasons in the standard normative sense are *external* reasons, such that to conclude that there are no *external* reasons is to conclude that there are no normative reasons at all.

The problem with the proposed interpretation of Parfit is that it is hard to see what the argument for this conceptual equivalence could be. Make no mistake: It's easy to see how one might argue *that there are external reasons*. To undertake this, the general method is to imagine cases in which it does *not* follow from someone's subjective motivational set that he or she has normative reason to act in a certain way, and then call upon people's intuitions to the effect that nevertheless the agent *does* have reason (in the standard normative sense) to act in this way. Parfit makes this kind of argument on a routine basis, throughout Part 1 and also in his discussion of Williams in Part 6. For example, in discussing Williams, Parfit imagines the case he calls *Early Death*, in which

> unless you take some medicine, you will later die much younger, losing many years of happy life. Though you know this fact, and you have deliberated in a procedurally rational way on this and all of the

---

[6] I am grateful to Matty Silverstein for pressing this objection.

other relevant facts, you are not motivated to take this medicine. (*OWM*, II, 432)

Parfit then calls upon the intuition that in such a case, you have decisive normative reason to take this medicine. While I don't find such arguments compelling or adequately developed, as I discuss elsewhere,[7] they are nevertheless clearly a way of bolstering the case *that there are external reasons*.

But an argument for *that* point isn't what we're looking for under the proposed interpretation of Parfit. Rather, we're looking for an argument that shows that it's a (presumably non-obvious) *analytic truth* that reasons in the standard normative sense are external reasons. This is a much stronger claim, and appealing to intuitions about cases like *Early Death* is insufficient to establish it. Indeed, even if one cites many cases of this form, as Parfit in fact does, this still does not establish that it is *analytically true* that reasons in the standard normative sense are external reasons. To establish that claim, one would have to do something much more ambitious; roughly, one would have to make the case that our "normative reasons discourse" is so shot through with the assumption that there are *external* normative reasons (and not just normative reasons$_{NEUT}$) that to give up on this assumption would be to vitiate the discourse so completely as to leave something unrecognizable as the same discourse. One would have to show, in other words, that to conclude that there are no *external* normative reasons would be to give up on a platitude so basic to our normative discourse that we would have given up on the idea that there are normative reasons at all.

I will argue in the next section that this is simply not so. It is not plausible to think that the conclusion that there are no *external* reasons would leave such a gaping hole in our normative discourse that the right conclusion would be that there are no reasons in the standard normative sense *at all*. For the moment, however, note that Parfit himself seems

[7] I explain what I think is wrong with arguments of this kind—and issue a plea that people stop making them, at least in the cursory form in which they're usually made—in "In Defense of Future Tuesday Indifference: Ideally Coherent Eccentrics and the Contingency of What Matters," *Philosophical Issues* (a supplement to *Noûs*), Vol. 19 on "Metaethics," ed. Ernest Sosa (2009): 273–98.

to agree with these very same points when they present themselves in a different terminological guise. In particular, in Part 1 of *On What Matters*, Parfit discusses what he calls the debate between *Objectivist* and *Subjectivist* theories of normative reasons. Parfit understands that debate as a substantive normative debate, arguing that Subjectivism is a substantively mistaken view about what normative reasons there are. In that context, Parfit agrees that one may deny the existence of *objective* normative reasons while still holding (as a Subjectivist) that there are normative reasons. The question here is: Why not similarly agree that one may deny the existence of *external* normative reasons while still holding (as an Internalist) that there are normative reasons? On the way of thinking about things that I've been suggesting, this is really just the same point.[8]

It is revealing that in his discussion of Williams, Parfit draws a contrast between what he calls *Analytical Internalism* and just plain *Externalism*. After all, one might have thought that the relevant point of contrast with *Analytical Internalism* would be not "Externalism" *simpliciter*, but *Analytical* Externalism. Talk of Externalism *simpliciter* is ambiguous between externalism conceived of as a substantive normative position and what we might call *Analytical Externalism*, the view that the concept of a normative reason and the concept of an external reason are one and the same. Parfit's way of dividing up the territory obscures a possibility to which we should be highly attuned, namely the possibility that *both* Analytical Internalism *and* Analytical Externalism are false. And why wouldn't this be the right view? It's plausible to think, after all, that some of the considerations that raise trouble for *Analytical Internalism*

[8] In other words, if we interpret the Internalism/Externalism debate as a substantive normative debate in the manner I've been suggesting, then there is no meaningful difference between the Internalism/Externalism debate and the Objectivist/Subjectivist debate as Parfit characterizes it in Part 1. This is not to say that there is *no* way to draw a distinction between the two debates. One way to maintain a distinction is to interpret the Internalism/Externalism debate not as a substantive normative debate, but rather as a conceptual debate—what I suggest in the next paragraph would more aptly be called the *Analytical Internalism/Analytical Externalism* debate. As I suggest below, though, the problem with the Internalism/Externalism debate so understood is that the two positions are not exhaustive. There is a third position available according to which *neither* Analytical Internalism *nor* Analytical Externalism is correct. And that's the position that I think is actually right.

might also, mutatis mutandis, raise trouble for *Analytical Externalism*. In other words, just as the expression "normative reason" does not (as Parfit puts it) *mean* "internal reason," the expression "normative reason" *also* does not *mean* "external reason." The expression "normative reason" means nothing more nor less than "normative reason"—exactly as Parfit himself insists in other contexts.

5. *We Can All Agree That There Are Reasons in the Standard Normative Sense*

The news so far is good for all concerned. There is a shared concept in terms of which Parfit and his antirealist opponents may continue to debate, without talking past one another, the important philosophical question that we all care about—namely whether, and if so, in exactly what way, normativity is an attitude-dependent phenomenon. Moreover, the shared concept turns out just to be the familiar one of a reason in the standard normative sense (understood as identical to the "thin" concept *normative reason*$_{NEUT}$). Having isolated the concept we need, let us drop the cumbersome terminology and hereafter just say *normative reason*.

The next question is how best to formulate, in terms of this shared concept, the fundamental debate about the attitude-dependence of normativity. Here there is space only to state, without defending, what I think is the best formulation. I'll call this debate the *realism/antirealism* debate, recognizing that the terminology is not ideal, but regarding it as the best (or anyway, one of the least bad) among a bad set of options.[9]

According to *realists* such as Parfit (and many others—including quasi-realists such as Blackburn and Gibbard when they don their hats

---

[9] As will be clear, the "realism/antirealism" debate as I formulate it is in the close neighborhood of both the "internalism/externalism" debate as I defined it in previous sections and the "objectivist/subjectivist" debate as Parfit defines it in Part 1 of *OWM*. While I can't defend the point here, I believe the refinements I've made in formulation are important. I also believe that the "realism/antirealism" terminology, while it has its own problems, is the least misleading. The "internalism/externalism" terminology is too closely associated with the assumption of a conceptual tie between normative reasons and motivation, and Parfit's "objectivist/subjectivist" terminology is misleading with respect to the antirealist's ability to capture a very healthy degree of objectivity.

as normative theorists[10]), there are at least some normative reasons such that some fact or consideration X is a normative reason for some agent A to Y, even though the conclusion that X is a reason for A to Y in no way follows, logically or instrumentally, from A's global set of normative attitudes in combination with the non-normative facts. Call such reasons *robustly attitude-independent normative reasons*. According to *antirealists* such as myself (and many others—including Kantian constructivists such as Korsgaard[11]), no such robustly attitude-independent reasons exist. Rather, according to the antirealist, there are plenty of normative reasons, but no fact or consideration X is ever a normative reason for a given agent A to Y unless the conclusion that it is such a reason follows, logically and/or instrumentally, from A's global set of normative attitudes in combination with the non-normative facts.

Returning to Parfit's *Early Death* case for the sake of illustration, suppose again that unless a man takes a certain medicine, he will later die much younger, losing many years of happy life. Call the man *Earl*, and let us stipulate that it in no way follows, logically or instrumentally, from Earl's global set of normative attitudes, in combination with the non-normative facts, that he has any normative reason to take the medicine. Indeed, let's suppose that he is ideally coherent in the sense that his global set of normative attitudes is internally perfectly logically and

[10] I say more about quasi-realism in "Mind-Independence Without the Mystery: Why Quasi-Realists Can't Have It Both Ways," in *Oxford Studies in Metaethics*, Vol. 6, ed. Russ Shafer-Landau (Oxford: Clarendon Press, 2011), 1–32. The fact that quasi-realists count as "realists" on my formulation of the debate is one of the ways in which the "realism/antirealism" terminology is potentially misleading, but (a) as is well known, non-naturalist realists and quasi-realists are increasingly having trouble distinguishing themselves from one another; and (b) it is a point of this paper, as well as the paper on quasi-realism, that even if the assertion of robustly attitude-independent reasons is understood as an "internal," substantive normative claim, it *still* causes epistemological trouble. The mysteries associated with positing robustly attitude-independent normative reasons can't be escaped by pointing out that in asserting their existence, one is making a substantive normative claim.

[11] For my reading of Korsgaard, see "Coming to Terms with Contingency: Humean Constructivism about Practical Reason," in *Constructivism in Practical Philosophy*, ed. James Lenman and Yonatan Shemmer (Oxford: Oxford University Press, 2012), 40–59. While I am skeptical that a Kantian version of constructivism can be made to work, such views show how one can be an antirealist while simultaneously arguing for a strong form of normative objectivity.

instrumentally consistent, and he is making no mistakes about the non-normative facts. As we're imagining the case, according to the standards "set" by *Earl's* normative point of view on the world, the fact in question provides no reason for him to take the medicine. The *realist* will say that Earl nevertheless has strong normative reason to take the medicine. The *antirealist* denies this, holding that if Earl's situation is indeed what we have stipulated it to be, then there is no normative reason for him to take the medicine.

This way of formulating the realism/antirealism debate raises many questions that I can't address here. A few basic comments will have to suffice.

First, on this formulation, the realism/antirealism debate is a *substantive normative debate*, conducted in terms of the shared, "thin" concept of a normative reason (once again, the concept **normative reason**$_{NEUT}$), which is understood as itself *neutral* on the realism/antirealism question. Thus, the antirealist agrees that as a *conceptual* matter, there could be robustly attitude-independent normative reasons; she agrees that nothing about the very idea of a normative reason rules this out. Put another way: The antirealist understands perfectly well the idea of a normative reason (of one thing's counting in favor of another), and she understands perfectly well the idea of robust attitude-independence. So when Parfit and other realists assert the existence of robustly attitude-independent normative reasons, she understands perfectly well what they are saying. She simply disagrees that there *are* any such reasons—much as one may understand perfectly well the idea of a witch, while holding that there aren't any.

Second, on this way of understanding the realism/antirealism debate, all parties to the discussion agree *that there are normative reasons*. Suppose again that taking a certain medicine will give someone many more years of a happy life. While the antirealist denies that this is a reason for *Earl* to take the medicine, she will insist as vehemently as anyone that this *is* a reason for *most actually existing human beings* to take the medicine. In other words, there are scads and scads of normative reasons, the antirealist agrees, and ordinary people's reasons to take life-saving medicines are just the tip of the iceberg. Thus, on this understanding of the realism/antirealism debate, both the realist and the antirealist are committed to a *non-skeptical position* about the existence of, and our ability to learn and know about, normative reasons. The antirealist merely denies the existence of a certain *subcategory* of normative reasons whose existence the realist insists upon.

Third, any remotely sophisticated antirealist is going to be able to capture the idea that human beings can and do make mistakes—and indeed, often large and tragic mistakes—about their own and other people's normative reasons. Antirealists (whose ranks include both Humean and Kantian constructivists of the kind I discuss elsewhere[12]) have an arsenal of simple but powerful resources for explaining why normative error is not only possible but rampant in human life. These include pointing to (a) ignorance of non-normative facts; (b) mistakes in logical and instrumental reasoning; (c) failures to draw out the full consequences of already existing commitments; and (d) all manner of other distracted, confused, and self-deceived human thought.

Fourth, while I can't defend the following claims here,[13] I argue elsewhere that drawing upon these and other resources, the antirealist can do just as good a job as the realist at capturing and explaining our views about the normative reasons of real human beings in real human life. Indeed, I argue, the realist's and the antirealist's verdicts about cases only clearly come apart when we leave real human beings behind and fix our attention on a cast of characters I call *ideally coherent eccentrics*, whose ranks include Earl as described above, Parfit's man with Future Tuesday Indifference, Gibbard's ideally coherent anorexic, and Gibbard's ideally coherent Caligula. Furthermore, when one does the necessary but often neglected work of considering in depth what such beings would actually have to look like in order to meet the stipulated conditions, it is no longer remotely obvious whose verdicts (the realist's or the antirealist's) about the reasons of these beings are more plausible.

Fifth and finally, let us return, in light of these points, to an idea we were considering in the previous section—the idea that *Analytical*

---

[12] I discuss these views in "What Is Constructivism in Ethics and Metaethics?", *Philosophy Compass*, 5 (2010): 363–84, and "Coming to Terms with Contingency."
[13] I defend them in "In Defense of Future Tuesday Indifference."

Externalism might be true. Here is a way of arguing that it can't be. I've just said that the realist and the antirealist can do an equally good job of capturing a huge swath of our intuitive judgments about cases, coming apart only with regard to esoteric ones imagined by philosophers, and in particular with regard to ideally coherent eccentrics. Now, I strongly agree with Parfit that these esoteric cases are philosophically pivotal; I by no means intend to diminish their importance, but on the contrary think they are essential to focus on if we are to get clear on the nature of normative reasons. My point is rather that *given how esoteric the cases are*—how unfamiliar they are to actual human life and the context in which the concept of a normative reason developed in the first place and is normally deployed—it is not at all plausible to think that *accepting the antirealist's verdicts about these cases* would (as Parfit seems to believe) vitiate our familiar, everyday concept of a normative reason so completely and terribly that the upshot would be that there are no normative reasons at all.

To put it another way, our normative discourse clearly presupposes the following idea: People can and often do go wrong, indeed very badly wrong, about their own and other people's normative reasons. Call this idea *modest attitude-independence.* Any theory of normative reasons that failed to capture *this* idea would certainly have failed to preserve anything recognizable as our current normative discourse. As we have seen, however, realists posit not only the *modest* attitude-independence of normative reasons (which antirealists are perfectly capable of accounting for), but also the *robust* attitude-independence of normative reasons. And while it's plausible to think that the assumption of modest attitude-independence is "built into" our concept of a normative reason, it is *not* plausible to think that the assumption of *robust* attitude-independence is "built into" the concept. The concept of a normative reason grew up and continues to thrive in the context of ordinary human beings—a context in which one never encounters ideally coherent eccentrics. It is therefore utterly implausible to suggest that one must agree with Parfit and other realists about such esoteric cases *in order recognizably to possess the concept in question*, or that to adopt the antirealist's view of such cases is to give up on the idea that there are normative reasons at all.

6. A Brief Return to Williams and Transition to Epistemological Worries

It is worth returning at this juncture to something that Parfit says about Williams, and then commenting on it. In puzzling over Williams's views, and continuing to insist that Williams lacked the concept of a purely normative reason, Parfit writes:

> When I have earlier claimed that Williams did not understand this external concept of a reason, some people have urged me to be more *charitable*. These people suggest that, like Scanlon, I should assume that Williams had this concept, and was merely making different claims about which facts give us reasons. But this assumption would, I believe, be *less* charitable. If Williams *did* understand the external normative sense, why does he so often call this sense mysterious and obscure? Though many of us misunderstand our own thoughts, I find it hard to believe, given his brilliance, that *Williams* could have been so muddled or confused. And, if Williams understood the idea that certain facts might count in favour of certain acts, some of his remarks would be baffling. It would be baffling, for example, why he claims that, in *Early Death*, you have no reason to take your medicine. How could Williams believe that though, as you know, taking your medicine would give you many more years of happy life, this fact does not count in favour of your acting in this way? (*OWM*, II, 434)

In this passage Parfit again seems to be failing to distinguish clearly enough between the concept of a reason in the standard normative sense (the concept **normative reason**$_{NEUT}$) and the concept **normative reason**$_{EXT}$. I think it's this conflation, in part, that makes it so hard for Parfit to understand why Williams says some of the things he does. For example, when Parfit writes "If Williams did understand the external normative sense, why does he so often call this sense mysterious and obscure?" he seems clearly to be wondering "If Williams did understand the concept of a reason in the standard normative sense, why does he so often call this sense mysterious and obscure?" Given what I have said to characterize *this* concept—as a concept that all of us are capable of acquiring in virtue of a certain kind of conscious experience that can be pointed at—it would indeed seem strange for someone to insist that they find it mysterious and obscure. As I've suggested, the concept is no more mysterious nor obscure than a color concept, or the concept of a certain taste or smell. But presumably what Williams was finding mysterious and obscure was not *this* concept—not what we are calling the notion of a reason in the standard normative sense—but rather the notion of an *external* reason in the standard normative sense.

Yet even here, Parfit is baffled. If Williams possessed the concept of a reason in the standard normative sense, then why on earth would he hold that in *Early Death* the fact that the medicine would save your life is not a reason for you to act that way? Here, though, as someone who believes the same thing as Williams about such a case, I can speak to Parfit's question of how someone could believe this. The answer is that someone could believe this because he or she thinks that taking the contrary view is unacceptable for *metaphysical and epistemological reasons.* In short, to posit that there is a reason to take the medicine in *Early Death* is to posit that there are normative reasons for action that exist attitude-independently in an extremely robust sense—such that a person can have a normative reason of a certain kind in a way that floats entirely free of his or her own normative responses to the world. But one might reasonably think (as I do) that to posit normative reasons of *this* kind—not just modestly attitude-independent, but *robustly attitude-independent* normative reasons—is what suddenly involves one in a host of problems, including, most notably in my view, an inability to account for how we could ever know about normative reasons of this sort.

When Parfit asks, "How could Williams believe that though, as you know, taking your medicine would give you many more years of happy life, this fact does not count in favour of your acting in this way?" the answer "maybe because he thinks metaphysical and epistemological worries force us to this view" does not, at that moment, even seem to be on Parfit's radar as a possibility. I take it that this is because Parfit is thinking of the claim in question—about our reason to take the medicine—as a substantive normative claim, and so more "meta-ethical" kinds of worries do not spring to mind as potentially relevant here. But what I hope this whole discussion shows—and what Parfit himself seems to acknowledge at other points[14]—is that there is ultimately no clean divide here between substantive normative issues and "meta-ethical" issues, such that the claim that the person has a normative reason in *Early Death* is immune to questioning based on epistemological worries. It is *not* so immune. The worry is that if you posit that there are normative reasons of this sort—robustly attitude-independent ones in the sense that they're there in a way that is *not* ultimately a function of the attitudes of the agent whose reasons are in question—then it suddenly becomes obscure what these things really could be, or how we could ever really know about them.

7. Why Parfit's Reply to the Evolutionary Debunking Argument Fails

In Chapter 33 of *On What Matters*, Parfit raises a battery of objections to my evolutionary debunking argument against realism.[15] Unfortunately there is not space to address all of them here, so I will limit myself to brief replies to three in particular. I single out these three because they seem to me the most important objections, and moreover they fail, in my view, in virtue of the same basic conflation I've been talking about throughout the paper.

7.1. First Objection

It is most efficient to quote Parfit directly:

> These [evolutionary debunking] arguments cannot succeed, since they have one premise which is much less plausible than the normative beliefs which they claim to undermine. (*OWM*, II, 522)

> Two such beliefs [that the skeptical arguments claim to undermine] are:
>
>> (U) When certain facts imply that some belief must be true, these facts give us a decisive reason to have this belief.

---

[14] See *OWM*, I, 109, where Parfit briefly acknowledges that meta-ethical considerations might be what push many people to subjectivism (which Parfit understands as a substantive normative position).

[15] For this argument, see especially "A Darwinian Dilemma for Realist Theories of Value," *Philosophical Studies*, 127/1 (2006): 109–66.

And

> (V) When certain facts imply that some belief is very likely to be true, these facts give us a robust reason to have this belief.

When normative skeptics challenge these beliefs, their arguments must assume that

> (W) We have no way of knowing whether such normative beliefs are true.

Of these three claims, much the least plausible is (W). If (W) were true, we could not know whether

> (X) we ever have any reasons to have any beliefs.

But we do know that we sometimes have such reasons. (*OWM*, II, 521–2)

7.2. Reply to First Objection

Nowhere in the evolutionary debunking argument is it assumed, and nowhere do I ever assume, that (W). I'm the first one to agree that we *do* have a way of knowing whether our normative beliefs (whether about practical or epistemic reasons) are true. Indeed, it's the very implausibility of (W) that, I argue, forces us to abandon *realism*—because it's the assumption of realism that gets us to (W) as a consequence. In other words, the question is not whether (U) and (V) are true, or whether we have any way of knowing they are; I completely agree that they're true and that we have a way of knowing they are. The point that's up for discussion is whether (U) and (V) are not just true, but true in a way that is *robustly* independent of our attitudes. And the view that they are *attitude-independently* true in Parfit's very robust sense, far from being an unshakable fixed point, is itself the esoteric assumption that is ultimately less plausible than any of the others in play.

7.3. Second Objection

Here again it is easiest to quote Parfit directly:

> On Street's account, the evolutionary forces caused us to have certain reproductively advantageous normative beliefs. We were led to

believe that pain and injury are bad, and that we have robust reasons to promote the survival and well-being of ourselves and our children... [W]e can reply that, even if [these beliefs] were [produced by natural selection], these beliefs are not badly mistaken, but correspond to some of the independent normative truths. Pain is bad, and we do have robust reasons to promote the survival and well-being of ourselves and our children. So even on Street's account, our normative thinking would have started with some true normative beliefs. The power of rational reflection could then have led us to believe other such truths. (*OWM*, II, 533)

7.4. Reply to Second Objection

This is completely inadequate as an answer to the evolutionary argument against realism. Consider an analogy. Suppose someone has just learned that his belief that Hayes was the twentieth president was implanted in him by a whimsical hypnotist. But suppose that he continues to insist that the hypnotist made him reliable with respect to the question of who was the twentieth president. When you ask him why, imagine he says "I know the hypnotist made me reliable because Hayes *was* the twentieth president, and that's exactly the belief the hypnotist implanted in me." It is obvious that this person has supplied no good reason whatsoever to think that the hypnotist has made him reliable on the question of who was the twentieth president. Parfit's answer here is of exactly the same form. Our question was: Why think evolutionary forces would have made us reliable with respect to independent normative truths of the kind Parfit posits? And Parfit's answer here is that "I know evolution made me reliable because pain *is* bad, and we *do* have robust reasons to promote the survival and well-being of ourselves and our children, and those are exactly the beliefs that evolutionary forces implanted in me." This is unacceptable in the same way that the reply in the hypnotism case is unacceptable.

7.5. Third Objection

Parfit anticipates such a reply, and objects next:

To answer her argument, Street...writes, we must show that the evolutionary forces have led us to form true normative beliefs, and we must defend this claim without making any assumptions about which normative beliefs are true. What Street here requires us to do is impossible. Some whimsical despot might require us to show that some clock is telling the correct time, without making any assumptions about the correct time. Though we couldn't meet this requirement, that wouldn't show that this clock is not telling the correct time. In the same way, we couldn't possibly show that natural selection had led us to form some true normative beliefs without making any assumptions about which normative beliefs are true. This fact does not count against the view that these normative beliefs are true. (*OWM*, II, 533)

7.6. Reply to Third Objection

This objection is based on a serious misunderstanding of what is being asked. Here again Parfit is failing to distinguish between the view *that there are normative truths and we have some idea of what they are*, which I agree with, from the view *that there are* robustly attitude-independent *normative truths and we have some idea of what they are*. It's the *latter* view that I am challenging, and which Parfit is not, in this context, simply entitled to assume without argument. I am by no means requiring that Parfit show us that evolution made us reliable about normative matters without making any assumptions about normative matters; I agree that *this* would be impossible. That is why Parfit is more than welcome to assume that pain *is* bad, and we *do* have robust reasons to promote the survival and well-being of ourselves and our children, and so on. I agree with all these claims (as applied to ordinary human beings in ordinary circumstances, anyway). The question we are considering is not whether we are reliable about these and other such normative matters— again, it is a key assumption of my own argument that we are. Rather, the question we are considering is whether, *on the assumption that normative truths are robustly attitude-independent*, we would have any reason to think that evolutionary forces shaped our normative beliefs in such a way as to make us reliable about them. It's in answer to *that* question that it is unacceptable to reply: "Yes, I do have reason to think that evolutionary forces shaped our normative beliefs in such a way as to make us reliable, because the *independent normative truth* is X, Y, and Z, and that's exactly what the evolutionary forces shaped me to think."

8. Realism, Theism, and Nihilism as a Causal Threat

If the argument of this paper has been successful, then we have located the conceptual space for a position that is skeptical about the existence of *robustly attitude-independent* reasons, but not about the existence of *reasons*. But locating this space doesn't mean that suddenly all our problems in life are solved, of course, nor does it mean, as we perhaps might have hoped, that there is nothing left to the deeper spirit of philosophical worries about nihilism. On the contrary, there's something big left to those worries.

The worry might be put this way: One way of reading Parfit is as holding the following *substantive normative position*:

> (P1) Nothing matters unless it matters in a way that is robustly attitude-independent.

Couple this with my contention that

> (P2) Nothing matters in a way that is robustly attitude-independent.

and you get the conclusion that

> (C) Nothing matters.

Now obviously I think P2 is right; that is the denial of realism. But I also reject (C): I think that many things matter—indeed, I think that many things matter a very great deal. I just think, of the things that matter, that their mattering ultimately depends on their mattering *to* beings like us. In other words, I think that things matter in *modestly* attitude-independent ways, not in *robustly* attitude-independent ways. What I want to reject, then, is P1. How might this go?

The thought is that P1 must be interpreted as a substantive normative claim that makes a claim about what matters and under what conditions. (I have argued that it cannot plausibly be understood as a *conceptual* truth.) But once one reads it as a substantive normative position, it becomes opaque why anyone would hold this substantive normative position—what reason there would be to think that something doesn't matter unless it matters (robustly) attitude-independently. Consider the analogy between:

(A) Nothing matters unless there is a god.

and

(B) Nothing matters unless there are robustly attitude-independent normative truths.

We (at least many of us engaged in secular meta-ethics) don't find (A) plausible (Parfit explicitly rejects this idea[16]), so the suggestion is why find (B) any more plausible?

The thing is, even if you agree with me that (B) is an implausible substantive normative thesis, it's still not true that there is nothing left to worries about nihilism. The whole idea behind antirealism is that things matter, but only ultimately in virtue of your thinking they do. The *causal* threat of ceasing to think things matter never goes away, and there's a kind of vertigo involved in recognizing that value is there only as long as you think it is and that you could slip into a state in which you stop thinking there is. But here it seems to me the only measures we can take against *that* possibility are causal—getting enough sleep, eating right, cultivating a wide and deep range of interests, and so on. We should fear the view that nothing matters not as a philosophical position that might, to our dismay, turn out to be correct, independently of what we think or hope—but rather as a state of mind we might fall into—false as long as we don't fall into it, but true as soon as we do.[17]

[16] See *OWM*, II, 444.

[17] For helpful comments on earlier drafts, I am indebted to Terence Cuneo, David Owens, Nishi Shah, Matthew Silverstein, David Sobel, David Velleman, and Jared Warren. I am also grateful for the feedback I received from audiences at Bowling Green University, Colgate University, the University of Kent, Rutgers University, Tulane University, UNC Chapel Hill, and the 2012 SPAWN Workshop at Syracuse University.

7

KNOWING WHAT MATTERS

Richard Yetter Chappell

1. Causal Origins-based Skepticism

1.1. The Naturalist Argument for Normative Skepticism

There are any number of logically consistent moral worldviews that a person might endorse. Many of us hold that pain is always and everywhere bad. But we can just as well imagine aliens who consider pain and suffering to be intrinsically good,[1] or 'Future Tuesday Indifferent'[2] agents who hold that pain only matters when experienced on days other than Tuesday. Such values strike us as bizarre, but we can nonetheless imagine agents who hold them sincerely, and who consider *us* bizarre for denying what seem to them 'obvious' facts about the value of pain. Call this the fact of *coherent moral diversity*.

According to Parfit's non-naturalist normative realism (hereafter, 'moral realism'), there's an objective fact of the matter about the dis/value of pain. There's one correct view, and all other possible views are—to a greater or lesser extent—mistaken. This then raises an obvious epistemological challenge for realists who also take a stand in favor of one

---

[1] I will continue to speak of 'pro-pain' agents, for vividness, but if you doubt the coherence of this particular example, feel free to substitute a less extreme case of moral error.
[2] D. Parfit, *Reasons and Persons* (Oxford: Oxford University Press, 1984), 124.

first-order moral viewpoint over others: Why think that *their* moral view, amongst all the coherent possibilities, is the correct one?

The problem is especially acute for those of us who share Parfit's view that the moral facts, being non-natural, are causally inert. For this means that we cannot consider our moral beliefs to be caused by the moral facts, the way we think that our perceptions of physical objects are typically caused by those objects. Such a causal connection could explain the reliability of our beliefs. In its absence, we seem to be left without any grounds for taking our moral belief-forming mechanisms to be at all reliable. After all, there is going to be some purely natural, causal explanation of why we've ended up with the particular moral beliefs that we have—perhaps appealing to evolutionary, psychological, or sociocultural factors—a causal explanation that at no point invokes the moral facts themselves as playing any role in shaping our moral intuitions. Call this *the causal irrelevance of the moral facts*.

Critics like Sharon Street then ask: Shouldn't we then think it extraordinarily *unlikely* that those natural causes would happen to lead us to the one true morality? Given the fact of coherent moral diversity, plus the causal irrelevance of the moral facts, realists seem forced to admit that it would be a 'striking coincidence'[3] if our moral beliefs turned out to be (anywhere near) correct. We shouldn't believe something so improbable. So if we accept moral realism, we're committed to thinking ourselves totally ignorant and incapable of grasping the moral truth. This argument is a version of what Parfit calls 'the Naturalist Argument for Normative Skepticism' (*OWM*, II, 513).

1.2. Parfit's Response

First consider how we could respond if the argument's target (whose reliability was in question) was not ourselves, but some alien species. In the absence of any more particular information, we have no *antecedent* reason for expecting some arbitrarily chosen alien species to be morally reliable. But rather than trying to assess their reliability more or less a priori, with little or no concrete information, we would do better to

---

[3] S. Street, 'Objectivity and Truth: You'd Better Rethink It' (ms).

inquire into their concrete circumstances. If we look and find that the aliens seem generally sympathetic and altruistic, concerned to promote the well-being and non-harmful life goals of other sentient beings, then we may be reasonably confident that they're on the (morally) right track, whatever the causal process that brought this about. If, on the other hand, they seem to enjoy gratuitous torture, then we'll judge them to be morally abhorrent.

Moving up a level of abstraction, we may also have some idea of what evolutionary and socio-cultural pressures are most likely to bring about these morally good practices in an intelligent species. For example, we may expect sympathy and altruistic norms to more likely arise in social animals where there are great gains to cooperation, and where pair-bonding and parental investment are important for long-term reproductive success. The precise details don't matter for my purposes. The point is just that, once we learn that a species lives in a certain kind of environment, it will no longer be a 'coincidence' if they turn out to have generally correct views about the value of friendship, love, sympathy, aversion to pain, etc.[4] And so it is for human beings: We (as observers, using our best moral judgment) may reasonably conclude that we (as anthropological subjects) are, for all our manifest faults, generally pretty reliable on moral matters!

Of course it sounds hopelessly circular to use our own moral judgments to assess our moral reliability like this, and it certainly won't persuade the skeptic—but trying to persuade the committed skeptic is a fool's game. It's logically impossible to give a non-question-begging justification to one who questions *everything*. So that cannot be our goal. A more appropriately modest philosophical goal is simply to provide an *internal* defense of our claims to knowledge, showing how the realist—given her starting assumptions—could reasonably fail to be swayed by the skeptic's argument. The question for us is thus not whether the skeptic must, on pain of inconsistency, grant the realist's claim to moral knowledge (of course he needn't), but whether the realist is forced to

[4] Cf. D. Copp, "Darwinian Skepticism About Moral Realism," *Philosophical Issues*, 18/1 (2008): 186–206, and D. Enoch, "The Epistemological Challenge to Metanormative Realism: How Best to Understand It, and How to Cope with It," *Philosophical Studies*, 148/3 (2010): 413–38.

accept the skeptical conclusion that she lacks moral knowledge. We have nowhere else to start but from the premises that seem to us to be true, and from this starting point there's nothing obviously self-undermining about the moral realist's worldview.

In his response to the Naturalist Argument for Normative Skepticism, Parfit similarly defends the need for making normative assumptions along the way:

> Some whimsical despot might require us to show that some clock is telling the correct time, without making any assumptions about the correct time. Though we couldn't meet this requirement, that wouldn't show that this clock is not telling the correct time. In the same way, we couldn't possibly show that natural selection had led us to form some true normative beliefs without making any assumptions about which normative beliefs are true. This fact does not count against the view that these normative beliefs are true. (*OWM*, II, 533)

After this point, however, Parfit takes an odd turn. He concedes to the skeptic that if our 'normative beliefs were mostly produced by evolutionary forces... that would count strongly against the view that we can respond to [their] intrinsic credibility' (534). He then spends several pages arguing that our normative beliefs are not plausibly explained by evolution.

This is puzzling, for two reasons. First, if evolutionary forces didn't cause our normative beliefs, that just means that some other natural cause did. This makes Parfit's fixation on specifically *evolutionary* causes baffling. Why should evolutionary forces be seen with any more or less suspicion than any other (equally non-moral) natural cause?

Secondly, the quoted passage makes it sound as though 'evolution' and 'intrinsic credibility' are two rival causal explanations for our normative beliefs. But Parfit acknowledges that intrinsic credibility is not causally efficacious (*OWM*, II, 502). Presumably the way that we respond to the intrinsic credibility of a proposition is by being psychologically constituted such that we are disposed to believe the right things (*OWM*, II, 503; see also §2.1). Evolutionary forces may well be a large part of the causal story of how we got to be so constituted. And if not, there will be some other, similarly natural, causal story. Either way, there's no necessary tension between having the right psychology and having an independent (non-moral) causal explanation for how we came to possess this psychology.

Parfit seems to recognize this in the case of evolution via group selection: 'When the acceptance of certain normative beliefs made some community or culture more likely to survive and flourish, this fact does not *as such* cast doubt on the truth or plausibility of these beliefs' (*OWM*, II, 537, emphasis added). But surely the point generalizes: it's just as unclear why other causal origins should *as such* be epistemically undermining, independently of the substantive content of the beliefs thereby produced. Some special explanation must be offered for treating different kinds of causes differently, given that they are alike in the salient respect of being natural rather than normative.

Perhaps Parfit is assuming that individual-level selection is more likely to yield selfish rather than pro-social norms. That is, holding fixed our understanding of what particular things are right and wrong, one might expect individual-level selection to cause creatures to endorse the latter rather than the former. But then it is really the (presumed) *content* of these norms, rather than their origins, that Parfit is objecting to. This would render unnecessary his argument that our pro-social norms aren't explained by evolution. So long as they have the right content, their origin shouldn't matter. Since we actually endorse pro-social norms, we know (trivially) that evolution did *not* lead us to endorse the contrary norms that we take to be wrong, so we have no content-based reason for taking our beliefs' possible evolutionary origins to be undermining. If evolution caused our actual beliefs, then the beliefs it caused are pro-social, for those are the beliefs that we actually have.

Parfit thus faces a dilemma. What he really needs is a purely *formal* reason for thinking that (individual-level) evolution, more than other natural causes, would likely have led us morally astray. But absent our substantive normative assumptions—from the perspective of a moral 'blank slate'—there would be no basis for any such judgment. On the other hand, given our *substantive* normative assumptions (and the psychological fact that those are our normative assumptions), such a claim is trivially unfounded.

I wish to propose a more flat-footed response on behalf of the realist. Rather than relying on this dubious distinction between evolutionary and other causes, and holding our moral epistemology hostage to the contingencies of an unsettled empirical question, realists should cut off the skeptic's argument at its root—namely, its assumption that the causal origins of our normative beliefs are ever *in themselves* epistemically undermining.[5] The basic response to the skeptic's argument is then simple: All things considered, in light of all that we know or believe to be true, we have every internal reason to retain our 'default trust' in our normative beliefs.[6] From our current standpoint, we have every reason to regard our pro-social evolutionary heritage as providing us with roughly correct moral intuitions (along with various biases which we can hope to identify and dispel by reasoning from our core moral commitments). So reflection on the causal origins of our moral beliefs is not in itself epistemically undermining. It would only be undermining if we accepted the skeptical principle that we need to provide an *independent* justification for our beliefs—a justification that would convince even one who has adopted a position of radical doubt towards the beliefs in question. But we should not accept such a skeptical principle. So it's not clear that there's any real force to the Naturalist Argument for Normative Skepticism after all.

1.3. *The Moral Lottery*

Street acknowledges that 'in seeking to answer the skeptical challenge...the normative realist is...entitled to offer an answer that is ultimately question-begging'.[7] However, she goes on to claim that the flat-footed realist reply 'provides no *reason* to think that the causal forces described by our best scientific explanations shaped our normative

---

[5] The italicized proviso is necessary to rule out trivial cases where, e.g., one is caused to believe a moral claim previously known to be false. In that case it is not the cause per se, but more fundamentally the resulting belief, that is the problem.
[6] On the importance of default trust, see P. Railton, "How to Engage Reason: The Problem of Regress," in *Reason and Value: Themes from the Moral Philosophy of Joseph Raz*, ed. R. J. Wallace, P. Pettit, S. Scheffler, and M. Smith (Oxford: Clarendon Press, 2004), and also §2.2.
[7] Street, OT, 26.

judgments in ways that might have led those judgments to track the truth; it merely confidently reasserts that they did'. Here the dialectic becomes murky: Given our prior belief that (e.g.) helping others is good, why does this not qualify as an internal reason to think that pro-social evolutionary forces put a species on the morally right track? It's not an independent or non-question-begging reason, granted, but that doesn't yet show that it is no reason at all.

Street's subsequent discussion of perceptual epistemology suggests the following view. We may seek to explain the accuracy of our mental faculties in either of two ways. Firstly, we might presuppose some particular, substantive claims in the domain in question, and then merely show how our mental faculties would lead us to believe those putative truths. This is the kind of explanation—call it *substantive explanation*—that the moral realist offers. By contrast, a *constitutive explanation* aims to show how our mental faculties can be reliable merely in virtue of general facts about the nature of the domain in question. For example, it is in the nature of concrete objects to have causal powers, which offers a general explanation of how we might reliably detect them. Similarly, on Street's constructivist anti-realism, it is in the nature of normative facts that they be coherent outgrowths of our core practical commitments, which suggests a general explanation of how reasoning from our core practical commitments might be expected to lead us to true moral beliefs. On Street's view, these constitutive explanations are epistemically legitimate (though the radical skeptic could deny even these), but substantive explanations are not. Call this *Street's principle*. My claim is then that moral realists should simply reject Street's principle. When engaging in wide reflective equilibrium we may appeal to *all* our beliefs, including our particular substantive beliefs within a domain, as providing (defeasible) internal reasons.

But even if the most general form of the skeptical argument thus fails, perhaps there are ways of expanding upon it to show that the realist is (by their own lights) in epistemic trouble. Street's lottery analogy suggests one such route:

> [The realist's response] is no better than insisting, without any non-trivially-question-begging reason to think so, that one has won

the New York Lottery. Given the odds we can reasonably suppose to be in play in this 'normative lottery' case, we should conclude that in all probability we *didn't* win—that, if there is indeed such a thing as the robustly independent normative truth we are positing as a substantive normative premise, then we are probably among the unlucky ones who (just like the ideally coherent Caligula, grass-counter, hand-clasper, and so on) are hopeless at recognizing it. (21)

To restate the argument: We all accept epistemic principles that disallow believing (a priori) oneself to have won the lottery against all odds. And, Street assumes, the fact of coherent moral diversity plus the causal irrelevance of the moral facts together establish that the non-skeptical moral realist is in an epistemically equivalent position of believing herself to have won the 'normative lottery' against all odds. So those same epistemic principles must similarly disallow the realist from complacently believing herself to be so lucky.

The main problem with this analogy concerns the 'odds' that we assign to the various outcomes. Given our understanding of the physical lottery mechanism, we know that we should assign equal odds to each possible outcome, and hence the odds we should assign to some particular ticket (#139583923, say) winning are extremely low. For Street's argument to work, it must be that we are similarly required to assign equal (or roughly equal) odds to the truth of each possible normative system. But *why think that*? I certainly have no antecedent inclination to assign equal odds to all possible normative systems—I think it's overwhelmingly more likely that pain is intrinsically bad than that it's intrinsically good, and I don't see anything in Street's argument that suggests I should change my mind. (It's not as though the normative truth was itself settled by a chance process that gave equal objective probability to each possible outcome.)

Street might try to push the analogy by asking us to imagine a lottery player who likewise insists that the (a priori) odds of ticket #139583923 winning are much higher than for any other ticket. There are a couple of things to say about this. Firstly, I agree that such a person would be crazy. But my reasons for thinking this depend on a fact specific to the physical lottery case, namely, the role of a chance mechanism in producing the outcome. A person who fails to assign equal odds across the possible outcomes of a fair lottery either doesn't understand the underlying physical mechanism, or else is violating the epistemic principle that we should apportion our credences to correspond to the objective chances.[8] But this reason doesn't carry over to the normative case, where the truth of the matter was not settled by a chance process. It's only by employing our normative judgment that we can draw any conclusions about the likelihoods of various normative claims.[9] That's the most important point. But the following consideration is also of interest: It's not entirely clear that the irrationality of the physical lottery player consists in *internal incoherence*; we may instead take them to be *substantively* irrational, as a matter of mind-independent normative fact, though of course Street cannot accommodate such a 'realist' thought.

So I think Street's argument strictly fails: There's nothing incoherent about assigning higher odds (a priori) to anti-pain normative systems than to pro-pain views. So the moral realist needn't conclude that she is 'probably' among the misguided when she holds to her anti-pain view. It's true that our views are structurally analogous to others (like the pro-pain view) that we hold to be mistaken. But there's nothing wrong with the *structure* of those other views—they're just wrong on the substance. So we shouldn't be particularly troubled to share the structure of the wrongheaded view, just with different substance. That's how the right view would *have* to look.

Suppose you grant that the realist *needn't* (on pain of incoherence) take herself to be 'probably' among the misguided. Still, you may think, perhaps it's still the case that she really *should*, as a matter of substantive epistemic rationality, conclude this. But now you're positing a mind-independent normative truth. And if the argument against normative realism depends upon the truth of realism, then that can't possibly be a sound argument!

---

[8] Cf. D. Lewis, "A Subjectivist's Guide to Objective Chance," in *Philosophical Papers*, Vol. 2 (Oxford: Oxford University Press, 1986).
[9] See also K. Schafer, "Evolution and Normative Scepticism," *Australasian Journal of Philosophy*, 88/3 (2010): 471–88.

2. A Positive View

2.1. Explication

We've seen that there's no sound argument against realism to be found here. But there is at least a *challenge* for the realist, to say more about how moral knowledge is possible on her view. I can't give a full answer here, but here's a rough sketch of a view:[10] There's a fact of the matter as to which psychologies qualify as *fitting* or 'substantively rational'. The fitting psychology might, among other things, endorse *modus ponens* as a valid rule of inference, accept inductive over counter-inductive norms, and take the badness of pain as a provisional moral datum. More generally: the fitting psychology is one that reflects or 'fits with' the objective normative facts, whatever they may be. So, if the truth of *p* would in fact be a reason to believe that *q*, then the fitting psychology is one that responds to the appearance of *p* with an inclination towards believing *q*. If some outcome *o* is intrinsically desirable, then the fitting agent is one who intrinsically desires *o*. Inferences drawn, and conclusions reached, by agents with fitting psychologies are, on this view, thereby justified— and, if true, eligible to qualify as knowledge.

That seems a coherent view, and one that allows for (fitting) agents to know the mind-independent moral facts. One might think of it as akin to a kind of reliabilism (the view that true beliefs formed via reliable methods thereby constitute knowledge). Simple reliabilism is clearly immune to Street-style skeptical arguments: The mere fact that there are *other*, less reliable, processes does nothing at all to undermine the process that I actually use. Even if I have no independent way of verifying that the process I use is one of the few reliable ones, all that matters is that it *is* reliable as a matter of actual fact. And this highlights the disanalogy with the physical lottery: Presumably there's no way to be a reliable predictor of lottery results, the way that an anti-pain moralist might be a reliable predictor of moral truths. Similar observations may be made when using the fittingness view in place of reliabilism.

---

[10] Of course, I don't mean to suggest that the view I go on to sketch is the *only* option for the realist.

One reason to prefer the fittingness view to traditional reliabilism is that the latter implausibly holds the justification of our beliefs hostage to purely external circumstances. The sensory 'perceptions' of a Brain in a Vat, for example, are not very reliable, but surely my BIV-duplicate is no less rationally justified in his beliefs than I am in mine.[11] The fittingness view, by contrast, is 'internalist' in the following important sense: Epistemic justification supervenes on one's mental states, so that any two intrinsic duplicates are alike with respect to the justificatory status of their beliefs. We might characterize the fittingness view as a priori *expected reliabilism*, whereby what matters is not whether my actual belief-forming mechanisms are reliable in the actual world, but rather whether my actual belief-forming mechanisms are *expectably* reliable, given the objective a priori probability distribution over possible worlds.[12] (This probability distribution, being a priori, does not differ depending on which world is actual. This is how the view manages to be 'internalist' in the above sense.)

The fittingness view can also comfortably grant that *mere* reliability is not enough.[13] For example, an agent who merely found themselves automatically parroting the claim that slavery is wrong, without any understanding of the reasons why, might well strike us as a poor candidate for moral knowledge. But the fitting agent is not so vacuous. Rather, she possesses a complex and interweaving 'web' of moral beliefs, accurately reflecting the explanatory relations that hold between the actual moral facts. She thus understands *why* slavery is wrong, such that she is reliably accurate not just on this precise question but also various permutations of the case. She knows what the morally relevant considerations are, and exhibits sensitivity to them in two crucial respects: (1) she recognizes when similar underlying moral considerations arise in superficially different cases, and (2) she recognizes when morally relevant differences

---

[11] S. Cohen, "Justification and Truth," *Philosophical Studies*, 46/3 (1984): 279–95.
[12] The idea of an a priori objective probability distribution is controversial, but I think it can do important explanatory work. The basic idea is that some possible worlds were, as a matter of brute fact, *more likely* to be actualized than others. For example, we may think that simpler and more uniform worlds are more 'eligible' or likely to exist, and this is why it is fitting to reason according to inductive rather than counter-inductive norms.
[13] Thanks to William Fitzpatrick for pressing me on this point.

should prompt different verdicts in superficially similar cases. Fill in further details of the fitting or 'substantively rational' psychological profile as you please. What matters for my purposes is, firstly, that such a psychological profile could emerge in an agent through purely natural causes, and secondly, that the true beliefs of such a broadly reliable— indeed, *wise*—moral agent plausibly constitute moral knowledge.

To wrap up: It may be epistemically undermining if *this psychology* I'm using was lucky to get things right. That casts doubt on the rationality of my psychological processes. But there's no such problem if I'm merely lucky to have *acquired* a rational psychology in the first place. That doesn't cast doubt on the rationality of the psychology I have; it merely suggests that I could easily have ended up with some other, less rational, psychology instead. To which the appropriate response is simply, 'Thank goodness I didn't!'

Non-skeptical normative realists are merely committed to the latter, unproblematic kind of epistemic luck. Given the fact of coherent moral diversity, and the causal irrelevance of the moral facts, there's no guarantee that agents will end up with substantively rational or normatively fitting psychologies. And there's no 'neutral', purely procedural way to test for substantive normative correctness. All that we can do is pursue wide reflective equilibrium, resolving the inconsistencies in our thoughts in whatever way strikes us as overall most plausible, and hope for the best.[14] When we consider all the possible ways of being crazy without realizing it, we may have a feeling of 'There but for the grace of God go I'. In this sense, we must consider ourselves 'lucky' to be rational: We can just as well imagine circumstances causing us to have substantively crazy normative commitments, and it was not in our control that we happened to be born into the good circumstances rather than the bad. But, crucially, none of this implies that we are *now* unreliable, or that *given our actual psychology* the odds of our answering moral questions correctly is low. Being in some sense 'lucky' to possess a reliable, rational, and competent psychology does not, of course, make one's actual psychology any

---

[14] That's not to say that reflective equilibrium is sufficient. What we really need, to be in a good epistemic position, is to pursue reflective equilibrium *from an objectively adequate starting point*. Cf. T. Kelly and S. McGrath, "Is Reflective Equilibrium Enough?" *Philosophical Perspectives*, 24/1 (2010): 325–59.

less reliable, rational, or competent. It most certainly does not imply that the correctness of one's conclusions is mere luck or accident, as opposed to being the expected result of one's rational competence. But that is the conclusion the skeptic needs to establish in order to undermine normative realism. Since they cannot establish this, the skeptical challenge is thus defanged.

2.2. Defense

While I haven't space here to offer a full-fledged defense of the above sketched view, let me offer a few quick comments to assuage the concerns of some who might initially regard it as excessively 'dogmatic'. So far I've shown that the view is internally coherent and defensible, even in the face of Street's arguments. I now want to suggest that many should find the view positively appealing, as the best way to render coherent our various common-sense commitments. Here are three considerations in support of this conclusion.

First, there is the Moorean point that we may reasonably be more confident in our first-order moral views than we are of any skeptical principle to the contrary, including Street's principle (from §1.3, that we should regard our moral faculties as unreliable unless we can give a constitutive, as opposed to substantive, explanation of their reliability). Street hopes that her constructivist anti-realism can accommodate enough of the moral data to provide a viable alternative to moral realism. I think it's far from clear that we should have greater credence in Street's principle than in the realist's datum that even pro-pain agents shouldn't engage in gratuitous torture. Regardless, as I'll now argue, we can rule out Street's constructivism on the stronger grounds that it is self-defeating.

Constructivism is the view that eligible normative judgments—those that 'withstand scrutiny' from the agent's normative standpoint—thereby constitute normative truths.[15] Call $S_{PROPAIN}$ the situation of making an eligible judgment that one ought to engage in gratuitous torture. Constructivism implies that any agent in $S_{PROPAIN}$ thereby really ought to engage in gratuitous torture. Yet many realists hold the contrary belief

[15] Street, OT.

that they shouldn't engage in gratuitous torture *even if* they found themselves in situation $S_{PROPAIN}$. If this normative belief of ours also withstands scrutiny, then constructivism will imply that it is true, thereby contradicting itself. Constructivists are thus committed to showing that moral realism is incoherent, or cannot withstand scrutiny from the normative standpoint of any possible agent.[16] But we've seen that moral realism is *not* incoherent (however substantively implausible some may find it), and so Street's constructivist alternative fails. This forces us back to the initial choice between flat-footed realism and skepticism, reinforcing the Moorean case for the former.

Second, the epistemologically awkward feature of moral realism—that any explanation of our reliability must presuppose substantive claims within the domain—is not unique to the moral domain. It seems equally true of our inductive norms, for example. We can imagine an internally-coherent 'counter-inductivist' who takes the sun's rising in the past as evidence that it will *fail* to rise in the future. There is not enough common ground to productively argue with a person who has such fundamentally different epistemic norms. Still, outside of the philosophy seminar room, few of us take the problem of induction at all seriously. The possibility of alternative inductive practices does not seem to undermine our confidence in our own inductive practices. If the possibility of fundamental epistemic diversity does not undermine our epistemic norms, it's unclear why the moral case should be so different.

Third, a general lesson from reflecting on radical skepticism is that we sometimes need to make our peace with having reached justificatory bedrock. We feel the pull of the Socratic ideal to 'question everything', and to defend our views against all comers with non-question-begging

[16] Street, OT, 36, explicitly accepts this point, though William Fitzpatrick has pointed out to me that a constructivist might avoid this challenge by restricting 'eligibility' to *judgments about one's own actual current circumstances*. But this would leave ungrounded the various normative truths about non-actual, non-current circumstances. If the constructivist offered their theory as a mind-independent account of what's *objectively* true of those cases, then their theory would fall victim to all the same arguments that Street offers against moral realism. As Street acknowledges, her arguments can only support a more thoroughgoing constructivism: one that holds itself to be the unique meta-ethical truth that would be constructed from any possible standpoint.

reasons. But this simply cannot be done, so we should not grant too much weight to our persisting sense of unease over this.

3. Actual and Possible Disagreement

So far I've argued that Parfit is too concessive to causal-origins-based skepticism. In this section, I will argue that he concedes too much to disagreement-based skepticism. In particular, I'll argue that Parfit's response to merely possible disagreement should also extend to relevant cases of actual disagreement. To support this argument, I'll offer an analysis of when it makes an epistemic difference for a disagreement to be actual, and show that the relevant moral cases do not possess this feature.

3.1. Parfit on Disagreement

Parfit characterizes the *argument from disagreement* as follows:

> If we had strong reasons to believe that, even in [procedurally] ideal conditions, we and others *would* have deeply conflicting normative beliefs, it would be hard to defend the view that we have the intuitive ability to recognize some normative truths. We would have to believe that, when we disagree with others, it is only we who can recognize such truths. But if many other people, even in ideal conditions, could not recognize such truths, we could not rationally believe that we have this ability. How could *we* be so special? (*OWM*, II, 546, emphasis added)

Parfit is clearly concerned about this argument, and immediately concedes that 'Intuitionists must defend the claim that, in ideal conditions, we and others *would not* have such deeply conflicting beliefs' (546, emphasis added). He spends the rest of the chapter defending this convergence claim, following in the vein of the first volume of *On What Matters* (which argued for the convergence of Consequentialism, Contractualism, and Kantianism).

As noted previously, Parfit does grant the fact of *coherent moral diversity*, that people *could* have radically divergent moral beliefs even in procedurally ideal conditions. But such *merely possible* disagreement does not bother him nearly as much. 'If we claim that we have some ability,' he writes, 'it is no objection that we might have lacked this ability' (545). This response is very much in the spirit of the epistemology I sketched in the previous section: What matters is just that we in fact possess a rationally fitting psychology, and are thereby capable of recognizing self-evident moral truths as such. So long as our moral belief-forming processes are indeed a 'fairly reliable way of reaching the truth' (545), it is of no matter that we—or others—could have possessed some *other*, less reliable, psychology. (It can be a little unnerving when we reflect on the fact that there's no non-question-begging way to *show* that our psychology is as reliable as we hope it is, but so it goes.)

But now note that this reliabilist response doesn't depend upon the non-actuality of the 'other, less reliable psychologies' in question. They could be actually realized—whether in our neighbours or distant aliens—and it would still make no difference to the reliability of our moral beliefs (assuming that we don't defer to those misguided others). If it's reasonable to consider ourselves morally reliable or 'special' compared to a hypothetical pro-pain agent, what difference should it make if the imagined agent turns out to actually exist? Conversely: If it's epistemically undermining to be faced with an internally coherent alternative to your present views, why should it matter whether the advocate of this alternative view really exists, or is merely a figment of your imagination playing devil's advocate?

One possibility is that Parfit is thinking of our moral belief-forming process in very coarse-grained terms, e.g. as '[b]elieving what seems self-evident, after [careful] reflection' (545), a process that might be shared by pro-pain and other thoroughly wrongheaded agents.[17] So whether this shared process qualifies as statistically 'reliable' or not depends on what proportion of actually existing agents have the right intuitions to begin with. If there turns out to be great diversity in what moral beliefs actually result from using this process, then it doesn't reliably yield *any* particular results, let alone reliably *correct* ones.

---

[17] Ashley Atkins and Sarah McGrath have suggested, in conversation, that a more plausible variant of this view might be restricted in scope to some more limited moral community—e.g. just other humans—leaving distant aliens aside. But my below objection still applies to this more moderate view.

However, as suggested in §2.1, the rational status of our beliefs should not depend in this way on how things are outside of our heads. This untoward consequence is avoided by more fine-grained approaches, such as the fittingness view, which see our starting beliefs and intuitions as an essential part of our overall belief-forming process. This means we should separately assess the reliability of pro-pain and anti-pain moralists, rather than indiscriminately lumping them all together into a single class of epistemically-equivalent agents. Given this more fine-grained categorization, we avoid the absurd result that the reliability of *our* moral belief-forming process depends on the absence of creatures with radically *different* intuitive starting points.

3.2. When Actual Disagreement Matters

There are clearly some cases in which actual disagreement matters. If we learn that my thermometer actually disagrees with yours about the temperature, that's epistemically significant in a way that merely imagining a divergent thermometer reading is not. But I think the sort of 'ideal disagreement' that meta-ethicists are interested in does not share this feature. So let me say a bit more about these two kinds of disagreement, and why the modal status of a disagreement (as actual or merely possible) makes no difference in cases of the second kind.

In cases of what we might call 'non-ideal' disagreement, there's a presumption that the disagreement is rationally resolvable through the identification of some fallacy or procedural mis-step in the reasoning of either ourselves or our interlocutor. The disagreement is 'non-ideal' in the sense that we're only disagreeing because one of us made a blunder somewhere. We are sufficiently similar in our fundamental epistemic standards and methods that we can generally treat the other's output as a sign of what we (when not malfunctioning) would output. The epistemic significance of the disagreement is thus that the conflicting judgment of a previously-reliable source is some evidence that we have made a blunder *by our own lights*, though we may not yet have seen it. Now, obviously, merely *imagining* a blunder-detector going off in our vicinity is no more evidence of an actual blunder on our part than is an imagined fire siren evidence of an actual fire.

The case of 'ideal' or irresolvable disagreement is rather different. In this case, both agents are (we may stipulate) logically omniscient and hence fully confident that they have not made any procedural blunder in their reasoning. The other's disagreement casts no doubt on this, because the disagreement is instead traceable to a much more fundamental divergence in starting assumptions.

Here the epistemic significance of the disagreement is more indirect. It's significant just in that it brings to our attention a fact that we might otherwise have neglected: *there's this internally coherent alternative world-view against which we can muster no non-question-begging argument*. But of course we might just as well be gripped and troubled by this fact even if there never actually existed any advocate for the view in question. The challenge is just: why accept our worldview rather than some other? Any answer we try to give will naturally draw on the assumptions of our own worldview, and hence prove dialectically unsatisfying. But given the inevitability of this, perhaps it shouldn't bother us too much.

4. Conclusion

We've seen that Parfit addresses skeptical arguments, whether causal-origins-based or disagreement-based, by conceding the first step to the skeptic and then trying to draw a line further down the track. But this proved to be a slippery undertaking. In the causal origins case, Parfit draws a line between evolutionary influences on belief and other causal influences, claiming that only the former are sure to be epistemically undermining. In the disagreement case, he distinguishes actual and possible disagreement, again claiming that only the former should concern us. In both cases, I have argued, these distinctions lack the epistemic significance Parfit attributes to them, and leave the realist needlessly vulnerable to empirical contingencies. If we are to defend moral realism against these skeptical challenges, we must instead address them at their first step. By appealing to a new kind of reliabilist moral epistemology, I hope to have shown how we can meet this deeper challenge.[18]

[18] Thanks to Ashley Atkins, William Fitzpatrick, Alex Gregory, Elizabeth Harman, Barry Maguire, Sarah McGrath, Karl Schafer, Peter Singer, Jack Spencer, Helen Yetter-Chappell, and audiences at <http://www.philosophyetc.net> and Princeton University, for helpful discussion and comments.

References

Cohen, S. 1984. "Justification and Truth." *Philosophical Studies*, 46/3: 279–95.

Copp, D. 2008. "Darwinian Skepticism About Moral Realism." *Philosophical Issues*, 18/1: 186–206.

Enoch, D. 2010. "The Epistemological Challenge to Metanormative Realism: How Best to Understand It, and How to Cope with It." *Philosophical Studies*, 148/3: 413–38.

Kelly, T. and S. McGrath. 2010. "Is Reflective Equilibrium Enough?" *Philosophical Perspectives*, 24/1: 325–59.

Lewis, D. 1986. "A Subjectivist's Guide to Objective Chance." In *Philosophical Papers*, Vol. 2. Oxford: Oxford University Press.

Parfit, D. 1984. *Reasons and Persons*. Oxford: Oxford University Press.

Parfit, D. 2011. *On What Matters*. Vol. 2. Oxford: Oxford University Press.

Railton, P. 2004. "How to Engage Reason: The Problem of Regress." In *Reason and Value: Themes from the Moral Philosophy of Joseph Raz*, ed. R. J. Wallace, P. Pettit, S. Scheffler, and M. Smith. Oxford: Clarendon Press.

Schafer, K. 2010. "Evolution and Normative Scepticism." *Australasian Journal of Philosophy*, 88/3: 471–88.

Street, S. (ms.) 'Objectivity and Truth: You'd Better Rethink It'.

8

NIETZSCHE AND THE HOPE OF NORMATIVE CONVERGENCE

Andrew Huddleston

"Those who can breathe the air of my writings know that it is an air of the heights, a *strong* air. One must be made for it. Otherwise there is no small danger one may catch cold in it. The ice is near, the solitude tremendous...Philosophy, as I have so far understood and lived it, means living voluntarily among ice and high mountains—seeking out everything strange and questionable in existence, everything so far placed under a ban by morality."

Nietzsche, "Preface" to *Ecce Homo*, 3

1. Introduction

Near the end of *On What Matters*, Derek Parfit offers a defense of what he calls the "convergence claim." According to this claim of Parfit's, we would all reach the same normative beliefs under certain idealized conditions (*OWM*, II, 570). Envisaging what would happen in such rarefied circumstances is not easy. Yet, insofar as we can get some clear sense of what would happen were the idealization conditions to obtain, Nietzsche, more than any other figure in the philosophical tradition, would seem to pose a serious challenge to any hope for this convergence. This is not just because Nietzsche disagrees with Parfit on the philosophical question of whether this convergence is likely, though surely he does. It is rather because Nietzsche scoffs at the moral values that to many of us can seem self-evident. In their stead, he proposes ideals imbued with a blend of aestheticism, elitism, and Homeric heroism, assigning these perfection-ist values a priority that is deeply alien to conventional moral sensibili-ties. The "most influential and admired moral philosopher of the last two centuries" (*OWM*, II, 570) would thus, at first glance, seem to be out of step with some of our deepest normative commitments. Parfit accord-ingly seeks to disarm this challenge that he takes Nietzsche to present. Nietzsche's normative pronouncements, he thinks, are either the product of psychological distortion, are contradicted by other things Nietzsche says, or else, on closer textual examination, are more moderate and con-siderably closer to Parfit's own view than one might at first expect from the strident and polemical tone that Nietzsche adopts.

In devoting several of the culminating chapters of his monumental book to Nietzsche, Parfit joins the gradually widening circle of anglo-phone moral philosophers who in the past few decades have taken Nietzsche's difficult and often shocking ideas as worthy of contempo-rary engagement and discussion. While Parfit is of course not a Nietzsche scholar, nor is he aiming to produce a piece of Nietzsche scholarship, his interpretation admirably avoids many of the crude caricatures of Nietzsche's ideas that surface even in serious academic works, and it pre-sents a nuanced reading, drawing on a wide range of textual evidence. Nonetheless, I will be arguing here that Parfit's interpretation is wrong on several key points. My interest is not primarily that of a philosophical historian, setting the record about Nietzsche straight for its own sake. Even less is my aim to defend Nietzsche's views as the correct alternative to Parfit's. But I *do* want to suggest that the Nietzsche that Parfit does outline, both because of the views that Parfit attributes to him and because of some difficult views that Parfit does not adequately grapple with, proves an easier challenge than Nietzsche should pose when it comes to the convergence claim.

I'll begin with two preliminary sections to set the stage: In the first of these, I spell out why the convergence claim matters to Parfit and why he takes Nietzsche in particular as someone whose views need to be dealt with. In the second of these, I'll briefly draw attention to a salient exeget-ical matter regarding Parfit's abundant use of Nietzsche's notebooks as textual evidence. After these two preliminary sections, I turn to a discussion of the two points on which I think Nietzsche's disagreement with Parfit is most serious and intractable—first, Nietzsche's denial that suffering is in itself bad and, second, Nietzsche's deep-seated anti-egalitarianism. On both fronts, Nietzsche has radical normative views that simply cannot be expected to converge with Parfit's. I then turn to a discussion of Parfit's account of Nietzsche's critique of morality and next, in the section to follow, to his consideration of Nietzsche's meta-ethics. Parfit's questionable interpretations, in attributing to Nietzsche a drastic rejection of ethical normativity, coupled with a similarly drastic rejection of any sort of remotely plausible realist grounding for values, makes Nietzsche far easier to dismiss than he might be.

2. *The Rules of the Game*

Parfit's argument would seem to presuppose the following conditional claim: If it turns out that there are deep and intractable normative disagreements between him and Nietzsche—disagreements that cannot plausibly be dismissed as the result of distorting factors or patent confusion—this would cast grave doubt on the convergence claim. It would take me too far afield, and it would probably require another whole paper, to deal with the philosophical underpinnings of the argument from disagreement in sufficient detail. So my strategy in this paper will be the more limited one of accepting the terms that Parfit has himself implicitly set and seeing whether he is successful in convincing us that Nietzsche is not a threat to the convergence claim after all.

It is worth briefly rehearsing, though, why Parfit cares about convergence in the first place: It is a protective measure on his part to buttress the sort of moral intuitionism he advocates. Parfit is especially worried about the challenge of an argument from disagreement. If normative truths, like the basic truths of mathematics, are out there to be intuited, then we should expect suitably well-informed people not to give incompatible accounts of what these truths are. Unless we can somehow explain away these conflicting reports, our confidence in our intuiting capacities should be shaken. If there is disagreement about normative matters in suitably idealized conditions and yet we stick to our guns about what we take to be the normative facts, "[w]e would have to believe that, when we disagree with others, it is only we who can recognize such truths. But if many other people, even in ideal conditions, could not recognize such truths, we could not rationally believe that we have this ability" (*OWM*, II, 546). Unless the convergence claim is true, the argument from disagreement, Parfit concedes, would have "great force" against his moral epistemology (*OWM*, II, 546).

Yet why does Parfit take *Nietzsche in particular* as a challenge? (As opposed to, say, any random crank who writes him a rambling email purporting to outline a normative alternative to his own?) Why, indeed, does Parfit focus on the position someone *actually held* as opposed to a hypothetical position someone could coherently hold? There would appear to be some idea of epistemic peer-hood in the background that leads Parfit to focus on salient cases of disagreement with past luminaries: "Nietzsche," Parfit writes, "was a brilliant thinker, who made many claims that are original, important, and true. We should ask whether our disagreements with Nietzsche give us reasons to doubt our own views" (*OWM*, II, 579). Parfit worries that philosophical giants, such as Nietzsche or Kant, seem to disagree with him on important normative issues, because, I take it, he thinks that they (unlike the random crank) are as epistemically well-placed as he is to intuit the normative reasons. In fact, their brilliance and historical stature amounts to a kind of meta-evidence, giving us further reason to take seriously views they in particular held, as opposed simply to coherent views that someone could potentially hold. Truly ideal conditions are no doubt beyond our ken, and we thus can't say with certainty whether there would be agreement or disagreement in these conditions (*OWM*, II, 570). But disagreement among those we take to be epistemic peers (maybe even epistemic superiors) in very good, but less-than-ideal conditions should at the very least shake our confidence not only about whether there would be agreement in ideal conditions, but also about what particular normative claims this agreement would encompass.

In order to dispel the challenge that he takes Nietzsche to pose, Parfit hopes to show either that Nietzsche (1) has beliefs that do not really diverge significantly from Parfit's; (2) is subject to distorting influences in the normative beliefs he does purport to have, so that these beliefs can be discounted as likely running afoul of the ideal conditions; or that, like the person insisting that in order for a given shape to be a triangle, it is not enough to be a closed three-sided figure, but it must also be sanctioned as a triangle by God, he (3) is subject to such serious conceptual confusion regarding the concept under discussion (there, triangularity— here, morality) that his disagreement can be written off as the result of confusion-provoked blindness to an important region of logical space. Parfit tries a combination of all three strategies. Before we turn to a discussion of some likely points of substantive philosophical disagreement between Nietzsche and Parfit, and to Parfit's interpretations and arguments, I want briefly to register a concern about the textual evidence that Parfit often cites.

3. *The Question of the Nachlaß*

The philosophical historian in me would be remiss in not mentioning an important philological issue that arises with Parfit's interpretation. Parfit draws very freely on the so-called *Nachlaß*, the collection of Nietzsche's notebooks that were published after his death. To the reader who does not consult the list of references at the end of *On What Matters*, and indeed to one who does and yet does not realize that Nietzsche never actually published a book called *The Will to Power*, it can seem that all these Nietzschean quotations cited by Parfit are on a par as positions behind which Nietzsche stood enough to publish them. This is not the case. In fact, more than a third of the quotations that Parfit cites— and many of the most important ones for his reading of Nietzsche—are drawn from these notebooks.

To be sure, Parfit is not alone in extensively citing the notebooks in this way. Following a model set by Heidegger, some of the best scholars of Nietzsche make considerable use of the notebooks in their interpretations, sometimes as the sole evidence that Nietzsche held a particular view.[1] I myself am quite reluctant to draw on the notebooks except where

[1] R. Schacht, *Nietzsche* (London: Routledge, 1983); A. Nehamas, *Nietzsche: Life as Literature* (Cambridge, MA: Harvard University Press, 1985); J. Richardson, *Nietzsche's System* (Oxford: Oxford University Press, 1996); B. Reginster, *The Affirmation of Life: Nietzsche on Overcoming Nihilism* (Cambridge, MA: Harvard University Press, 2006).

they augment or clarify a position also clearly found in the works
Nietzsche himself published or prepared for publication before his mental collapse in 1889, but I recognize that sensible arguments can be given
for using the notebooks in a more permissive way.[2] In any event, the
contemporary interpreters who use Nietzsche's notebooks typically have
the positive aim of showing that there are coherent and interesting philosophical positions to be found when we look to this notebook material.[3]
These contemporary interpreters think it would be a shame to neglect
what in their philosophical opinion are important claims and insights
that Nietzsche didn't ever publish.

Yet Parfit, by contrast, most often draws on the notebooks with the
negative aim of *casting doubt* on Nietzsche and his positions. To this
end, he cites passages from the notebooks as evidence that Nietzsche is
saddled with implausible commitments and moreover as evidence that
Nietzsche contradicts himself. But it seems to me quite unfair to establish either point, and especially the latter, by drawing on material that
Nietzsche never chose to publish. After all, Nietzsche may not have published this material precisely because ultimately he did not agree with it.
Many of the ideas from the notebooks are ill-considered or overreach-
ing; they are, after all, *notebooks* where Nietzsche was trying out ideas,
not setting them down for perpetuity. We don't moreover know his purposes in writing down a given idea: it could well be an idea he endorses,
either fully or tentatively. Or it could be a view he doesn't agree with *at
all* and wants to subject to further scrutiny. But putting aside the fairness
to the historical Nietzsche of this interpretive practice, Parfit, in drawing
on this often dubious material from the notebooks in the way he does,
ends up making Nietzsche out to be a less threatening philosophical
opponent than he might otherwise be. The Nietzsche that we should
care about here is not the man scribbling half-baked ideas, some inspired
and some ridiculous, in his notebooks, but the more formidable philosopher who comes into view when we interpret his polished—and published—corpus of work with an eye to a charitable reconstruction. The

---

[2] Cf. Reginster, *The Affirmation of Life*, 16–20.
[3] Heidegger and his interesting, but self-serving interpretation of Nietzsche is a rather
more complicated matter.

most serious challenge comes from the opinions of the latter. Although this "Nietzsche" is in *some* sense a hermeneutical construct, even when faced with this figure, we are still much closer to an issue of actual as opposed to merely hypothetical disagreement. We are not inventing these philosophical positions afresh, but are extracting them from an existing body of canonical texts that Nietzsche himself carefully crafted. Our interpretation, accordingly, must be constrained by the require-ment of textual fidelity, not by the limits of anything we can coherently imagine as a normative position. I'll wait to go into specific positions attributed to Nietzsche and their textual support in the *Nachlaß* until the sections to follow, but I want to flag this issue before moving on.

4. *Nietzsche on the Value of Suffering*

In the chapter leading up to his discussion of Nietzsche, Parfit has argued for what he calls the "double badness of suffering" (*OWM*, II, 565), by way of the dual claims that (a) it is in itself bad to suffer and that (b) it is bad when people suffer in ways that they do not deserve. Just let us focus our attention on Nietzsche's position with respect to (a).[4] Does Nietzsche agree that it is *in itself* bad to suffer? Nietzsche, as Parfit notes, does laud suffering time and again (e.g. BGE, 225; GS, 338).[5] Yet Parfit wants to

[4] As for (b), Nietzsche, along with Parfit, is skeptical of the whole notion of people deserving to suffer. Nietzsche, though, is less interested in approaching this sort of ques-tion head-on than he is interested in various anthropological and psychological ques-tions surrounding punishment and desert, namely (a) why people have come to hold others accountable for the actions they are alleged "freely" to do, and (b) why people (Christians, in particular) concoct perversely elaborate stories explaining why it is that they deserve the suffering that is their lot.

[5] Works by Nietzsche are cited by section number (with one exception noted below) using the following abbreviations and translations, which I have modified where I have thought appropriate. A = *The Antichrist*, trans. Walter Kaufmann; BGE = *Beyond Good and Evil*, trans. Walter Kaufmann; BT = *The Birth of Tragedy*, trans. Ronald Speirs; D = *Daybreak*, trans. R. J. Hollingdale; EH = *Ecce Homo*, trans. Walter Kaufmann; GM = *On the Genealogy of Morals*, trans. Walter Kaufmann; GS = *The Gay Science*, trans. Walter Kaufmann; HH = *Human, All Too Human*, trans. R. J. Hollingdale; LNB = *Writings from the Late Notebooks*, trans. Kate Sturge, ed. Rüdiger Bittner [n.b.: this volume is cited by *page* number]; TI = *Twilight of the Idols*, trans. Walter Kaufmann; UM = *Untimely Meditations*, trans. R. J. Hollingdale. In works that comprise several individual essays, after the abbreviation is the essay number (as a Roman numeral) and section number (as

establish that appearances to the contrary, Nietzsche proves no serious challenge to convergence on this score.

But first of all, what, we should ask, would it take to deny that suffering is in itself bad? Parfit elucidates this badness-in-itself claim by noting that "[a]ll suffering is, in this sense, bad *for the sufferer*" (*OWM*, II, 565). No doubt, there is *some* sense in which suffering is just *by definition* something bad for the sufferer in that it is that which, among other things, is characterized by feeling bad to the one who undergoes it. If this is all Parfit is claiming in noting that suffering is in itself bad, his claim could in principle brook no disagreement from Nietzsche or anyone else. In attempting to deny that suffering has an unpleasant phenomenal character, and therefore is *to some disagree* bad for the sufferer, one would, it seems, just be denying that the state in question was even suffering at all. Parfit, I take it, shouldn't want the claim that suffering is bad in itself to be this trivial. And what Parfit goes on to write suggests that he really has a deeper, more substantive point in mind. "Instrumental" seems to be the key point of contrast with "in itself" when Parfit notes the following: "Though suffering is always *in itself* bad, some suffering has good effects which may make it on the whole good, as when the pain that is caused by some injury prevents us from acting in ways that would increase this injury" (*OWM*, II, 565).[6] The suffering would appear to be worthwhile *only* in virtue of its downstream beneficial effects, not on its own account. Thus Parfit's view is best read, I think, in the following way: Instances of suffering never have anything more than this sort of instrumental value for the sufferer and thus, considered "in itself"—that is,

---

an Arabic numeral). For example, GM, I:2 is *On the Genealogy of Morals*, Essay I, Section 2. In works that include titled main sections, I include a key word for that section, followed by sub-section numbers, if applicable. For example, TI, "Socrates," 1 is the *Twilight of the Idols* section "The Problem of Socrates," Sub-Section 1.

[6] Parfit could in principle be pressing the view that suffering is "in itself" bad where "in itself" means intrinsically (where that is meant as the opposite of extrinsically). But given that the point of contrast he sets up is with suffering being instrumentally good, this does not appear to be the right interpretation. Even if Parfit did intend the "in itself" claim to be a point about intrinsicality/extrinsicality, Nietzsche would still not be in agreement. Given the holistic tenor of Nietzsche's axiology (presupposed, e.g., in TI, "Errors," 8), we cannot correctly assess the value of things in isolation from the relations they bear to a larger whole; intrinsically, an instance of suffering is neither good nor bad.

apart from this instrumental value—suffering is not ever good for the sufferer.

Parfit rightly observes that often what Nietzsche is actually celebrating in praising suffering is simply this instrumental value of suffering (BGE, 225; cf. HH, I: 235). This would not be in tension with Parfit's own view, because one could still think of suffering as the regrettable cost of other important things—for example, the great symphony achieved through tremendous labor and psychological turmoil.

Yet Parfit observes, also rightly, that Nietzsche often appears to go beyond this instrumental point to deny that suffering is always in itself bad. What could Nietzsche mean in claiming this? His idea, I think, would need to be that instances of suffering are themselves *constitutive elements* of the good life. Even holding fixed all the other goods (exceptional achievement, for example) that suffering instrumentally makes possible, removing suffering from a life would render that life less good. Put differently: If one made a list of the features of a life that render it good—climbing a mountain peak, producing a masterpiece—instances of suffering would also be on that list of good-making features.

Parfit attributes to Nietzsche two claims that might be thought to lend support to this rather surprising view, and he then tries to show that once we see the dubious claims that are allegedly underwriting it, Nietzsche's position on suffering is not going to be a challenge to the convergence claim. On Parfit's interpretation, Nietzsche is doubtful that suffering is in itself bad because he accepts "the wider view that *everything* is good" (*OWM*, II, 571), a claim Parfit takes Nietzsche to hold in tandem with the response-dependence style claim that "we can make any event good by *affirming* or welcoming this event" (*OWM*, II, 571). The latter claim would just be a concession on Nietzsche's part that suffering is bad, because it stands in need of being made good in this way. And the Panglossian delusion that "*everything* is good" can be understood, and dismissed, Parfit thinks, as the product of psychological distortion, the response of someone who suffered in the prolonged and intense way that Nietzsche did (*OWM*, II, 572). Recall the rules of the game I set out earlier. Parfit here is trying to establish that (1) Nietzsche agrees with him in important respects, and insofar as Nietzsche disagrees, his beliefs (2) can be written off as the product of psychological distortion.

Let us not linger on the exegetical issue of whether Nietzsche should be interpreted as accepting either extreme view that Parfit attributes to him as the scaffolding for the claim that suffering is in itself good. The best evidence Parfit cites is from the notebooks, and even here, it is difficult to tell where Nietzsche stands vis-à-vis the viewpoints he is toying with.[7] The important question for us should instead be this: Are these extreme positions, which it is not even clear that Nietzsche should be read as accepting, the only anchors in Nietzsche's work for the claim that suffering might constitutively render a life better? Or is there a more modest and philosophically-attractive Nietzschean position to support the claim that suffering is not always in itself bad? More, it seems to me, can be said in Nietzsche's favor.

According to one important recent interpretation suggested by Bernard Reginster, Nietzsche's main objection to the moral tradition (including Christianity) is that its ideal of life is of one that is free from suffering.[8] Whereas, on Nietzsche's view, Christians, Schopenhauerians, utilitarians and others think that suffering with no instrumental payoff is thereby always objectionable, Nietzsche, by contrast, thinks that suffering is *itself* part of what makes this life and world good, in addition to the further

---

[7] Parfit's interpretation relies on two notebook passages, where Nietzsche can appear to press this sort of cosmodicy (LNB, 207; LNB, 135–6). Putting aside all issues about the textual status of the notebooks, the support that even these notebook passages lend is questionable. Parfit condenses one notebook entry to read: " 'Everything actually happens *as it should happen*... every kind of "imperfection" and the suffering that result are also part of the *highest desirability*' " (OWM, II, 571). But this misleadingly makes it seem as though Nietzsche is *asserting* this in his notebook, when, judging by the context, that is far from clear. Nietzsche, quoted in full, writes: "To attain a height and bird's eye view where one understands how everything actually runs *as it should run*: how every kind of 'imperfection' and the suffering that results are also part of the *highest desirability*...." Nietzsche's ellipses leave unclear what his own stance toward this evaluative perspective is. He might well reject it as the tendentious position of those deluded Christians seeking to give a theodicy. This is the danger of drawing so freely on the notebooks. In the work he chose to publish, which Parfit cites as the third and final piece of evidence for his interpretation (OWM, II, 572, citing EH), Nietzsche opts for the more modest view that it a worthwhile and admirable trait of strong, life-affirming, and self-reverential human beings that they will have such an attitude toward their lives and toward the world. But we should not assume that because Nietzsche thinks this attitude is valuable, he thinks such an attitude is *correct*, since he thinks many of the most worthwhile beliefs for people to hold are false (BGE, 4).

[8] Reginster, *The Affirmation of Life*, 176.

goods that suffering instrumentally secures. Notice that this claim is far more modest than the radical one Parfit has attributed to Nietzsche. It is not saying that all instances of suffering are good, or even more absurdly that everything whatsoever is good. It is simply saying that suffering itself, apart from what it makes possible, is *sometimes* a good-making feature of a life. Now what grounds could Nietzsche possibly have for thinking this, other than the ones mentioned by Parfit?[9]

It seems to me that the best Nietzschean argument in support of this point is one that draws on his rich analogy between lives and works of art (BT, 5; GS, 290). Part of what makes one's life a better life, judged by this distinctively aesthetic metric, may be *precisely* the suffering it contains, especially when the suffering is an aspect of a compelling narrative of adversity and achievement. Other philosophical perspectives, Nietzsche thinks, fail to notice the fact that suffering can be valuable in this way, because they assume that once isolated from that which it instrumentally makes possible, suffering can be judged, and a negative verdict on it rendered, on account of its unpleasant *phenomenal* character alone. But this is an assumption that Nietzsche rejects: "Whether it is hedonism or pessimism, utilitarianism or eudaemonism—all these ways of thinking that measure the value of things in accordance with *pleasure* and *pain*, which are mere epiphenomena and wholly secondary are ways of thinking that stay in the foreground and naïvetés on which everyone conscious of *creative* powers and an artistic conscience will look down not without derision, nor without pity" (BGE, 225). The person living the heroic life will of course experience great suffering, but he may also be living the best sort of life *for him*, not despite, but partly in virtue of his suffering, because that suffering itself contributes to a better life *qua*

---

[9] On Reginster's interpretation, Nietzsche holds that the process of reaching a goal is constitutively valuable, in addition to just the goal itself. One vital element in making this process valuable is that it is *not* easy. It involves overcoming resistance—and, according to a certain Schopenhauerian backdrop Nietzsche is working with, that will thereby involve suffering as an essential ingredient. See *The Affirmation of Life*, 194. Although I agree with Reginster that Nietzsche regards suffering as also valuable in this way just sketched, I'm not sure this particular Nietzschean argument will go far enough in questioning Parfit's contention that suffering is only ever instrumentally valuable. The alternative line of argument from Nietzsche that I develop in what follows is one that I think will more directly address this point of Parfit's.

Nietzschean life-as-a-work-of-art. If we just subtracted the suffering from the life of Odysseus in those long years of journeying, imagining him a person alike in all other respects, but who couldn't feel the suffering as suffering, that would not render his life better *even for him*. It is better to be a suffering hero than an anesthetized one.

Notice that the suffering is not here instrumental to making the life-qua-artwork good, as typically would be, say, drinking enough water to be able to do the interesting and important things that would make one's life good as a work of art. The suffering is instead partly constitutive of the life's goodness, being itself a good-making element of the life considered in this aesthetic way. These features come as part of a holistic package, and accordingly, they cannot be adequately judged in isolation from other elements of the life. But just because some element (a beautiful patch of color in a painting or an instance of suffering in a life) is *extrinsically* valuable in this way, it doesn't follow that its value is merely instrumental. Nor is the suffering valuable simply on account of affording *others* aesthetic pleasure. It may well do that. But the aesthetic value inheres in one's life itself, insofar as it has the aesthetically commendable features it does—the features which would warrant the aesthetic response others might have to it.

I think, in short, that there is an intelligible Nietzschean position here on which one denies that suffering is only ever instrumentally valuable. And I would hasten to add that it would be ill-advised to dismiss Nietzsche's position as the product of psychological distortion, at the risk of throwing stones from one's glass house. For Nietzsche might just as well claim, perhaps with even more justice, that the people who denounce suffering as always in itself bad are equally beset by a serious form of psychological distortion. Their weakness and "softening" (TI, "Skirmishes," 37) make them fetishize the phenomenal character of suffering and lead them to focus on *that alone* as what makes it always a part of a life that is of negative value. This is the understandable result of a desperate desire to avoid all pain. But it leads them to prefer what might not be the truly preferable life for them, judged in aesthetic terms.

This Nietzschean ideal of life is of course born of a sort of arch-Romantic aestheticism, but it is important to recognize that despite its extremity, it is vastly more plausible than the view that Parfit has attributed to Nietzsche. It preserves the possibility that many things are bad (including a great many instances of suffering). And it doesn't reduce the value of suffering to simply an instrumental vehicle for securing other things. It is not my aim to establish that Nietzsche is right or that his view is free from problems, only that he has an interesting position that will push back against Parfit's claim that suffering is always in itself bad. The threat of disagreement still looms.

5. Nietzsche on Egalitarianism

Few writers in the history of philosophy are as (apparently) elitist and anti-egalitarian as Nietzsche.[10] Parfit acknowledges this seeming anti-egalitarianism, writing:

> Since Nietzsche gives supreme weight to the greatest creative achievements in art, science, and philosophy, he also gives supreme value to the existence and well-being of the few people who are capable of these achievements. Nietzsche believes that these few people, whom we can call the *creative elite*, should be given special rights. When he makes such claims, Nietzsche may seem to be denying that everyone's well-being matters equally. That would be a deep disagreement with what most of us now believe. (*OWM*, II, 590)

There are three separate anti-egalitarian positions on Nietzsche's part that should be distinguished. Nietzsche would appear to be:

(1) doubting that all humans have equal worth and dignity;
(2) counting the well-being of some more than that of others in the reckoning of what matters; and
(3) believing that the elite should be given special rights.

Parfit seeks to dispel the appearance of deep disagreement with Nietzsche on these matters. While Parfit admits that Nietzsche makes

---

[10] Brian Leiter has noted that the "egalitarian premise of all contemporary moral and political theory—the premise, in one form or another, of the equal worth and dignity of each person—is simply absent in Nietzsche's work." B. Leiter, *Nietzsche on Morality* (London: Routledge, 2002): 290; cf. A, 43; A, 57.

some anti-egalitarian-sounding remarks, he argues that Nietzsche also holds some "strongly egalitarian beliefs" nonetheless (*OWM*, II, 591). Yet Parfit's interpretation, it seems to me, does nothing to dislodge (1)–(3) as the right interpretations of Nietzsche, nor does he establish that Nietzsche held countervailing egalitarian beliefs in any significant sense of the word "egalitarian."

Parfit seeks to soften the blow of Nietzsche's anti-egalitarianism by noting that although Nietzsche makes some "rude and dismissive remarks about the mediocre" (*OWM*, II, 591), Nietzsche nonetheless thinks the elite are obligated not to mistreat them. He cites a passage in *The Antichrist* where Nietzsche writes that "when the exceptional human being treats the mediocre more tenderly than himself and his peers, this is not mere courtesy of the heart—it is simply his duty" (*OWM*, II, 591, citing A, 57). Since Nietzsche opts for the word "duty" [*Pflicht*], the Kantian overtones might be taken to suggest that Nietzsche thinks these claims of duty are grounded in the equal moral status of the "mediocre" human beings that are thus to be treated tenderly. That would cast doubt on whether he accepts (1).

Yet this remark of Nietzsche's from *The Antichrist*—the highly condescending tone of which should itself give us pause about Parfit's tack—is taken from a section in which Nietzsche has been noting with approval the intense stratification present in the caste-based Laws of Manu. Far from thinking these are rooted in an arbitrary social convention that contravenes the fact that all people are of equal worth and dignity, Nietzsche calls this stratification a "sanction of a *natural order*" (A, 57). Some people, he appears to think, *really are* of higher worth than others, and it is these people who have, as he says, the privilege of "represent[ing] happiness, beauty, and graciousness on earth" (A, 57). In fact, in the paragraph prior to the one from which Parfit has drawn this quotation about treating the mediocre tenderly, Nietzsche echoes Aristotle's infamous and disturbing remarks about natural slavery from the *Politics* (1254a18–23), noting, "To be a public utility, a wheel, a function, for that one must be destined by nature: it is *not* society, it is the only kind of *happiness* of which the great majority are capable that makes intelligent machines of them" (A, 57). From the fact that Nietzsche thinks the elite are duty-bound to treat these "intelligent machines" tenderly, it does not follow that he thinks they are of equal moral status as the elite to whom this requirement is directed.

Nor does it follow that the elite and the peons should have equal social and political rights either. For Nietzsche goes on to write later in the same passage: "Whom do I hate most among the rabble of today? The socialist rabble, the chandala apostles, who undermine the instinct, the pleasure, the worker's sense of satisfaction with his small existence— who make him envious, who teach him revenge. The wrong [*Unrecht*] lies not in unequal rights but the claim of 'equal rights'" (A, 57). Parfit notes that with these unequal rights come unequal responsibilities, with more being expected of the elite (*OWM*, II, 590–1). But this lends no succor to reading Nietzsche as more of an egalitarian with respect to (3); it just shows that, on the subject of rights, he is an anti-egalitarian with a correlative commitment to *noblesse oblige*.

Parfit seeks to question (2) by claiming that Nietzsche is an "egalitar-ian" about the badness of suffering, because he "does not seem to believe that suffering is in itself less bad when it is endured by mediocre human beings" (*OWM*, II, 591–2). The idea of this suffering being "less bad" admits of a few different readings, and I suspect that Parfit may here be equivocating among them. Suffering to degree x, he could be claiming, feels bad to degree x regardless of who the sufferer is. That claim is in itself bordering on the trivial. Unless it is supplemented with ancillary theses about what *follows from this* with respect to what is impersonally good, it has no bearing on issues of egalitarianism. Parfit could also be claiming that suffering is an equally "bad-making" feature of a life regardless of who the particular sufferer is. Now Nietzsche *would* allow that suffering in this respect is no less bad for the mediocre—and indeed may be worse for them, especially if, like the lower animals, they are unable to incorporate it into some heroic narrative of their lives. But the thesis that Parfit really needs is something far more ambitious, so as to put pressure on (2). What (2) attributes to Nietzsche is the view that it is more important, from the impersonal axiological standpoint, that a few select beings flourish than that the mass of mankind do so. Noting that suffering is no less bad (and maybe even worse) in *personal terms*, when endured by the "mediocre" does not undermine this claim. The argu-ment equivocates on the respect in which it is worse—for the sufferer in particular or from the standpoint of the whole. And the standpoint of the whole may of course regard with callous indifference the fact that many people's individual lives will go worse.[11]

Parfit's best argument is to question (2) by noting that the exceptional achievements of the few are of benefit not just to that select few, but to humanity as a whole. This is an important point, and it has not been stressed enough in interpretations of Nietzsche's ethics and social philosophy. The exegetical strategy for Parfit would thus be to say that (2) is rightly attributed to Nietzsche, *only because* Nietzsche thinks this focus on the creative elite is in everyone's interest and that ultimately no one person's interest is more important than another's. But I don't think this follows: Just because Nietzsche thinks that everyone gets some benefits from the perfectionistic achievements of the few, it doesn't follow that he holds that everyone's well-being matters *equally*, as would be needed for the egalitarian claim to be significant. Mice may benefit from the crumbs that fall from exalted tables, but this doesn't have any bearing on the question of whether the well-being of the diners and the mice is on an axiological par.

Parfit's arguments, in short, are unconvincing in dislodging Nietzsche from the ranks of the entrenched anti-egalitarians. Parfit himself suggests that claims (2) and (3), if Nietzsche is indeed making them, are in deep disagreement with Parfit's own view (*OWM*, II, 590). And surely Parfit must think (1) is as well. But Parfit has not given us good reason for thinking that Nietzsche's apparent acceptance of these claims is an exegetical illusion or that it is contradicted by other things Nietzsche says. As with the issue about the badness of suffering in itself, Nietzsche, it seems to me, will continue to disagree with Parfit on these issues of egalitarianism.

---

[11] On Nietzsche's own reckoning of what matters, the existence of a few great types is of vastly greater importance than the "well-being" of the rest of mankind. Nietzsche notes how much "one would like to apply to society and its goals something that can be learned from observation of any species of the animal or plant world: that its only concern is the individual higher exemplar, the more uncommon, more powerful, more complex, more fruitful" (UM, III:6). The goal of a species' evolution lies "not in the mass of its exemplars and their wellbeing...but rather in those apparently scattered and chance existences which favourable conditions have here and there produced" (UM, III:6).

One could, I suppose, accuse Nietzsche of being subject to a distorting influence because he has beliefs that favor a creative aristocracy in which he would place himself. (As one example of a distorting influence, Parfit cites the "knowledge that, if other people accepted and acted on some normative belief, that would give special benefits to us" (*OWM*, II, 547).) But Nietzsche might just as well accuse egalitarians as subject to a "distorting influence" in their endorsement of egalitarian ideas. Consider things, Nietzsche might ask, from the perspective of the most lowly and powerless: If others (particularly the strong) acted on the belief that everyone is of equal worth, and that all are deserving of equal rights and of equal respect, that would be a tremendous boon for the lowly and powerless.

Would these benefits they thus gain be relevantly "special" (*OWM*, II, 547)? We must be careful here. For there is a way of reading "special" so as just to beg the question in favor of egalitarianism in the statement of the ideal conditions; any *unequal* distribution of rights and benefits is "special" and any normative beliefs favoring the unequal distribution thereby count as "distorted." But if we want to resist smuggling our normative commitments into the ideal conditions themselves, we should opt for a neutral way of reading this term "special": Any distribution of rights and benefits counts as "special" when it diverges from what one actually merits or deserves. This formulation is compatible with everyone deserving the same moral status, rights, and benefits. But this is *also* compatible with their *not* deserving the same moral status, rights, and benefits. Yet if we take *this* reading of "special" that I am proposing—the reading that doesn't beg the question—then if we think, as Nietzsche does, that the lowly and powerless are *not* deserving of the same status, rights, and benefits as the noble and the well-constituted, then the lowly and powerless are indeed in favor of normative beliefs that confer "special" benefits on them.

We should not forget how central this egalitarianism is to Parfit's own project. Take the sort of "Triple Theory" that Parfit has argued for, in which Kantianism, rule consequentialism, and Scanlonian contractualism are supposed to converge. The true moral theory, he thinks, is made up of the optimific principles that, in conditions of full information, *everyone* could rationally choose and that *no one* could reasonably reject

(*OWM*, II, 245). And yet why, Nietzsche might ask, is it being assumed that everyone has rights that are absolute side constraints, so that they get a say and get veto power in this highly democratic fashion? This whole approach, like much of modern moral philosophy, begs the question from the start about the equal moral status of all people, by making it seem as if it is a neutral deliverance of the moral theory, when in fact it is an entrenched and self-ratifying presupposition of it.

Parfit believes that "there has been slow but accelerating progress towards the beliefs that everyone's well-being matters equally, and that everyone has equal moral claims" (*OWM*, II, 563). Like Parfit, I also believe that, and the readers of this paper probably believe that too. But we do a disservice to the truth if we project our views onto Nietzsche. Nietzsche harbors doubts about whether this greater inclusiveness *does* mark normative or epistemic progress. Nietzsche relishes playing the provocateur, drawing our attention to the extraneous ideological factors that might account for this radical change toward egalitarianism, so as to undermine our confidence that our beliefs arose as the result of a cool apprehension of the moral facts. However confident we may feel in writing off his views as the product of distortion, he wants to insinuate that *our* views are just as likely to be the products of distortion.

In doubting some of our deepest normative convictions, Nietzsche may make us uncomfortable. We may even despise him as a reactionary monster. But we should not make his views out to be more egalitarian than they really are. When it comes to (1)–(3), it is doubtful that we would arrive at normative convergence with Nietzsche. Once again, the threat of disagreement looms.

6. Nietzsche's Critique of Morality

Now that we have considered two important points of disagreement between Nietzsche and Parfit when it comes to certain egalitarian ideals and to the value of suffering, I'd like to turn to Parfit's account of Nietzsche's criticism of morality. Nietzsche, Parfit's interpretation claims, does not have anything approaching our non-theological concept of what we ought morally to do. Nietzsche neglects this possibility, Parfit thinks, because he is subject to a form of conceptual confusion that ties morality inextricably together with God. This confusion results in a blindness on Nietzsche's part to a whole realm of logical space that his distorted concept of morality will not allow him to bring into view. He is, to use my earlier example from Section 2, supposedly like the person who insists that in order to be a triangle a closed figure must not just have three sides, but must also be *sanctioned by God* as a triangle. This extraneous requirement is one that fastens on to something that is just irrelevant to the concept of triangularity. If a person is skeptical about the existence of triangles on this perverse basis, his opinions can simply be discounted. It is a similar situation, Parfit thinks, with Nietzsche's concept of morality and his critique thereof.

On Parfit's reconstruction of his view, Nietzsche's doubts about morality are rooted in conceiving of it as a system of commands issued by God. It is something having normative authority only if there is a God to issue these commands (*OWM*, II, 584–9). Nietzsche's objection, on this construal, is that the norms of morality are bankrupt with no God to stand behind these commandments. Nietzsche, if this reading is correct, thus overlooks the possibility of a non-theological, non-imperatival morality. After all, the claim "person *x* ought to φ" needn't take an imperatival form, let alone be the imperative of God, in order to be a true norm of morality. Because Nietzsche's critique allegedly depends on this simplistic misunderstanding, Parfit thinks that we needn't put any stock in Nietzsche's vociferous criticisms of morality. "Nietzsche's claims cannot straightforwardly conflict with our beliefs about what we ought morally to do," so long as our conception of morality is not tied to these dubious theological and imperatival underpinnings (*OWM*, II, 589). Yet in interpreting Nietzsche in this way, Parfit makes Nietzsche into too easy a target; whatever the ultimate merits of Nietzsche's criticisms of morality, they cannot be so easily brushed aside as this elementary confusion.

The first thing to note is that in "deny[ing]" morality (D, 103), or purporting to be an immoralist (EH, "Destiny," 4), Nietzsche is not rejecting the very idea of ethical normativity. His target is a more specific family of worldviews, offering themselves as the correct account of what matters and of what actions and ways of living are appropriate or inappropriate.[12] In the seminal passage from *Daybreak* that Parfit cites as evidence for Nietzsche's thorough opposition to morality, Nietzsche indeed writes: "I deny morality as I deny alchemy, that is I deny their premises" (D, 103). Just as alchemy presupposes that one can turn baser metals into gold, morality—Parfit takes Nietzsche to think—presupposes that certain things are genuinely right and wrong only in virtue of being commanded by God.[13] Yet *just after* the bit of text from *Daybreak* that Parfit cites as evidence that Nietzsche gainsays morality, Nietzsche continues: "It goes without saying that I do not deny—unless I am a fool—that many actions called immoral are to be avoided and resisted, or that many called moral are to be done and encouraged—but I think the one is to be encouraged and the other avoided *on different grounds than hitherto*" (103).[14] Since he thinks that there really are things to be done and avoided and since he thinks that there is no God (cf. GS, 108; 125), clearly he cannot think this ethical normativity depends on the commands *of God*. What Nietzsche is doubting is a certain family of normative claims—and in particular, the *grounds* supporting these claims—not the very idea of things that are to be done and avoided.[15]

---

[12] This point has been noted by a number of scholars: see Schacht, *Nietzsche*, 466–9; R. Geuss, "Nietzsche and Morality," in his *Morality, Culture, and History* (Cambridge: Cambridge University Press, 1999), 170; Leiter, *Nietzsche on Morality*, 74.

[13] It is doubtful that Nietzsche thinks this. He seems on the contrary to think it is a false belief held by certain proponents of morality (TI, "Skirmishes," 5). For helpful discussion of this issue, see T. Shaw, *Nietzsche's Political Skepticism* (Princeton: Princeton University Press, 2007), 83–8.

[14] The German reads: "Ich leugne nicht, wie sich von selber versteht—vorausgesetzt, dass ich kein Narr bin—, dass viele Handlungen, welche unsittlich heissen, zu vermeiden und zu bekämpfen sind; ebenfalls, dass viele, die sittlich heissen, zu thun und zu fördern sind,—aber ich meine: das Eine wie das Andere *aus anderen Gründen, als bisher*."

[15] This supposed misunderstanding on Nietzsche's part stems from a feature of the German word "sollen," Parfit thinks. Unlike the English "ought," "sollen" can both "express commands" and "state normative claims" (OWM, II, 584). Parfit further uses this passage to imply, though not directly to argue, that Nietzsche thinks there are no *moral* truths, because morality, being a set of commands, cannot in principle be true or false (OWM, II, 585). "Don't kill," *qua* command, is not of course the sort of thing that can be true or false. Nietzsche, according to Parfit, overlooks the possibility that morality might state normative propositions that can be true or false.

This is a questionable line of interpretation on a number of levels. First, Nietzsche apparently thinks in the very passage that Parfit himself cites (D, 103) that there are things "to be

Parfit's interpretation taps into the widespread misunderstanding that because Nietzsche is critical of "morality," he thinks everything is permitted. Yet Nietzsche's criticisms of morality are in fact motivated by his own profound normative commitments. Indeed, he at times even suggests that these criticisms of his are founded upon a different and *"higher"* sort of morality (BGE, 202), by the lights of which he finds the "herd animal morality" holding sway in Europe deeply problematic (cf. D, 4).[16] He thus would seem to believe that there is such a thing as morality, in some very broad sense of the term, but the systems *purporting* to be morality—the "harm no one" ([*laede-neminem*], BGE 186) moralities championing equal rights for all, pity for the destitute, self-deprecating humility, disdain for the powerful, bovine contentment, contempt for the body and for this earthly world, and the elimination of suffering are all pretenders to the claim of being the true morality (cf. EH, "Daybreak," 1). Rather than rejecting anything that could go under the name "morality," Nietzsche is rejecting *various versions* of morality—and he is rejecting them as normatively wanting by the lights of his own morality or ethics.[17]

done" and "to be avoided," and he conveys this *without ever* using a form of the word "sollen." Second, even about "sollen" and its forms in particular, Nietzsche has no thoroughgoing doubts to the effect that it is moot without theological backing. Earlier in *Daybreak*, he notes that the "du sollst" [you ought/thou shalt] speaks to Godless Nietzschean immoralists too (D, "Preface," 4). Third, it would be odd if he thought there were things to be done and avoided, but no truths about these matters, at least from his own evaluative perspective.

[16] Unfortunately for his more philosophically minded readers, Nietzsche does not use the term "morality" consistently. (*Moral, Moralität*, and *Sittlichkeit* are all words he uses, and there is this same lack of consistency in the German too.) Sometimes he speaks as if morality is something to be rejected wholesale as mistaken or dubious (TI, "Improvers," 1). But when he says this, he is clearly talking about a narrower system than ethical normativity *tout court*.

[17] Nietzsche realizes the danger of misunderstanding brought in tow by his "dangerous slogan" that is the title of his famous book *Beyond Good and Evil* (GM, I:17). He takes pains to note in this section of the *Genealogy* that at least this phrase does not mean "beyond good and bad." "Good" and "evil," Nietzsche thinks, are creatures of a certain normative framework that he sees as having replaced a Greco-Roman ethics of "good" (in a different sense of the word "good") and "bad." At one time, the "good" (in the Greco-Roman sense) were the strong, the proud, the noble, the healthy, and the beautiful, and the "bad" were the weak, the humble, the base, the sick, and the ugly. With the "slave revolt" (GM, I:10), the worth of these qualities gets inverted and those who were previously the "bad" get the title of the "good"; those who were previously "good" now get villainized as the "evil." The poor and meek were not always due to inherit the earth.

But what does Nietzsche make of the standing of these values of his own? Does he think they are borne simply of his own idiosyncratic taste? Or might they be grounded in some more secure claim to meta-ethical authority? To this difficult exegetical issue, I want now to turn.

7. Meta-Ethics and Meta-Axiology

Parfit attributes to Nietzsche several meta-ethical or meta-axiological suggestions. (Given that Nietzsche concerns himself with "values" broadly—where that includes ethical values along with aesthetic values— "meta-axiology" may be the most appropriate term instead of meta-ethics, so that is the one I shall use.) I take it that Parfit's strategy here is to show that Nietzsche has incompatible meta-axiological views—and thus that he contradicts himself. Nietzsche, on Parfit's interpretation, holds one of three views. He is either a misguided realist, who thinks that "life" or the "will to power" provide the ultimate grounding of value, or he is a sort of constructivist or subjectivist who thinks that value derives from us in some meta-axiologically ambitious way, or he is a projectivist, who holds that judgments of value are simply the expressions of evaluative attitudes. These readings are all anchored in less-than-decisive textual evidence.

The realist interpretation builds on Nietzsche's remarks about the will to power being the ultimate basis of value (*OWM*, II, 597–8, citing LNB, 215 and 119). First of all, it is difficult to tell whether Nietzsche means to offer this as a reductive theory of the property of being valuable or instead as a theory of what things have the property of being valuable.[18] Yet even if this is intended as a meta-axiological claim, Nietzsche *never*

---

[18] The closest we get in Nietzsche's published work is A, 2. Here Nietzsche writes, "What is good? Everything that heightens the feeling of power in man, the will to power, power itself. What is bad? Everything that is borne of weakness." Here Nietzsche is not giving a *definition* of all that is good, let alone a meta-ethical claim about its grounding, but describing a certain broad class of things that are good. And when it comes to his description of them as good, he leaves it unclear whether they are unconditionally good, conditionally good, *prima facie* good, *pro tanto* good, and so on. It is highly unlikely that his position in *The Antichrist* or elsewhere is that the will to power is unconditionally good, since he devotes a considerable portion of the book to abusing St. Paul and the priestly inventors of Christianity for the particular exercise of their will to power (e.g. A, 26, 37, 55).

published this silly idea, and the most reasonable inference to draw from the fact that he did not is that he was dissatisfied with it.[19]

The second position attributed to Nietzsche is that he thinks values are created (*OWM*, II, 600–1, citing e.g. GS, 301, BGE, 211). The trouble here is that Nietzsche uses "value" and "values" in two quite different senses.[20] One sense is more social and anthropological. The other sense is more axiologically loaded. Nietzsche takes the "value of these values" (GM, "Preface," 6) as a serious question to be considered, and not as a pleonasm, precisely because these two different senses of "value" are at work. It is an open question for Nietzsche whether certain "values" (in the social/anthropological sense) are really valuable (in the axiologically loaded sense). We should then ask: In the places where he talks about values being created, what sense of values does he have in mind? As social or anthropological entities, values do indeed get created when people, normative systems, and societies *take* or *proclaim* things to be valuable. Such "values" needn't have any meta-ethical or meta-axiological import; Christianity and slave morality are systems of values in just such a sense. While Nietzsche could *also* have in mind something very axio-logically ambitious in his talk of the creation of values, we needn't extract this dramatic meta-axiological theory from the text. For it is far from clear that Nietzsche thinks *the value* of these values (that is, the fact of their really being valuable) is *itself* something that gets created. Sim-ilarly, when he raises doubts about whether values are part of the mind-independent fabric of reality (e.g. GS, 301), what sense of values does he have in mind? As social or anthropological entities, values surely cannot be wholly independent of the activities and practices of human beings, any more than the institution of money can. But what of the fact of certain values *really being* valuable? Can *that* be independent of human practices of valuing? Again, it is difficult to know what he thinks.

---

[19] We should not, however, prejudge the issue of whether he was dissatisfied with *all* potential forms of value realism.

[20] Maudemarie Clark and David Dudrick are sensitive to a similar distinction. See their "Nietzsche and Moral Objectivity: The Development of Nietzsche's Meta-ethics," in *Nietzsche and Morality*, ed. Brian Leiter and Neil Sinhababu (Oxford: Oxford University Press, 2007). See also Schacht, *Nietzsche*, 348.

Yet we should be careful not simply to assume that he is making meta-axiological claims, when it is not clear from the texts whether he is.

There is related conflation of these two different senses of "value" in the attributions of blanket value projectivism to Nietzsche (*OWM*, II, 601). When Nietzsche sees values as expressive of people's preferences or attitudes, is he making a claim about values in the social or anthropological sense (that is, a claim about what people and societies *regard* as valuable)? Or is he making a deflationary claim that this is *all there is* to values in the other apparently more axiologically loaded sense? Once again, it is difficult to know.

These cursory remarks of mine are just meant to show that none of these three interpretations is decisive in pointing to a meta-axiological view that Nietzsche clearly held. There are indeed many passages in Nietzsche's work that can be read as suggestive of meta-axiological views. But in the recent anglophone secondary literature, Nietzsche has been attributed the gamut of views by various interpreters, sometimes by taking passages that are not obviously addressing these issues and finding evidence for some fairly complex meta-axiological position in them. The texts, it seems to me, leave issues of meta-ethics and meta-axiology seriously underdetermined. That is a more sweeping and ambitious claim than I can substantiate here, but my point is simply that we needn't read Nietzsche as *contradicting* himself in putting forward a set of three apparently incompatible meta-axiological views. We can instead read him as just not particularly focused on what we would now classify as distinctively meta-ethical or meta-axiological questions and making remarks that are addressing different sorts of questions entirely.

When it comes to Parfit's own interpretation, it is difficult to know exactly what bearing these meta-axiological issues are supposed to have on the convergence claim. Even assuming for the sake of argument that Nietzsche's views about meta-axiology are self-contradictory, does this give us reason for discounting his *first-order* views about the value of suffering or about egalitarianism? That is far from clear.

Another way of understanding Parfit's strategy of argument would be along the following lines: He thinks that *whatever* meta-axiology of these three Nietzsche holds (assuming, charitably, that he holds just one), he has no recourse to a "reason-implying" concept of what matters

(*OWM*, II, 600).[21] Thus, even if he did have first-order claims diverging from Parfit's, these would founder for want of real meta-axiological support. Perhaps so. But of what relevance is this? Nietzsche's meta-axiological views, assuming any can be pinned on him, would have little bearing for the purposes of the convergence claim, where it is his first-order normative views that matter. And, as we have seen in the foregoing sections, when it comes to the important points where Nietzsche and Parfit disagree, in no case would Nietzsche's first-order normative views seem to be driven by his (supposed) meta-axiological commitments.

Let us imagine, though, a Nietzsche who thinks that there are "reason-implying" (*OWM*, I, 38) senses of good and bad. Such a Nietzsche would be an even more formidable opponent for Parfit. He would think, in Parfit's terms, that there genuinely are good and bad things, better and worse lives. And it is not that the desires or attitudes of person x are the decisive factor in making this the case for x. It is not that there is the *ex nihilo* creation of these values either. Nor is it that there is some reductive naturalistic basis for these values in "life" or "the will to power." Such a Nietzsche would share a Parfitian meta-axiology. But there would be a brute clash of intuitions about what matters. Now it is not clear that Nietzsche either accepts *or* rejects this robust sort of realism. But it is, I think, a position that his texts do not foreclose either.

8. Conclusion

Parfit hopes to show that, despite appearances very much to the contrary, Nietzsche was not—if I may draw on Parfit's image at the heart of *On What Matters*—climbing a different mountain. I have tried to argue here that Parfit's case is not successful. On two important normative issues, Nietzsche and Parfit cannot be expected to agree. Nor should we draw hasty conclusions about Nietzsche's critique of morality or his meta-ethics and dismiss his views accordingly. For even if Nietzsche were subject to the confusion that normative claims only have force if

---

[21] I take it that Parfit considers the brand of realism he attributes to Nietzsche (making "life" or the "will to power" the ultimate basis of value) to be a form of reductive naturalism. Accordingly, by Parfit's lights, it would be meta-axiologically wanting (*OWM*, II, Chs. 24–7).

they are the commands of God, and even if he were beholden to a meta-ethical view that undermines the normative standing of his own pronouncements, the fact remains that his value assessments radically diverge from Parfit's—and from nearly all of modern moral philosophy. The point is not to prove that Nietzsche is right. It is instead to question whether we can expect Nietzsche and Parfit to converge in their normative judgments in ideal conditions. Such convergence is unlikely. As we see in the epigraph I used at the beginning of this paper, Nietzsche, like Parfit, casts himself as a metaphorical climber of mountains (EH, "Preface," 3; *OWM*, I, 419). But at the top of *his* mountain Nietzsche expects to find icy solitude, not the company of many others who have been climbing on the other side. And whatever else Nietzsche is wrong about, about that I suspect he is right.[22]

[22] My thanks to Sarah McGrath, Peter Singer, and Jack Spencer for their helpful comments on earlier drafts of this paper.

9

IN DEFENCE OF REDUCTIONISM IN ETHICS

Frank Jackson

This essay is concerned with Derek Parfit's critical discussion of naturalism in *On What Matters* (Vol. 2, Chs. 25, 26, and 27).[1] I explain why I am a naturalist and why I am unmoved by his criticisms of the kind of position I like. Why does the word 'reductionism' appear in the title of this essay rather than the word 'naturalism'? I will explain in due course, but to give you a sense of the reason: I agree with Parfit that what he calls soft naturalism is no advance on what he calls hard naturalism.[2] I start by noting some points of agreement.

1. *Common Ground*

Like Parfit, I am a *cognitivist* in ethics. Cognitivists hold that when we affirm an action, X, to be morally right, we are making a claim about X's nature, about how X is. We are, in consequence, ascribing a property to X, that of being morally right. *Mutatis mutandis* for claims that something

---

[1] I am indebted to more discussions than I can possibly recall, but must mention Michael Smith, Simon Blackburn, Daniel Wodak, Philip Pettit, and Tristram McPherson. None should be held responsible for anything.

[2] He says, e.g., 'Soft naturalism is, I believe, an incoherent view', Ch. 27, §97, p. 365.

is morally good, or required, or that some character trait or law is morally evil, etc. Cognitivists are, therefore, believers in ethical properties. My disagreement with Parfit is over the nature of these ethical properties. Moreover, like Parfit, I am a realist: I think that the moral properties are, on occasion, actually possessed by actions, laws, character traits, etc. This indeed is how affirmations of the form 'X is right', 'T is immoral', etc. get to be true when they are true. 'X is (morally) right', for instance, gets to be true just when X has the property of being right, in the same way that 'X happened last Friday' gets to be true when X has the property of happening last Friday. Moreover, to believe that X is right is to believe that X has the property of being right, and it is a true belief just when X does in fact have the property.

The contrast is with a range of views that deny, in one way or another, that ethical sentences ascribe properties. *Non-cognitivism* can take a number of forms but the currently most discussed version is a style of expressivism according to which ethical sentences express certain pro and con attitudes without reporting them, or indeed reporting anything at all. They aren't, according to expressivism, in the business of saying how things are; they are instead in the business of expressing attitudes. In this sense, they are akin to expressions of approval like 'Hooray', and expressions of disapproval like 'Boo'. Parfit argues against non-cognitivism in detail in *On What Matters*.[3] In this essay, we will be taking the cognitivist position as given common ground with Parfit.

Let's now look at the case for naturalism, or if you prefer for reductionism, in ethics. It takes off from what we learn from the combination of two plausible theses, which I will call *Grounding* and *Supervenience*.

2. *The Argument for Necessary Co-Extension*

Grounding says that it is impossible to have an ethical property without also having a non-ethical property. Ethical properties are grounded in non-ethical properties. Every right act has, of necessity, properties in addition to being right that can be expressed in non-ethical terms—

---

[3] In Vol. 2, Ch. 28, and Ch. 29, §102. Simon Blackburn's chapter in this volume is a reply to Parfit's arguments against expressivism and non-cognitivism more generally.

perhaps the act leads to an increase in happiness, or is the honouring of a promise. It is important here that the 'grounding base' be specified in negative terms, as that which is *non*-ethical. If, for example, one expressed Grounding as the doctrine that it is impossible to have an ethical property without also having a *physical* property, where a physical property is specified as the kind of property physicalists about the mind are thinking of when they declare themselves to be physicalists, one would make Grounding false. There are worlds where physicalism is false—indeed, dualists think that our world is one of them—and among these worlds will be ones with items possessing ethical properties but lacking physical properties. Their moral nature will be grounded in the 'ectoplasmic' properties they possess.

Supervenience says that, across logical space, there is no difference in ethical nature without a difference in non-ethical nature. It isn't just that *within* any possible world, there is no difference in ethical nature without a difference in non-ethical nature. The thesis is that, for any x and y, be they in the same world or not, if they differ in ethical nature, they differ in non-ethical nature. Of course, the difference may in some cases lie in non-ethical differences in how they are related to other items in the worlds they belong to, not in themselves. It may be that for some x in world W_1, and y in world W_2, where x and y differ in ethical nature, the difference in non-ethical nature between them lies in differences in the non-ethical nature of W_1 and W_2, respectively. As was the case with Grounding, it is important that we do not read non-ethical as a surrogate for physical or anything in that line of country. It is false that, across logical space, there is no difference in ethical nature without a difference in *physical* nature. In Cartesian worlds, the good angels may differ from the bad ones without a difference in physical nature: the non-ethical difference demanded by Supervenience may lie in differences in their 'angelic' natures.

Grounding and Supervenience combined give us an argument to the conclusion that ethical properties are necessarily co-extensive with non-ethical properties. I will develop it for the property of being a (morally) right act. It will be obvious how to extend the argument to moral properties more generally. Grounding tells us that every right act, r_1, $r_2, \ldots$, in logical space has a non-ethical nature. Let $n_1, n_2, \ldots$, be the non-ethical natures of r_1, r_2,..., respectively. Supervenience plus Grounding then tells us that x is right if and only if x is n_1 or n_2 or n_3 or... is necessarily true. Grounding gives us the necessity from left to right (remember we included every right act in logical space); and Supervenience gives us the necessity from right to left, for otherwise we could have two acts alike in having n_1, or alike in having n_2, or alike in having n_3, or..., but unlike in that one is right and the other is not.

What's the significance of this little proof that being right is necessarily co-extensive with a certain infinite disjunction of the non-ethical? We will say a fair bit about this shortly, but first we need to connect the discussion with naturalism, and also to head off an objection that sometimes comes up in discussion. I used 'n' above for 'non-ethical', but we can equally think of it as 'natural', *provided* we give 'natural' the negative reading of not being ethical. If we give it some positive content, as would be the case if we read it in the way common in the philosophy of mind, where it often figures as a surrogate for 'physical' with a nod to the idea that we should divorce the relevant notion of the physical from too close a link to physics, we would threaten the truth of both Grounding and Supervenience, as observed above. (I think that this is likely the reading of 'natural' that G. E. Moore had in mind when he insisted that goodness was a *non-natural* property.[4] He wasn't, as many note, saying that goodness was a *supernatural* property, in the sense of a property of something outside nature. He was insisting that goodness could not be identified or analysed in non-ethical terms.) From here on, I will use the word 'natural' in the sense of 'non-ethical'. Thus, our discussion to follow will be framed in terms of the significance (or otherwise) of the equivalence of being right with an infinite disjunction of natural properties. But first that objection.

3. Leibniz Law Trouble?

If we read naturalism in the negative way just outlined, one might wonder— and some have in discussion—whether naturalism can possibly be true. We would seem to have a violation of Leibniz's law that if x is identical

[4] G. E. Moore, *Principia Ethica* (Cambridge: Cambridge University Press, 1929).

with y, then x and y are alike in all their properties—a law that applies to properties just as much as it applies to objects, events, or whatever. For isn't it a core thesis of naturalism that ethical properties are *identical* with natural properties? Naturalists disagree about the possibility of analysing the ethical in natural terms, and about what to say about ethical concepts and ethical language, but they agree that ethical properties are identical with natural ones. But if we cash out natural as non-ethical, this sounds awfully like identifying ethical properties with properties that aren't ethical, and that would be a violation of Leibniz's law. Ethical properties cannot be identical with properties that aren't ethical.

The simplest way of seeing what is wrong with this perhaps tempting line of objection is in terms of an example. Analogues of Grounding and Supervenience are true for density. *Grounding$_D$* says that, necessarily, every object with a density has properties that are not density (mass and volume, in fact). *Supervenience$_D$* says that, necessarily, if objects o_1 and o_2 differ in density, they differ in properties that are not density (in fact, they differ in volume or mass). All the same, there is no violation of Leibniz's law in identifying density with mass divided by volume. We don't identify density with a property that isn't density; we identify it with a property that can be specified in terms that do not mention density—in particular, we identify density with a pattern in properties that aren't density, namely, the ratio of mass to volume.[5] It is in virtue of this fact that we can think of the identification of density as a *reductive* account. In this sense, what's on offer is a reduction of density (though of course there are other senses of reduction in the philosophical literature).

It is worth noting that putting the point in terms of a pattern in properties that aren't density makes it clear that the claim about density isn't a claim about words. It is a claim in metaphysics. Although we may and often do put the claim using words like 'density can be identified with a property that *can be specified in terms that do not mention* density', it isn't a claim about language. The possibility of so specifying rests on the metaphysics of the situation. Likewise, when we naturalists agree that ethical

---

[5] The need for a notion of density *at a point* means that things are a bit more complicated than this but not in ways relevant to the philosophical point.

properties are natural properties and explain the notion of the natural in the negative way outlined earlier, what we affirm is that ethical properties are identical with properties that can be specified in non-ethical terms (and so, are offering a reductionist account, in one good sense of that notion). But the possibility of so specifying isn't a thesis about ethical words (although some of us, myself included, do hold relevant theses about ethical words, more on this anon); it is a thesis about the metaphysics of ethical properties. The possibility of specifying them in non-ethical terms rests, we naturalists say, on the metaphysics of ethical properties.

Now I can say why I agree with Parfit that soft naturalism is no advance on hard naturalism. Both claim that ethical properties are identical with natural properties. Soft naturalism insists that ethical terms cannot be analysed in natural terms. But if ethical properties are one and all natural properties, and given our account of what is (ought to be) meant by a natural property in the context of discussions in ethics, it must be possible, at least in principle, to *specify* ethical nature in non-ethical terms.[6] Or is soft naturalism really some sort of *unsayability* doctrine? If it is, it would seem to me to be an implausible one, and essentially one about words and not about matters central to ethics as such.

There is, however, something important Parfit gets wrong, or so it seems to me. He is right, I have said, to insist that naturalists should allow that ethical terms are dispensable. However, he conflates this with the view that we can do without ethical *concepts* (see especially his discussion of Richard Brandt in §98). However, doing without terms and doing without concepts are two quite different matters. The laws of flotation can be expressed without using a term for density. For, at the cost of a bit of complexity, one can replace terms for density by terms for volume and mass in those laws. But that isn't doing without the concept of density: the concept of density *is* that it's what you get when you divide mass by volume. Or think of the concept of a nondenumerably infinite set. When we specify it in terms of the impossibility of putting the members of the set in 1:1 correspondence with the natural numbers, we clarify what the concept is, we open up a way to show that some set

---

[6] Parfit, Ch. 27, §97, quotes me (and Nicholas Sturgeon) as saying essentially this.

is or is not nondenumerably infinite, and we show how one might do without the *term* (the *word*). But one thing we do not do is show that the *concept* is dispensable.[7]

4. The Significance of the Necessary Co-Extension of Ethical and Natural Properties

I think the necessary co-extension of ethical and natural properties provides a strong reason to identify them, strong but not apodictic. However, one thing we cannot say, it seems to me, is that ethical properties match up with pattern-less, infinite disjunctions of natural properties. We cannot say that the right-hand side of the necessarily true bi-conditional given earlier: 'x is right if and only if x is n_1 or n_2 or n_3 or...' is a pattern-less infinite disjunction. If it were, we couldn't make sense of the way we draw ethical conclusions from information couched in non-ethical terms, something we do all the time. A big part of inferring the ethical way things are from the natural way things are involves latching on to the patterned connections between the ethical and the natural.[8] Some reply to this point by insisting that we never in fact infer ethical nature from purely natural information; the inference is always from a combination of the ethical and the natural. Don't think, they say, of the inferences in question as of the form: N, therefore, E. Think of them as of the form: N, E_1, therefore, E_2. But this cannot be right. The second inference can be re-written: N, therefore, if E_1 then E_2.

So there must be a pattern, just as there is with an example like: x is a circle if and only if x is p_1 or p_2 or p_3 or..., where each p_i is a location of points that make up a circle. The p_is aren't a pattern-less disjunction. Of course, the pattern will be harder to spot in the ethics case but it will be there (must be there) to be spotted all the same. Call the pattern in the ethics case, N. The question on the table now becomes whether or not

---

[7] So, for the record, when Parfit says, 'We don't need normative concepts, Jackson claims...', Ch. 27, §98, p. 376, this isn't my view.

[8] For more on this issue, see Frank Jackson, Philip Pettit, and Michael Smith, "Ethical Particularism and Patterns," in *Moral Particularism*, ed. Brad Hooker and Margaret Little (Oxford: Oxford University Press, 2000), 79–99.

we should identify being right with N. Being right is necessarily co-extensive with N, but is it identical with N?

Here is why I think we should say that being right is identical with N, and in what follows I'll be repeating things I (and others) have said before. I will include some commentary bearing on Parfit's reservations, but I think Parfit's major objection to the kind of naturalism I like is his triviality objection (it is after all the title of a whole chapter, Ch. 26), and that objection gets, as it should, a separate section in this essay.

First, there are a number of examples of properties that are necessarily co-extensive, where the right thing to say is that 'they' are one and the same—or, perhaps better, this is the right thing to say if one is thinking of properties in the way we are in this essay (and the way that Parfit thinks of them, it seems to me). Being an equilateral triangle in Euclidean space is necessarily co-extensive with being an equiangular triangle in Euclidean space.[9] One might say that there are two properties here, for can't you believe that a triangle has one property without believing that it has the other? But surely both properties are a certain shape, and we don't have two shapes. That is, what is true is something like: being an equilateral triangle in Euclidean space = shape S, and being an equi-angular triangle in Euclidean space = shape S. But then the transitivity of identity delivers the conclusion that being an equilateral triangle in Euclidean space = being an equiangular triangle in Euclidean space. What we have aren't two properties but two different ways of representing the same property. Philosophers (and the folk, the jargon to follow isn't local to the academy) often speak of properties as ways *things* might be; the phrasing signalling that properties are being thought of as pertaining to the nature of what's to be found in our world, and this is how we are thinking of properties. Our concern, and Parfit's, is with the *nature* of the acts, motives, laws, etc. that makes them right, evil, or whatever. Given this perspective on properties, surely the right thing to say is that we have one property in the triangle example.

Parfit mentions cases in logic and mathematics (Ch. 25, §87) where it is plausible that we have two distinct but necessarily co-extensive

---

[9] Thanks to Gil Harman for reminding me (telling me?) that one needs to include 'in Euclidean space' in this example.

properties. Fair enough. But I think it is also fair enough to observe that the whole question of the ontology and metaphysics of mathematics and logic is deeply mysterious and highly controversial, whereas, in ethics, we are addressing the question of the properties of entities that we come across every day and that have a location in space-time. For example, we see and bring into existence actions that have one or another moral property, the morally evil consequences of a bad law will start at some point in time and (hopefully) end at some later time, and so on. Also, many examples in mathematics of necessarily co-extensive properties *are* cases where it seems clearly right to insist that there's just the one property. A set has infinitely many members if and only if, for any natural number z, the set has more than z members. The suggestion isn't that those sets with the property of having infinitely many members also have the distinct property that, for any z, they have more than z members.

Second, if being right and N are distinct properties, how could we be justified in believing that some action had the property of being right in addition to having N? Its being right would—could—make no distinctive contribution to our experience of the action or to our thought about the action (how could our neural states track these extra properties?). Of course we can ask the same question about our knowledge of the properties of, e.g., numbers, but, to repeat the point made earlier, when we ask about the properties of actions, we are asking about the properties of concrete items in space-time. We want—indeed, need—the moral properties to be accessible in some relatively straightforward sense. If we deny that they are, I cannot see how we can have any good reply to the kind of scepticism about moral properties embraced by J. L. Mackie,[10] and Parfit most especially wants to hold that this would be very bad news.

The complaint I am making here is, of course, a common one. (Parfit mentions a number of authors who have made it, in one form or another.) And, interestingly, one of the features of Parfit's discussion of personal identity that impressed many, myself included, was his insistence that there was 'no further fact' that constituted being the same person over

[10] J. L. Mackie, *Ethics* (Harmondsworth: Penguin, 1977).

time, in addition to the well-known continuities.[11] I find it strange that he should be so prepared to countenance further facts when the topic is ethics instead of personal identity.

Third, any account of being right needs to *make sense* of someone's being motivated to do what is right. I am not saying that there is some kind of conceptual connection between, e.g., judging that x is right and being motivated to do x. For all I say here, maybe there is, maybe there isn't. Equally, I am not appealing to a Humean or neo-Humean doctrine to the effect that all that can motivate an agent must, in one way or another, relate to what the agent desires, or would desire, or would ideally desire, or would desire to desire or.... For all I say here, maybe that is right, maybe it isn't. I am making a 'it's not arbitrary' point. Children sometimes go to some trouble not to walk on the cracks in the pavement (as do some adults, I am told). There can be a good reason to avoid walking on the cracks: perhaps they are unstable, maybe avoiding them makes a walk more fun or there's a reward for avoiding them. But suppose that nothing like this is true. The choice between avoiding them and not avoiding them is a matter of whim. Perhaps the child tossed a coin to make the decision. That's fine in a case like this. But it isn't fine when we address the question of the relationship between an action's being right and one's doing it. But if we think of being right as some kind of unanalysable property that necessarily goes along with N but is quite distinct from it, how could we give an account of why being motivated by it is non-arbitrary? How could adding this property to N make a difference to the case for performing an action that has N? The difference between doing what's right and doing what's not right cannot be like that between avoiding and not avoiding stepping on the cracks.

Some may insist that there's an easy response available to Parfit.[12] He can appeal to the existence of a priori true conditionals that go from an antecedent that mentions one or another moral property to a consequent that concerns action. One might quarrel about the details of proposed candidate conditionals, swapping intuitions about test cases. I am not going to enter that minefield. I think there is a problem of principle

---

[11] Derek Parfit, "Personal Identity," *The Philosophical Review*, 80/1 (1971): 3–27.
[12] Thanks to Barry Maguire for forcing me to think about this style of response.

with this kind of response. To the extent that one finds one or another conditional framed in terms of 'right' a priori, that places a constraint on the interpretation of the term; it constrains what the property of rightness, according to you, might be. (And, if it comes to that, the same is true for moral terms in general, and for statements other than conditionals: to the extent one finds statements framed in moral terms a priori that constrains the interpretations of those terms.) If Fred insists that it is a priori that anyone who judges that x is right is strongly motivated to do x, he had better offer an account of what the property of being right is that allows that claim to be a priori. This means that the mooted response gets things backwards. Any putative a priori conditional highlights the problem; it doesn't solve it.

There are signs that Parfit has some sympathy with some of these concerns.[13] He resists because he is persuaded by the triviality argument. He clearly regards this as a master argument against any form of naturalism. I also speculate that he is moved by a way of thinking about the nature of disagreement in ethics that seems to me to underlie the concerns that so many have about the kind of naturalism that I like. I will start with the triviality argument.

5. Parfit's Triviality Argument

The argument is simplicity itself. Take any putative identification of being right with natural property N. If it is correct, saying that an act which is N is right will be trivial. But it manifestly isn't. For example, suppose the naturalistic candidate for being right is maximizing happiness, then, he argues, the claim that it is right to maximize happiness will be trivial. It can come to nothing more than the claim that being right is being right, or that maximizing happiness is maximizing happiness. But no one thinks that. Many think the claim that being right is maximizing happiness is false, and those who think it is true agree it needs argument and, moreover, think it is important to tell people about its truth. How then could the claim be trivial?

[13] See the sentence that starts, 'Though these last two claims are plausible…', Ch. 98, §27, p. 377.

Some naturalists reply to the argument (and its close cousin the open question argument) by affirming the importance of the distinction between soft and hard naturalism, and arguing that the triviality objection is only a problem for hard naturalism. I cannot make this response. As I say above, I think Parfit is right that soft naturalism is no advance on hard naturalism. What I will say in reply is along the lines of some traditional replies to the open question argument, although I will say things in my own way.

My reply takes off from a point that will, I hope, be relatively non-controversial. The most attractive approaches to ethics start by making rather general claims that are urged to be self-evident, or a priori, or constitutive of the moral, or justified by the way they make sense of our most firmly held moral convictions, or.... What's right is what's in accord with norms that no one could rationally object to; what's right is what satisfies desires that are fully universalizable; what's right is that which maximizes the good, where the good is that which is desirable, or ideally desirable, or desired to be desired, or that which it is rational to desire...; what's right is what we have most reason to do when acting on desires that treat everyone as an end, not a means; what's right is that which satisfies the golden rule in all its forms; what's right is that which satisfies as many as possible of the virtues; etc. Speaking for myself, I like to think of the set of general claims as a theory, folk morality, akin in some ways to folk psychology,[14] but that's not important here. What is important is that we start from rather general claims that, for one reason or another, are thought to be compelling enough to be the starting point for an ethical theory. They give naturalists their riding instructions, as we might put it. The naturalists' task is then to find an identification of, let's say, being right in terms of a natural property that makes true the general claim or claims in question. If there is no way to do this, Mackie threatens. Indeed, the case for Mackie's error theory is a simple application of the approach to finding an ethical theory that we are talking about. The general claim that founds Mackie's error theory is, to put it roughly, one about the good being a 'necessary attractor', and the empirical contention is that there exists, in nature, no necessary attractor.

---

[14] See, e.g., *From Metaphysics to Ethics* (Oxford: Oxford University Press, 1998), Ch. 6.

The implication of this picture is that any identification of being right will be an unobvious one. It takes real work to move from the general claim or claims to a thesis about which property fits the bill. Indeed, this is obvious from the fact that books and articles on ethics can be quite long.

Moreover, the situation can be complicated by the need to draw a role-realizer distinction. Depending on the nature of the general claim or claims from which our theorist launches their theory, it may be that those claims specify a job description that rightness (to stick with that example) needs to satisfy, where it is *contingent* which property satisfies it. For example, if part of the job description gives a central place to what's desired in ideal circumstances, and allows that what's desired in ideal circumstances is contingent, then the property that fills the job description for rightness may vary from possible world to possible world. We will need, in this case, to distinguish the property that fits the bill—something that may vary from one world to another, from the property of being the property that fits the bill—something that is constant across worlds. The first is the realizer property, the second is the role property.[15] To which property does our little proof earlier that being right is necessarily co-extensive with some natural property apply? The role property, for that's the property shared by all right acts across logical space. The other possibility is that the general claim or claims from which our theorist launches their theory are such that which property satisfies the job description is not a contingent matter. In this case, there's no need to draw a distinction between the role property and the realizer property. From now on, we'll mean by being right the role property, in cases where there's a need to distinguish the role property from the realizer one.

The fact that naturalists must and do allow that it takes real work to find the natural property to identify with being right means that the identification isn't trivial. The situation will be akin to that which obtains in discussions of randomness in probability theory and statistics, and data fitting in the philosophy of science.

---

[15] Analogy: suppose that red is the king's favourite colour. In this example, red is the realizer property and being the king's favourite colour (whatever it may be) is the role property.

The concept of a random sequence is of central importance in probability theory and statistics. In consequence, what it takes to be a random sequence is an important foundational question. It is also a controversial and difficult one, and different accounts are on offer. Finding the right account is very far from trivial. All the same, when someone offers an account of what it takes to be a random sequence, the proposal isn't that there are *two* properties, that of being a random sequence and that of being so and so, where so and so is the account on offer—two distinct properties that are somehow glued together of necessity. There's one property. All the same, someone who says that being a random sequence is being so and so isn't saying nothing more than that being a random sequence is being a random sequence, or that being so and so is being so and so.[16]

Much the same applies to the problem of data fitting. Long books and articles have been written on the problem of what it takes to be the hypothesis that best fits a given set of data points. How big a role does simplicity play? Can there be two distinct but equally good 'curves' that each fit all the data points? How theory laden is the data itself? And so on. The solution to the problem will be a claim of the form: the hypothesis that best fits a given set of data points is such and such (or maybe, if ties are possible: *an* hypothesis that best fits a given set of data points is *an* hypothesis that is such and such). The claim won't be that there are two properties that necessarily go hand in hand. The claim will be that being the (or an) hypothesis that best fits the data points *is* the (or an) hypothesis that is such and such. But no one thinks that because there is just the one property, the claim is trivial. ('If only it were', those struggling to find the answer may well say.)

The triviality argument is Parfit's master argument against naturalism, as we said. However, I think that there is another argument—or maybe line of thought best describes it—hovering in the background which is playing a role in making him so sure that naturalism is a big mistake. My

[16] Perhaps there are different concepts of randomness in different parts of statistics. In that case, what we say needs to be complicated but the essential point remains: it will be that being a random$_1$ sequence is being so and so isn't trivial, despite the fact that the claim is that being a random$_1$ sequence and being so and so are one and the same property.

reason is partly that when I present the kind of response just bruited to his attack on naturalism, those sympathetic to Parfit's position often quickly move to this other argument.[17] Also, I know that something similar often happens when naturalists reply to the open question argument, which, as we've remarked, is a close cousin of the triviality objection. Finally, there is Parfit's discussion of disagreement in Ch. 25, §87, some of which seems to rest on the argument I am about to criticize. I will call this argument: *the argument from real disagreement*. It is the last topic of this essay.

6. *The Argument from Real Disagreement*

Not all disagreements are real. Sometimes what appears to be a disagreement is, when one does some digging, really a case of two people talking past each other. They use the one term 'T' to make what appear to be inconsistent claims—'x is T' and 'x isn't T', as it might be—but it turns out that they understand 'T' differently, in a way that means it is possible for x to be T on the one understanding, while failing to be T on the other. Perhaps this happens more often than we philosophers (who love an argument) admit. All the same, some disagreements are real and, surely, runs the argument from real disagreement against naturalism, two naturalists in ethics must allow that sometimes when one of them says that being right = N_1, and the other says that being right = N_2, where $N_1 \neq N_2$, they are disagreeing. Maybe sometimes they mean something different by 'morally right' and so are talking past each other, but it isn't plausible that this is always the case or must be the case. But how can they, on the naturalists' own picture, be in real disagreement? Doesn't real disagreement here require that there be one property about which they are taking different views? But what might that one property be? Being right, you might say. But our two naturalists agree on at least this much—either N_1 is being right or N_2 is. What's more, they agree that $N_1 = N_1$, $N_2 = N_2$, and $N_1 \neq N_2$. Where's the single property about which they are disagreeing? Somehow it has vanished from the scene. That's the challenge to naturalism from the argument from real disagreement.

[17] This happened at a graduate seminar at Princeton; I am indebted to that discussion.

I grant the initial appeal of this line of argument but think it embodies a confused way of thinking about disagreements about the identity of properties. Philosophers disagree, really disagree, about the nature of motion. Let Dr Relational be our representative of the school that insists that motion is a relational property. She holds that motion is a relation between an object's position at a time and its position at earlier and later times. On this view, an object's velocity at time t is nothing over and above the value the rate of change of position over time takes at t (ds/dt, in obvious notation). Professor Intrinsic agrees that objects change position over time but he insists that motion is that which *explains* change of position over time, and so is distinct from change of position over time. It is an intrinsic property, I, which explains the relational property R.

This is a real disagreement and one that generates vigorous discussion at conferences. But what is the single property about which they are disagreeing? Motion, one might say. Doesn't one theorist think motion = R, and the other that motion = I. But what is this single property about which they take different views? There would appear to be just the two possible candidates to be that one property about which they disagree, namely R and I. But they agree that R = R, I = I, and that R ≠ I. Where's the property about which they take different views? What's more, although Dr Relational thinks that Professor Intrinsic is mistaken, she doesn't think that he's so confused as to think that R = I. But R is motion according to her. So, by her lights, Professor Intrinsic doesn't believe that motion is an intrinsic property after all! What then is going on when she gets up at a conference and declares that Professor Intrinsic wrongly thinks that motion is an intrinsic property?

There is much that could be said about this kind of puzzle in general.[18] But I think, in the broad, it is reasonably clear what needs to be said. Motion plays a role in our theory of the world we occupy. It plays a role in folk physics; it plays a role in the big improvement on folk physics that gets taught in physics departments. Dr Relational and Professor Intrinsic disagree about which property it is that plays that role. Their disagreement is not so much about the nature of some given property, but about which property *has some further property*—in this case, the property of

[18] See, e.g., David Lewis, "Noneism or Allism," *Mind*, 99/393 (1990): 23–31.

playing a certain role. It is like the disagreement between someone who thinks that Oxford blue is light blue, and someone who thinks it is dark blue. They are in real disagreement, but it isn't the case that there's a colour such that one person holds it is dark blue and the other that it is light blue. Rather one person thinks that light blue has the property of being the colour with a special association with Oxford University, whereas the other thinks that it is dark blue that has that property.

Ethical naturalists can and should say the same about the disagreement between those who hold that being right $= N_1$, and those who hold that it $= N_2$. There is no property the one holds to be N_1 and the other holds to be N_2. Their disagreement is over which property has the property of playing the role we give being right when we engage in moral theory.

References

Jackson, Frank. 1998. *From Metaphysics to Ethics*. Oxford: Oxford University Press.

Jackson, Frank, Philip Pettit, and Michael Smith. 2000. "Ethical Particularism and Patterns." In *Moral Particularism*, ed. Brad Hooker and Margaret Little. Oxford: Oxford University Press.

Lewis, David. 1990. "Noneism or Allism." *Mind*, 99/393: 23–31.

Mackie, J. L. 1977. *Ethics*. Harmondsworth: Penguin.

Moore, G. E. 1929. *Principia Ethica*. Cambridge: Cambridge University Press.

Parfit, Derek. 1971. "Personal Identity." *The Philosophical Review*, 80/1: 3–27.

10

WHAT MATTERS ABOUT META-ETHICS?

Mark Schroeder

1. *Why Parfit's Life Has Not Been Wasted*

According to Part Six of Derek Parfit's *On What Matters*, some things matter.[1] Indeed, there are normative *truths* to the effect that some things matter, and it matters that there are such truths. Moreover, according to Parfit, these normative truths are cognitive and irreducible. And in addition to mattering that there are normative truths about what matters, Parfit holds that it also matters that these truths are cognitive and irreducible. Indeed this matters so much that Parfit tells us that if there were normative truths, but that these truths were non-cognitive or reducible, then he, Sidgwick, and Ross "would have wasted much of our lives" (*OWM*, II, 367).[2]

---

[1] Subsequent references to *On What Matters* will be given in-line, with reference to the appropriate volume.

[2] Parfit advises me that since he doesn't think "truths" even *could* be non-cognitive, he believes this is an infelicitous way of formulating his view. However, as I have argued elsewhere (Schroeder [2009]), it is safe to assume that if meta-ethical non-cognitivism is true, then some kind of non-cognitivism about truth must be true as well. (Indeed, I argued in Schroeder [2010] that truth is itself a much more promising application for expressivism than meta-ethics is.) So if non-cognitivism is true at all, then it is in fact accurate to say that there are "non-cognitive truths." This is one of many examples where it doesn't turn out that a view is incoherent simply because Parfit believes that one of its commitments is false.

That it would be a consequence of the thesis either of non-cognitivism or of reductive realism that Parfit would have wasted his life is, of course, no evidence against either thesis; it is perfectly possible even for the most brilliant thinkers to waste their lives. Indeed, as any of the students from my introductory ethics course would be quick to point out, it is very difficult to think clearly and objectively about a question in which you take yourself to have a large personal stake. My undergraduates readily agree that the steak they have is enough to complicate their thinking about moral vegetarianism; so certainly explosive expressions like "wasted my life" give Parfit the kind of loaded stake in meta-ethical questions that should make us cautious of trusting his intuitive verdicts in meta-ethics. Fortunately, as I will argue in this paper, Parfit has not wasted his life, and he would not have wasted his life, even if either non-cognitivism or reductive realism turned out to be true.

In arguing that Parfit has not wasted his life, independently of the answer to any meta-ethical question, I am, of course, arguing against Parfit's own conception of what makes his life worthwhile. This makes my argument, in a certain way, very presumptuous. Parfit clearly believes that the worthwhileness of [much of][3] his life turns on the answer to questions in meta-ethics. But even brilliant thinkers can be wrong, and they are more likely to be wrong both about topics that are relevantly distinct from the topics to which they've applied their greatest brilliance, and when their approach to these topics is colored by a deep sense of a personal stake in them. Still, I admit that it is a bold thesis to claim that someone else's conception of what makes their own life worthwhile is incorrect.

But fortunately, it is no more bold—indeed, it is less bold—than Parfit's own pronouncements to the effect that other philosophers have not understood or believed their own views. For example, about me, Parfit says, "Schroeder's worries seem to show that he does not really accept his own view," on such paltry evidence as that I acknowledged the intuitive force of apparent counter-examples to that view and took steps to explain that intuitive force away (*OWM*, II, 361). It is a pessimistic vision indeed for the possibility of philosophical progress, if it turns out

---

[3] I'll be ignoring this qualification from here forward for illustrative purposes.

that theorists cannot agree about the intuitive force of examples and offer competing theories about where that force comes from! Whereas Parfit's argumentative strategy in Part Six of *On What Matters* requires showing that everyone who seems to disagree with him either does not have the right concepts to disagree at all, or that they do not really accept their own views (Mackie and Williams apparently fall on the former fork, while I fall on the latter—Nietzsche conveniently slips the forks of the dilemma by going insane), my argumentative strategy only requires establishing that the significant value of Parfit's life has not depended on the answer to central meta-ethical questions. All I claim, therefore, for my presumptuous argument in this paper, is that I am on better grounds to claim that Parfit is wrong about what makes his life worthwhile than Parfit is to claim that I don't really believe my own philosophical views.

Let me begin, therefore, with my master argument that Parfit has not wasted his life. It goes like this:

(1) *Reasons and Persons* constitutes one of the most important contributions of the last century to making progress in our thinking about substantive normative ethics [premise].

(2) Making progress in our thinking about substantive normative ethics is one of the things that matters most [premise].

(3) Parfit is the author and creator of *Reasons and Persons* [premise].

(4) So Parfit is the author and creator of one of the most important contributions of the last century to one of the things that matters most [from (1), (2), and (3)].

(5) No life which involves creating one of the most important contributions in a century to one of the things that matters most has been wasted [premise].

(6) So Parfit's life has not been wasted [from (4) and (5)].

Where could this argument go wrong? It is valid, and has only four premises, one of which is that Parfit is the author of *Reasons and Persons*, which seems difficult to reject. Moreover, the only cause Parfit could have to reject premise (1) would be modesty; indeed the Oxford promotional materials for *On What Matters* describe *Reasons and Persons* as "one of the landmarks of twentieth-century philosophy." Since substantive normative ethics is only one branch of twentieth-century philosophy, and an underappreciated one, at that, it is safe to conclude that any contribution to substantive normative ethics that is also a landmark of twentieth-century philosophy full-stop is one of the greatest contributions to substantive normative ethics.

Premise (5) also looks unassailable; surely if any lives are not wasted, it is lives which make epochal contributions to the things that matter most. And yet premise (2) can hardly be said to be a weakness of the argument, either, for it is hard to see why Parfit himself would have spent so much time preoccupied with the attempt to make progress in substantive normative ethics—both his books are preoccupied with the possibility of such progress—unless he himself agreed that this matters. So I conclude that the argument is sound. Parfit has not wasted his life.

Of course, Parfit may agree with me that his life has not been wasted, for he believes that there are *irreducible, cognitive* normative truths about what matters, and he maintains only that his life *would* have been wasted, if it turned out that either non-cognitivism or reductive realism were true. What is at stake isn't *whether* Parfit's life has value, but *what gives it* value—the fact that he has authored one of the most important contributions to one of the things that matters most, or this somehow coupled with the fact that truths about mattering are cognitive and irreducible. Still, how, then, could things go wrong with my argument, if it turned out that there are normative truths, but those truths are either reducible in some way, or require a non-cognitivist interpretation? My argument doesn't say anything about issues meta-ethical. So where do they come in?

Well, it seems safe to assume that meta-ethical debates will have no bearing on whether Parfit is indeed the author of *Reasons and Persons*, and so premise (3) looks safe. But there are two possible ways in which one might think that a problem could arise for one of the other premises, on the basis of meta-ethical views. First, if there can be no such thing as progress in substantive normative ethics, then premise (1) couldn't be true since it says that *Reasons and Persons* was a great contribution to such progress. And second, if nothing at all matters, then it follows that either premise (2) or premise (5) is false. Which is false will depend on whether we interpret the expression "one of the things that matters most" so that if nothing matters, then everything is among the things that matter most—i.e. not at all. If we so interpret it, then if nothing mattered, premise (2) would be trivially true, but premise (5) would be false, since some lives are indeed wasted. Whereas if we interpret this expression so that it entails that something actually matters, then premise (2) would clearly be false if nothing mattered. Either way, the view that nothing matters would plausibly make trouble for my argument.

Fortunately for Parfit's concern that whether his life would have been wasted turns on matters meta-ethical, there seem to be meta-ethical views with each of these consequences. By the lights of the sort of crude emotivism espoused by a number of the logical positivists in the 1930s, for example, which is clearly a meta-ethical view, there does not seem to be anything worth calling "progress" in normative ethics. Indeed many of the logical positivists were of the opinion that there was no properly philosophical discipline of normative meta-ethical inquiry at all—again, clearly a meta-ethical view. Similarly, global error theories seem to be committed to the view that nothing really matters, any more than anything is right or wrong, or good or bad. I don't say that if either of these meta-ethical views turned out to be true, then Parfit's life would indeed have been wasted, because my argument considers only one sufficient condition among, perhaps, very many, for this to be false. But certainly my explanation of why Parfit's life has not been wasted would run into trouble if either of these meta-ethical theories turned out to be true. So in that respect, meta-ethics does look like it matters.

However, now we run into yet another problem. For Parfit claims not only that it matters that certain meta-ethical views are false. He appears to think—indeed, he could have saved hundreds of pages and many hours of his readers' time if he did not—that it matters that *all* meta-ethical theories other than his own cognitivist non-reductive realism are false. But so far we've only seen that there are certain meta-ethical views which are committed to rejecting one of the premises of my argument— we've hardly seen that *all but one* meta-ethical view is committed to rejecting one of the premises of my argument. Yet that seems to be what Parfit must think. How could that be so?

2. Conservative Reductive Realism

For concreteness, and because we know from the text that mine is one of the meta-ethical views which Parfit believes it matters to refute, let's take the case of the sort of conservative, non-analytic, reductive realism that I've defended in previous work. According to this view, some things matter—indeed, there are normative truths about what matters. But this view hypothesizes that there is an interesting question about *what it is* for something to matter—a question that can be answered in non-normative terms. It is no part of this view that we could do away with normative talk and thought about what matters and replace it with non-normative talk and thought. Similarly, it is no part of this view that substantive normative inquiry into what matters is not an autonomous and important domain of genuine inquiry. It is only a theoretical hypothesis about what it is to matter.[4]

Indeed, it is intended to be a conservative theoretical hypothesis. If any particular hypothesis about what it is to matter turns out to be inconsistent with other particularly indubitable truths, the proponent of this sort of meta-ethical view sees that as a strong argument against that particular hypothesis. And if every particular hypothesis about what it is to matter turned out to be inconsistent with other particularly indubitable truths, the proponent of this sort of view would cease to advocate it. Nothing about the outlook of this sort of view is intended to undermine or upset ordinary normative ideas; on the contrary, the

---

[4] In his response to this paper in this volume, Parfit characterizes me, apparently on the basis of the preceding paragraph, as defending "soft naturalism." This is the view that "[t]hough all facts are natural, we need to make, or have strong reasons to make, some irreducibly normative claims" (*OWM*, II, 365). However, I am clearly not a soft naturalist. I do not believe that we need to make or ever have reasons to make irreducibly normative claims. Indeed, I do not even believe that there are such things as irreducibly normative claims. I only believe that there are normative claims, which some people—Parfit among them—erroneously believe to be irreducibly normative. It is part of my view—part of conservative reductive realism—that we can and should make normative claims. It's part of my view that some things matter, and it's part of my view that we couldn't easily dispense with words like "matter" and still succeed at saying all of the interesting things that we want to say about what matters. But it is no part of my view that we should make irreducibly normative claims, or even that there are such things as irreducibly normative claims for us to make.

whole idea is to hold fixed ordinary normative ideas and try to answer some *further* explanatory questions in a way that is particularly theoretically satisfying.

As I have noted, it is part of the conservative outlook underlying the idea that the reducibility of the normative to the non-normative is a potentially fruitful explanatory hypothesis that no particular reductive hypothesis will count as satisfactory, unless it is consistent with independent truths. That at least some things matter, that there can be progress in substantive normative ethics, and that among the things that matter most is such progress, and that lives that make seminal contributions to what matters most are not wasted, are the right sorts of truths to serve as constraints, on this view. The conservative reductive realist is more confident in these truths than she is in the reducibility of the normative. That is what makes her view conservative. But it does not follow from this that she does not believe in the reducibility of the normative after all, as Parfit claims about me. It simply follows that she believes that there is at least one hypothesis about how the normative could reduce to the non-normative that is compatible with all of the most important such independent truths.

Now it may be that the reductive realist has been over-optimistic, and that she is wrong about this. Indeed, there is much that I am inclined to think that I was over-optimistic about in my own first book. (There is always a danger, for ambitious explanatory theories, of falling victim to optimism.) If so, then it may be that on the best available hypothesis about how the normative could reduce to the non-normative, it follows that certain fairly plausible independent normative truths are false, and hence there would be excellent grounds to reject the reducibility thesis. But it is certainly part of the conservative reductivist's *view* that there is an available reductive hypothesis which will *not* predict the falsity of any important independent truths. So if this sort of conservative reductivism were true, then some things would still matter, among them making progress in substantive normative ethics, and such progress would still be possible, as evidenced by, for example, *Reasons and Persons*. The bar is low for a reductive view to be able to explain why Parfit's life has not been a waste; it needn't be consistent with all of the important independent truths; only with those articulated by premises (1), (2), and (5).

It is worth comparing the conservative reductive realist to the flamboyant reductive realist. Whereas the conservative reductive realist is more confident in a range of important independent truths than she is in the reducibility of the normative to the non-normative, and more confident in the reducibility thesis than in any particular hypothesis about how it works, the flamboyant reductive realist is more confident in his reductive hypothesis than in a range of important apparent truths with which it might come into conflict. The conservative reductive realist's attitude toward normative inquiry is that there are other good theoretical questions that are also worth asking. In contrast, the flamboyant reductive realist's attitude is that meta-ethical problems are so pressing that virtually any plausible answer is worth giving up antecedently compelling normative views, if necessary.

The flamboyant reductive realist may or may not hold that my premises (1), (2), and (5) are compatible with his reductive theory. If he does, then even if his view were true, Parfit's life would still not be a waste. But there is a natural sense in which the compatibility of premises (1), (2), and (5) with his view is not itself a particularly important part of the flamboyant reductivist's view, for he would be happy to reject these premises if it turned out that he was not able to maintain them. Although this doesn't exactly get us the conclusion that were the flamboyant reductivist's view true, my argument would be unsound, it is not exactly comforting, either. It is therefore understandable why Parfit would want to reject the position of the flamboyant realist, because like the conservative realist, his confidence in truths like premises (1), (2), and (5) is high. It is much less clear, however, why it is important whether the conservative reductivist is wrong.

Just to be perfectly clear about the structure of this point, we may characterize conservative reductive realism as the conjunction of the following four theses:

CRR1 Some things matter, there can be progress in substantive normative ethics, and lives that make seminal contributions to what matters most are not wasted.

CRR2 There is an analysis of what it is to matter that ultimately bottoms out in non-normative terms. This analysis lets us answer explanatory questions that Parfit does not appear to be interested in.

CRR3 If theses (CRR1) and (CRR2) are incompatible, then thesis (CRR2) is false.

CRR4 Theses (CRR1) and (CRR2) are not incompatible.

Because conservative reductive realism is the conjunction of these four theses, in order to observe what implications it has for my argument about the value of Parfit's life, we need to think about what follows if all four of these theses are true. But if all four of these theses are true, then I think it clearly follows, as I've already demonstrated, that my argument goes through. So it is clear that the value of Parfit's life cannot turn on the question of whether conservative reductive realism is true.

Obviously, Parfit believes that my thesis CRR4 is false. Because he believes this, and because he presumably takes comfort in arguments similar to mine that his life has not been a waste, it is rational for him to hope that my thesis CRR2 is false, and that there is no analysis of claims about what matters that ultimately bottoms out in non-normative terms. But conservative reductive realism is a package view, and there is no rational cause for Parfit to hope that the package turns out to be false.[5]

3. *The Triviality Objection*

Parfit does offer an argument which is presented as an argument against any form of (non-analytic) reductivism. He appears to be quite taken with the argument, as it recurs repeatedly. Moreover, since he devotes six whole pages of *On What Matters* to rehearsing how the argument applies to my view in particular, as a general principle of charitable interpretation, I take it that it is safe to assume that Parfit believes that this argument does, in fact, apply to me, or at least show something instructive

---

[5] In his response to this paper in this volume, Parfit mistakenly claims that I have said that I am "not really committed to [my] reductive view." This is based on a clear misreading; on the contrary, I am both committed to my reductive view and to the thesis that this view is consistent with the fact that many things matter. The fact that I have the second commitment, which Parfit thinks is an error, does not show that I do not have the first commitment. Indeed, most interesting disagreements among philosophers involve disagreeing about two or more things at the same time. I suspect that a great deal of *On What Matters* could have benefited from greater appreciation of this important fact.

about the views that I have defended.[6] The argument is called the "triviality objection," and it is very simple. Parfit begins by defining "positive" so that if (A) is a generalization of the form, "When Bx, Dx," where B is a condition spelled out in non-normative terms and D is a normative condition, (A) counts as "positive" just in case (A) states or implies that when x is B, x also has some other, different, normative property. Similarly, although it plays no direct role in the argument, Parfit defines *substantive* to apply to (A) just in case we might disagree with it, or it might tell us something that we didn't already know (*OWM*, II, 343).

With these definitions in hand, Parfit's main presentation of the triviality objection considers the example of reductive utilitarianism, but assures us that his argument can be extended to other reductive theses. Since reductive utilitarianism is not, I think, a very plausible view, defending it is not, I think, very interesting for our purposes. Of course, there is a long and venerable tradition in meta-ethics of arguing against reductivism in general by arguing against straw men and then baldly asserting that one's arguments generalize, but it would not do for us to indulge Parfit in perpetuating this tradition.[7] So since Parfit claims that

---

[6] Actually, Parfit goes on to say that the triviality objection applies only to *soft* naturalists (*OWM*, II, 344), and does not apply to *hard* naturalists. See note 4 for Parfit's definition of soft naturalism, and my explanation of why I am not a soft naturalist. According to *hard naturalism*, "Since all facts are natural, we don't need to make such irreducibly normative claims. The facts that are stated by such claims could all be restated in non-normative and naturalistic terms." Parfit treats his distinction between hard and soft naturalism as exhaustive, but insofar as I understand this definition, I do not believe that I am a hard naturalist, either. At least, though I do not believe that we need to make any irreducibly normative claims, that is only because I do not think there is any such thing as irreducibly normative claims to make. I do not accept many of the claims accepted by Sturgeon, Jackson, and Brandt that Parfit goes on to criticize in his discussion of hard naturalism (*OWM*, II, 368–77). What I do believe, is that all normative properties and relations have analyses that ultimately bottom out in non-normative terms. So I suspect that here, as throughout Part Six of *On What Matters*, Parfit is arguing more by consideration of paradigms than by elimination.

[7] Michael Huemer (2005) takes this tradition to new heights:

> On the face of it, wrongness seems to be a completely different kind of property from, say, weighing 5 pounds. In brief:

1. Value properties are radically different from natural properties.
2. If two things are radically different, then one is not reducible to the other.
3. So value properties are not reducible to natural properties.

the same style of argument can be extended to any reductive view, it will be far more instructive for our purposes to consider the general form of the argument. Hence I will assume, in setting out the argument, that we are dealing with an arbitrary reductive view, according to which to be D is just to be B. He calls this thesis (C), and calls the corresponding thesis that "When Bx, Dx," (A). He then argues:

(1) (A) is a substantive normative claim, which might state a positive substantive normative fact.

(2) If, impossibly, (C) were true, (A) could not state such a fact. (A) could not be used to imply that, when some act would [be B], this act would have the different property of being [D], since (C) claims that there is no such property. Though (A) and (C) have different meanings, (A) would be only another way of stating the trivial fact that, when some act would [be B], this act would [be B].

Therefore this form of Naturalism is not true. (*OWM*, II, 343–4)

I have to confess that Parfit's triviality objection is one of the most puzzling arguments I have ever encountered in philosophy. It is true that according to (C), (A) could not be used to imply that when some act would be B, it would have the different property of being D, because according to (C) B and D are the same property. But that is neither here nor there, because premise (1) does not entail that (A) must be able to imply that when some act would be B, it would have the different property of being D. It only entails that when some act would be B, it would have *some* other, different, normative property. This needn't be the property of being D at all. So ignoring the fact that Parfit's second premise gratuitously presupposes that the conclusion of the argument is not only true, but necessarily true, the argument is not even valid.[8]

> To illustrate, suppose a philosopher proposes that the planet Neptune is Beethoven's Ninth Symphony. I think we can see that that is false, simply by virtue of our concept of Neptune and our concept of symphonies. Neptune is an entirely different kind of thing from Beethoven's Ninth Symphony. No further argument is needed. (94)

[8] In his response to this paper in this volume, Parfit suggests that by clarifying how his argument works, we can see that it is clearly valid:

Moreover, the fact that Parfit seems to treat this argument as if it were valid, by assuming that premise (1) really entails that the "different normative property" which (A) states or implies must be the property of being D, makes the argument look trivially question-begging. I grant that Parfit is very confident that no reductive theory is true, and that gives him great confidence that for any reductive hypothesis (C), the corresponding statement (A) will state or imply that when x is B, it has the *different* property *of being D*. But what is at issue here is precisely what rational grounds there are for this sort of confidence. And it is very hard to see where any rational grounds for confidence in Parfit's premise (1) are supposed to come from, that do not stem directly from confidence that being D is not the same as being B. And so it is very difficult to see how this argument is supposed to give us any leverage in evaluating whether the reductive hypothesis could be true.

> (1) (A) is a substantive normative claim which might state a positive substantive normative fact.
>
> (2) If, impossibly, (C) were true, (A) could not state such a fact.
>
> Therefore
>
> (C) is not true.
>
> As Schroeder would agree, this argument is valid. If we knew both that (A) might state such a normative fact, and that if (C) were true (A) could not state such a fact, we could infer that (C) is not true. (Parfit [Forthcoming 2])

Let's again ignore that this argument is made valid by virtue of Parfit's gratuitous inclusion of the presupposition that its conclusion is necessary in premise (2), and assume that what is at issue is whether the argument is valid in some way that non-trivially involves a role for premise (1). Parfit here seems to be suggesting that what does the work in this argument is not the assumption that (A) *does* state a positive substantive normative fact, but only that it *might* do so. But now again we may observe that this argument is not valid (ignoring the illicit presupposition of premise (2)), for yet a different reason. Suppose that Derek was in either Hawaii or Alaska last week, but we don't know which. We do know this: if he was in Alaska, then he could not have been in Hawaii. But of course, we don't know where he went. So he *might* have been in Hawaii. From this we cannot infer that he was not in Alaska—only that he *might* not have been in Alaska. What this case illustrates is the general and familiar fact that *modus tollens* is not valid for conditionals with modals in their consequents. So similarly, all we can conclude from the argument if we understand premise (1) in this way is that (C) *might* not be true. But of course, that is where we started—in ignorance of whether (C) is true. So this accomplishes nothing. It is genuinely bewildering to me what this argument is supposed to accomplish.

Still, since even if the argument is effectively question-begging, it is not even valid, we can grant Parfit's premise (1) without trouble, so long as attributions of "D" carry implications that attributions of "B" do not. If any of these implications are normative, then "When Bx, Dx" would be positive after all, in Parfit's stipulative sense—even if the reductive thesis is true. In fact, this is a direct consequence of a view for which I've argued in a number of places—namely, that claims about reasons carry *pragmatic* implications about the *weight* of those reasons (which is a normative matter).[9] There is no reason why claims about what would be part of the explanation of why the object of someone's desire would be promoted by her doing something would carry this same pragmatic implication.

In his helpful elaboration of how the triviality argument works against my view, Parfit contends that if I wish to accept that the "When Bx, Dx" claim corresponding to my view is positive by his definition of "positive,"

> Schroeder would then face the Lost Property Problem. It is hard to see what this other property could be. And if Schroeder could find some other property that could be the normative property...he would have to apply his Naturalism to this other property. The Triviality Objection would then apply to this other claim. This objection would not have been answered. (*OWM*, II, 359)

This sounds on the face of it like quite an impressive problem—that it should be both difficult to see what the "Lost Property" might be, and that even were I to say what it is, we would simply be off on a regress.

Fortunately, however, as I've already noted, it is not difficult to see what other property might be implied by generalizations about reasons, at least according to the views I've already defended in print; it is the property of being a relatively *weighty* reason. And I have in fact already applied my reductivism (unlike Parfit I don't use the term "Naturalism," which I find unhelpful) to this other property; I've given a reductive account of the weight of reasons in terms of reasons in Chapter 7 of *Slaves of the Passions*. Contrary to Parfit, moreover, this does not start

---

[9] See especially Schroeder (2007), Ch. 5.

the dialectic about the triviality objection all over again with the other property, because on my view, there is only one reduction of a normative property or relation in non-normative terms. The "Lost Property" that is implied is one that reduces in non-normative terms only *by way of reducing to reasons*. In fact, I've argued elsewhere that *all* promising reductive views should adopt this structure.[10]

Consequently, we may safely reject Parfit's triviality objection. It neither provides evidence against conservative reductive realism like that I've defended, nor grounds to think that it matters whether such reductivism is true or false.

4. Orogeny of the Mountain

Up to this point in this paper, I've argued that Parfit's life has not been a waste, admitted that the soundness of my argument depends on the falsity of *some* meta-ethical views, and maintained that it does not depend on the falsity of all alternatives to Parfit's own meta-ethical view, but only on the falsity of certain, particularly flamboyant, meta-ethical theses. And I've shown that Parfit's central argument against reductive theories, in particular, is highly problematic.

Fortunately, there is no reason to think that the sort of reductive theory that would be incompatible with one of the assumptions of my argument that Parfit's life has not been wasted is more likely to be true, or would be more likely to be true, if reductive realism were true, than the sort of reductive theory that would be compatible with those assumptions. Moreover, there are excellent reasons—all of the reasons making the key assumptions of my argument so compelling—to think that a reductive theory that is compatible with those assumptions is much more likely to be true than a reductive theory incompatible with them. In short, among the available reductive theories, some are better than others, being better candidates for the truth. The better reductive theories are the ones that agree about the important claims that my argument assumes or presupposes.

---

[10] See Schroeder (2005).

The same distinction, among better and worse theories—a distinction that we can make by appeal to their fit with independently compelling claims—applies to non-cognitivist theories. Just as reductive realists can be flamboyant or conservative, likewise for non-cognitivists. Whereas Carnap and Schlick made flamboyant claims, most contemporary non-cognitivists share a strikingly conservative orientation. Rather than seeking to derive stunning or unintuitive consequences, they aim to preserve all of the important claims—normative and otherwise—that Parfit emphasizes are so important, and to go on to ask a set of further, explanatory, questions. It's possible to be interested in these further explanatory questions because you find it puzzling *whether* there are any normative truths. But it's also possible to simply be curious about *how* there are normative truths, and find non-cognitivism a promising approach for providing a particularly satisfying answer.

Like the distinction among reductive realist views, there are excellent grounds—grounds provided by a lot of independently compelling truths—to hold that conservative non-cognitivist views are much more likely to be true than flamboyant ones. Holding this does not require holding that conservative non-cognitivist views will be able to bear all of the fruits which they promise—like the reductive realist, the conservative non-cognitivist may be over-optimistic about the resources of her view. Indeed, at times conservative non-cognitivism has largely consisted of optimism.

But even if we are pessimistic about the conservative non-cognitivist's aspirations for success in her conservative ambitions, that's not quite the same as it *mattering* that she fails. We should distinguish *predictions* that conservative non-cognitivism will fail from Parfit's apparent *hope* that it will, and similarly for conservative reductivism. It hasn't been my aim in this paper to defend either reductivism or non-cognitivism. It has instead been my aim to lower the stakes of the discussion so that we can evaluate these theories in reasonable and objective ways, treating them as what they are—theories. Certainly they may be false. But if they turn out not to be, everything will still be okay, so long as some things really matter and moral progress really is possible. And I think we should all have pretty high confidence that *if* any reductive or non-cognitivist theory is true, it is one that is not inconsistent with the fact that many things matter.

The fact that some reductive theses are better than others should look familiar, for readers of parts two, three, and five of *On What Matters*. For in parts two and three Parfit argues that some Kantian views are better than others, and in parts three and five he argues that some Contractualist views are better than others. Together with his view that some Consequentialist views are better than others, this leads to the result that any Kantians, Contractualists, and Consequentialists who share Parfit's confidence in the data that motivate discriminating these better versions of these views from the worse versions have much to agree about. Rather than arguing against Kantianism or Contractualism *as such*, Parfit argues only against the versions of Kantianism and Contractualism which fall astray of this core set of data. What turns out to be important, for the Parfit of the core chapters of *On What Matters*, is not which of Kantianism, Contractualism, and Consequentialism is true, but the core theses which their best versions share.

Another similar phenomenon arises in one of the most surprising twists of the entire book, on page 467, just a few pages into his discussion of the metaphysical objections to non-reductive normative realism, when Parfit launches into a criticism of *actualism* and defense of *possibilism*. This is not a defense of the view in ethics known as "possibilism," but of the thesis from the metaphysics of modality that there are *possibilia* which don't actually exist. Since possibilism is typically seen as a particularly ontologically extravagant thesis, this is hardly the move one expects in a chapter whose ostensible purpose is to persuade us that Parfit's view is metaphysically innocuous. Yet including Appendix J, Parfit spends a full forty pages attempting to defend this view, even going so far (don't be surprised) as to allege that "though Plantinga claims to be an Actualist, that is not really true" (*OWM*, II, 739).

One leaves the appendix with the distinct impression that the thesis that Parfit cares about is simply not the thesis over which participants in the debate in the literature on the metaphysics of modality between actualism and possibilism disagree. Rather, what Parfit seems to think is important, and the reason why he seems to think that Plantinga is really a closet possibilist, is merely that there be a way for us to talk about the different options that an agent could take in a choice situation—something that actualists and possibilists might make sense of in different ways.

In much of part six of *On What Matters*, I'm tempted to suspect that something very similar has happened, for meta-ethical inquiry in general. There is something important that Parfit is concerned about, and there are real views in meta-ethics that are inconsistent with the results that he needs—views on which, in particular, my argument that Parfit's life has not been wasted is unsound. But I'm inclined to think that the important issue about which Parfit cares is not quite the same as the issues that have been pursued in contemporary meta-ethical inquiry under the headings of reduction or non-cognitivism. Rather, if what Parfit cares about is right, then though many meta-ethical views are indeed false, there is still a striking range of what I've called *conservative* meta-ethical theories—views which share a relatively common picture of the data, but offer competing explanations of it. Though all but one of these views are false, which one turns out to be true would not affect whether Parfit's life has been wasted, and will have no consequences for Parfit's arguments in the core chapters of *On What Matters*.

Like the convergence between Kantian, Consequentialist, and Contractualist approaches to normative theory, the conservative approaches to meta-ethics which I've been discussing here share a common conception of some of the data. But I don't believe that they could merely be complementary paths toward the same truth (although contrast Gibbard [2003]). Rather, they are loosely like different orogenies for the same mountain—different theories about where it came from.

If what you are primarily interested in, like Parfit, is how to get to the top of the mountain, then you may not care where the mountain came from. And if most of the people you talk to who do care where it came from are mostly concerned to try to convince you that since they can't understand where it came from, it must really be a flat plain, or that since they can't understand how you could have gotten so high, you must not be climbing the same peak as anyone else, you are not likely to find orogeny very worthwhile. But it doesn't follow that the mountain has no history. Even fellow climbers can pause, every once in a while, to admire the sweeping vistas, to rest up for the next leg of the journey, and to ponder whether this mountain was formed by subduction, volcanic action, or in some other way. It is true that many contributions to meta-ethics are like the orogenist telling Parfit that there is no mountain, or that everyone has her own mountain. But at its best and most interesting, meta-ethical inquiry needn't be like that at all. It has room for many questions which can be pursued with an open mind even by mountaineers who share Parfit's quest for the peak.

References

Gibbard, Allan. 2003. *Thinking How to Live*. Cambridge, MA: Harvard University Press.

Huemer, Michael. 2005. *Ethical Intuitionism*. New York: Palgrave Macmillan.

Parfit, Derek. 1984. *Reasons and Persons*. Oxford: Oxford University Press.

Parfit, Derek. 2011. *On What Matters*. 2 vols. Oxford: Oxford University Press.

Schroeder, Mark. 2005. "Realism and Reduction: The Quest for Robustness." *Philosophers' Imprint* 5/1: <http://www.philosophersimprint.org/005001/>.

Schroeder, Mark. 2007. *Slaves of the Passions*. Oxford: Oxford University Press.

Schroeder, Mark. 2009. *Noncognitivism in Ethics*. New York: Routledge.

Schroeder, Mark. 2010. "How to be an Expressivist About Truth." In *New Waves in Truth*, ed. Nikolaj Jang Pedersen and Cory Wright. New York: Palgrave Macmillan.

11

A DEFENSE OF MORAL INTUITIONISM

Bruce Russell

Of my reasons for becoming a graduate student in philosophy, one was the fact that, in wondering how to spend my life, I found it hard to decide what really matters. It was disappointing to find that most of the philosophers who taught me, or whom I was told to read, believed that the question "What matters?" couldn't have a true answer, or didn't even make sense.

(Parfit, Preface, xl)

I became increasingly concerned about certain differences between my views and the views of several other people. We seemed to disagree not only about what matters, but also about what it would be for things to matter, and about whether anything could matter.

(*OWM*, II, 427)

Derek Parfit is an intuitionist in his moral and practical epistemology and a non-naturalist in his moral and practical metaphysics. I am going to defend his intuitionism against non-cognitivists like Allan Gibbard who see a different role for intuitions in moral thinking. Next, I turn briefly to the worry that disagreement in moral intuitions supports anti-realism, and to the special worry that says we cannot tell intuitions that have evidentiary weight from those that do not. I will then criticize Parfit's arguments against what he calls Analytic Naturalism and what he calls Non-Analytic Naturalism. I do not argue that one of these forms of Naturalism is true, only that Parfit's arguments against them are unsound.

By "intuition" I will mean the psychological state people are in when some proposition seems true to them solely on the basis of their understanding that proposition.[1] If "all bachelors are unmarried" or "no object can be red and green all over at the same time" seems true to you solely on the basis of your understanding the proposition that the sentence expresses, you are having an intuition that the proposition is true. Intuitions are non-inferential, that is, are not the conclusion of some argument. They are propositional like beliefs (intuitions are intuitions *that* something is the case), but are not beliefs. In general, intuitionism is the view that intuitions are evidence for the truth of the propositions that are their objects, though perhaps only under certain ideal conditions. Moral intuitionism is the view that moral intuitions are evidence for the moral propositions that are their objects. So if "it is wrong to torture babies to death just for the fun of it" seems true to you solely on the basis of your understanding that proposition, then you are having a moral intuition and, according to moral intuitionism, that intuition gives you some reason to believe that the proposition that is its object is true (at least if the intuition is had under relevant ideal conditions).

Like Parfit, I use "true" in a non-deflationary sense. When I say that "genocide is wrong" is true, I mean that it has the property of being wrong. When I say with Parfit that " 'there is reason to avoid agony' is true," I mean that the property of there being a reason to avoid it is possessed by agony. Like Parfit, I do not use "true" in a minimalist sense. Parfit writes that if you say, "Milk chocolate and honey meringues are disgusting," he might say, "That's true!" as a way of expressing the same dislike (*OWM*, II, 381; cf. 265, 380, 396, 405). But in that context he is

---

[1] I follow George Bealer in identifying intuitions with *intellectual seemings* that he argues are distinct from beliefs, though they are often the basis of corresponding beliefs. He also argues that they are distinct from "judgments, hunches, and guesses." Bealer has many essays on intuition and a priori justification, and there is an enormous amount of overlap between them. What he takes intuitions to be can be found in his "Intuition and the Autonomy of Philosophy," in *Rethinking Intuition: The Psychology of Intuition and Its Role in Philosophical Inquiry*, ed. Michael DePaul (Lanham, MD: Rowman & Littlefield, 1998), 201–39, esp. 207–14, "Phenomenology of Intuitions," for a discussion of the nature of rational intuitions. Parfit might call what I am calling *intuitions* mental states of *seeming self-evidence*, which serve as the foundations of a priori justification and arise from a person's full understanding of a proposition (*OWM*, II, 508).

using "true" in a deflationary sense. However, when Parfit and I say that it's true that causing gratuitous cruelty is wrong, and that there is a reason not to cause it, we are not merely expressing a dislike of such cruelty. We are also claiming that causing such cruelty has the property of being wrong, and the property of there being a reason to avoid it. We see moral and practical judgments like the judgments of some hypothetical rock dwellers who *typically warn* others when they say, "The rocks are slippery!" but *also attribute the property* of being slippery to the rocks. When people make moral and practical judgments they both *typically do* something (express some commitment or state of mind) *and always ascribe a property*.

I will defend moral intuitionism by first comparing moral intuitions to epistemic intuitions, which seem to provide evidence for the non-deflationary truth of epistemic propositions regarding knowledge or justified belief that are their objects. I will then consider, and criticize, a non-cognitivist's approach to the role of intuitions in justifying both moral and epistemic judgments. Barring other objections to the evidentiary force of moral intuitions, or intuitions in general, the analogy with epistemic intuitions supports moral intuitionism. Next, I briefly take up the objection from disagreement in intuitions, which says that intuitions can't provide evidence because they are so unreliable, and a special worry regarding our inability to distinguish trustworthy from untrustworthy practical and moral intuitions. Finally, I present, and then criticize, Parfit's arguments against Analytic and Non-Analytic Naturalism.

1. Intuitions in Epistemology and in the Practical Realm

Intuitions, or rational insights, are often appealed to in epistemology to defeat certain theories and confirm others. Gettier cases are famous and seem to refute the idea that, necessarily, a justified true belief is knowledge (the JTB theory). One such example that we might call *Sheep* supposes that there are animals in a field that look just like sheep, though they are really poodles bred and clipped to look like sheep. On the basis of seeing these animals from the road, you form the belief that there are sheep in the field and, as it turns out, there are—but they are lying down out of sight behind a large boulder in the far corner of the field. So you have a justified true belief that there are sheep in the field. However, *intuitively*, you don't know that there are sheep in the field.[2] So the JTB theory is false.

Or consider examples used against reliabilism either about knowledge or justification. Some people hold that you have knowledge, or at least a justified belief, if your belief is the result of a reliable belief-producing mechanism, that is, one that, for the most part, yields true beliefs. However, Laurence BonJour has offered an example of a clairvoyant he calls Norman whose clairvoyance is a reliable belief-producing mechanism even though he has no evidence or grounds for thinking it is.[3] He does not have a tested and remembered track record to confirm the reliability of his clairvoyance. Now suppose Norman has his first clairvoyant experience, and because his visual image of the President in NY is so vivid, he can't help believing that the President is in New York. Assume that it's true that the President is in NY. Still, *intuitively*, Norman does not know, and is not justified in believing, that the President is in NY.

Keith Lehrer offers a similar example involving someone he calls Truetemp who has the ability to reliably tell the temperature of her brain due to a temperature device (a "doxatemp") that has been implanted in it while she was having surgery to remove a brain tumor. The doctors did not tell her that they would implant the "doxatemp," and she has no grounds for believing that she has this ability. *Intuitively*, when Truetemp first correctly believes that the temperature of her brain is, say, 98 degrees, she does not know that it is, nor is she justified in believing that it is.[4] So reliability is not sufficient for either knowledge or justification.

---

[2] I adapt this example from George Bealer's example given in his "On the Possibility of Philosophical Knowledge," in *Philosophical Perspectives 10, Metaphysics*, ed. James Tomberlin (Oxford: Basil Blackwell, 1992), 1–34, esp. 3–4 for his example of the poodles that look like sheep.

[3] Laurence BonJour, *The Structure of Empirical Knowledge* (Cambridge, MA: Harvard University Press, 1985), 41–5.

[4] See Keith Lehrer, "Proper Function versus Systematic Coherence," in *Warrant in Contemporary Epistemology: Essays in Honor of Plantinga's Theory of Knowledge*, ed. Jonathan L. Kvanvig (Lanham, MD: Rowman & Littlefield, 1996), 25–45, esp. 31–3 for the example of Truetemp. Imagine that Norman and Truetemp have a son, Truenorth, who has a reliable sense of direction. He is able to accurately tell north from south and east from west by some internal means. When someone first asks him where north is he gets

Demon-world and Matrix examples show that reliability is also not necessary for justified belief. In the Matrix (as portrayed in the movie of that name) people have the sort of perceptual experiences people in the real world would have, and so are justified in believing that the world is pretty much the way they think it is. However, in reality they are floating in a gelatinous liquid in rows of pods, hooked up to supercomputers that get electricity from them and, in turn, cause them to have the experiences they have. Their perceptual experiences are unreliable, but *intuitively* they are justified in believing just the sorts of things we are justified in believing on the basis of our perceptual experiences. So it is false that reliability is necessary for justification.

A final example from epistemology. Coherentists claim that a person is justified in believing some proposition if it coheres appropriately with other things he believes. There are various accounts of coherence that yield different species of this view, but I believe there are examples that count against all of them. For instance, suppose I believe that intelligent beings on Gliese 581d are sending me telepathic messages about what goes on on their planet, and on that basis, I form a complex and coherent set of beliefs about what the planet is like and what the Gliesians do. I also believe that no one else receives these messages because I'm the chosen one, worshiped by the Gliesians. Of course, all this is a figment of my overactive and creative imagination. *Intuitively*, I am not justified in believing any of the things I do about Gliese 581d, and, if miraculously, they all turn out to be true, I would not have knowledge of those truths. So it is false that coherence is sufficient for epistemic justification, and also false that when combined with true belief and some condition to handle Gettier problems, it is sufficient for knowledge.[5]

---

it right, but not having any evidence of his reliability about directions, he does not know, nor is he justified in believing, which direction is north.

[5] See my "Rock Bottom: Coherentism's Soft Spot," *Southern Journal of Philosophy*, 50 (2012): 94–110. This example is inspired by one given by George Bealer in his "The Philosophical Limits of Scientific Essentialism," in *Philosophical Perspectives I: Metaphysics*, ed. James E. Tomberlin (Atascadero, CA: Ridgeview, 1987), 289–365, esp. 329. His example involves "perverse scientists" who produce in some "poor soul" a coherent set of false beliefs about what things are like on some distant planet.

In *On What Matters*, Parfit relies heavily on appeal to intuitions to defeat both substantive normative views about what there is reason to do and moral views about what makes actions right or wrong. Subjective theories of practical reason say that what we have most reason to do is what would best fulfill our intrinsic desires, sometimes requiring that they are the desires we have that are not based on false beliefs or that we would have after fully informed and procedurally rational deliberation, etc. Against all such desire-based theories Parfit offers the examples of *Agony, Anorexia, Early Death, Revenge*, and *Burning Hotel*. Parfit imagines that even after ideal deliberation, he has no desire to avoid agony, understood to be a sensation that for no reason he intensely dislikes (*OWM*, I, 56 for the definition of "agony"; 73–4 for the example and also *OWM*, II, 360). However, in the circumstances, "all subjective theories imply that I have no reason to want to avoid agony, and no reason to try to avoid it if I can" (*OWM*, I, 74). But *intuitively* everyone has such reason. Hence, all subjective theories of reasons for action are false. In *Anorexia*, a young woman with anorexia "knows that she could live a long and rewarding life, but her horror of gaining weight makes her prefer to starve herself to death," even when she is ideally situated (*OWM*, II, 369). *Intuitively*, her preference is not rational but subjectivism implies that it is.[6] In *Early Death*, "after ideal deliberation, you are not motivated to take the medicine that you know would give you many more years of happy life" (*OWM*, II, 281). Subjectivism implies that you have no rea-

---

[6] I would say that this example shows that subjectivism is false; Parfit says that it shows that the subjectivist's way is "not the best way to use" the words "rational preference" (*OWM*, II, 369; see also 370, 375). Interestingly, Allan Gibbard discusses a case of anorexia in his *Wise Choices, Apt Feelings* (Cambridge, MA: Harvard University Press, 1990), 165–6. He says that according to the norms we accept, it is irrational for the woman to starve herself to death and that those norms imply that it is irrational even if she has a coherent set of preferences that require her to starve herself to death. He says that our norms also imply that if we came to have her norms we would have become irrational. In other words, our norms, or acceptance of them, contain self-affirming and alien-condemning elements. He gives other examples of what he calls self-evident normative judgments, e.g. the fact that I would enjoy something is a reason to do it (177), it's monstrous to admire gratuitous cruelty (196), an excellent sun tan is not all that matters in life (227), and it is wrong to torture people for amusement (287, 321).

son to take the medicine, but *intuitively* you do. So *Early Death* also shows that subjectivism is false. In *Revenge*, even after fully informed and procedurally rational deliberation you want to kill someone who insulted you, knowing that if you do you will be "arrested and punished with hard labor for the rest of your life" (*OWM*, II, 281). Subjectivism implies that you have decisive reason to kill the person who insulted you, but *intuitively* you do not. In *Burning Hotel*, your hotel is on fire and if you don't jump from its top story into a canal below you will be burned to death (*OWM*, II, 283–4, 292, 326–7, 386–9). We can imagine that even after fully informed and procedurally rational deliberation someone who is deathly afraid of heights might prefer to burn to death rather than jump. Then subjectivism would imply that that is what there is most reason for him to do, but *intuitively* it is not. All of these examples seem to be counter-examples to subjectivism in the same way that Gettier examples are counter-examples to the Justified True Belief account of knowledge. Because Gettier examples refute the JTB account of knowledge, these examples refute subjectivism about practical reason.

Parfit also offers examples that evoke intuitions that refute certain moral theories. Suppose we take Kant to be asserting the following principle:

> *Mere Means Principle*: It is wrong to treat anyone as a mere means. (*OWM*, I, 212)

Parfit imagines a case where some Egoist "saves some child from drowning, at great risk to himself, but that his only aim is to be rewarded" (*OWM*, I, 216; also, 228). He says that the Egoist treats the child as a mere means (to receive the reward), but *intuitively* he does no wrong. So the *Mere Means Principle* is false.

Of course, Kantians might defend some "cousin" of the *Mere Means Principle*, say, what Parfit calls *The Harmful Means Principle*, which says,

> It is wrong to impose such a serious injury [such as losing a leg] on someone as a means of benefitting other people [by saving their

lives]. (*OWM*, I, 361; see also, 229, 361–2 and *OWM*, II, 47 (n. 9), 55, 146–7, my brackets)

Parfit admits that *intuitively* it seems wrong to him to cause someone to fall in front of a runaway trolley in order to stop the trolley and thereby save five other innocent people (*OWM*, II, 154). But he thinks the intuition is not strong enough to support *The Harmful Means Principle*, even though it does support it to some extent (*OWM*, II, 154). Kantians might disagree, and it's a difficult question about *how much* evidentiary weight particular intuitions have.

Transplant is a famous example in the philosophical literature in which you must kill and then cut up one innocent person for his vital organs that are needed to save, say, five other innocent people. This example is often taken to be a counter-example to Act Utilitarianism, though Parfit does not think it is a counter-example to Rule Utilitarianism.[7] Allan Gibbard grants that Act Utilitarianism has some counter-intuitive implications, but he thinks that classical decision theory clashes with those intuitions. He sees classical decision theory "as a systematic development of intuitions about what to do and why" and so sometimes "some of our strong intuitions will have to go whatever we hypothetically decide to do."[8] In the end, he thinks that the arguments in favor of classical decisions theory have more weight than the anti-utilitarian intuitions like those that arise in *Transplant*. As with Kantianism, it's a difficult question about *how much* evidentiary weight particular intuitions have.

My main aim of this section is to argue that if the appeal to intuitions is legitimate in epistemology, it is also legitimate when it comes to theories about what reasons there are to want or do certain things, and to theories about what makes actions right or wrong. We should treat intuitions in ethics and epistemology the same.

---

[7] Parfit writes of *Transplant*, "But the saving of these extra lives would be outweighed by these ways in which it would be bad for us and others if, as we all knew, our doctors believed that it could be right to kill us secretly in this way. We can call this the *Anxiety and Mistrust Argument*" (*OWM*, I, 363; Parfit's italics).

[8] *Reconciling Our Aims: In Search of Bases for Ethics* (Oxford: Oxford University Press, 2008), 26 for the first quote; 29 for the second.

2. *The Non-Cognitivists' View of Intuitions and Their Role*

Allan Gibbard grants that intuitions are relevant to answering both practical and epistemic questions. However, being a non-cognitivist in both realms, he (like Simon Blackburn) does not think that intuitions are evidence for the truth or falsity of either epistemic or moral claims, assuming that the truth of some claim implies that there is some moral, practical, or epistemic property that is possessed by what is being judged (an action, a desire, an intention, a trait of character, a belief, etc.). Blackburn thinks that when someone *says* he knows something he is expressing confidence that he can rely on that belief, whether what he *claims* to know is practical (say, that pain, or anguish, is intrinsically bad) or not practical (say, that some building is on fire).[9] Blackburn says,

> I believe that the primary function of talking of "knowledge" is to indicate that a judgement is beyond revision. That is, we rule out any chance that an improvement might occur, that would properly lead to revision of the judgement. Attempts to say just what counts as improvement and when revision is "proper" lead to the post-Gettier salt mines in epistemology.[10]

Blackburn does say that for him "improvement" includes increases in "maturity, imagination, sympathy, and culture" as well as "information, sensitivity, and coherence."[11] While *a* primary function of knowledge talk may be to express the confidence that what you say will not be given up in the face of new evidence in "nearby" worlds, another primary

[9] See Gibbard's "Knowing What To Do, Seeing What To Do," in *Ethical Intuitionism*, ed. Philip Stratton-Lake (Oxford: Clarendon Press, 2002), esp. 224–8.
[10] See Simon Blackburn's *Ruling Passions* (Oxford: Clarendon Press, 1998), 318; also, 307. Gibbard footnotes this passage in the essay referred to in the previous note, p. 226. I believe that by "post-Gettier salt mines in epistemology" Blackburn is referring to attempts to account for the elusive anti-luck "fourth condition" of knowledge in terms of when a subject would cease believing what he does. Such accounts appeal to counterfactual conditionals and so (on many accounts) to the notion of "nearby" worlds.
[11] *Ruling Passions*, 310 for the first quote; 318 for the second. See also Blackburn's "Securing the Nots," in *Moral Knowledge? New Readings in Moral Epistemology*, ed. Walter Sinnott-Armstrong and Mark Timmons (New York: Oxford University Press, 1996), 82–100, esp. 87–8, 93, and 95 for his discussion of "improvement."

function seems to be to attribute a property to your belief. The analogy with the rock dwellers who say, "The rocks are slippery," is apt here, too (see p. 233).

Like many epistemologists, Gibbard thinks that knowledge is justified true belief where "the truth of the belief is no fluke."[12] But being a non-cognitivist, his account of epistemic justification and "no fluke" will be non-standard. For him,

> The concept of justification we can explain by repeating old expressivist slogans in new variants: questions of what beliefs are justified are questions of what to believe, and a view on what to believe, a normative epistemology, amounts to a contingency plan of what to believe when.[13]

A contingency plan of what *to do* when is of the form: do A1 in circumstances C1; do A2 in circumstances C2...; do An in circumstances Cn, and so on indefinitely. A contingency plan of what *to believe* when is of the form: believe B1 in circumstances C1; believe B2 in circumstances C2, and so on, where the circumstances can include reference to the subject's mental states (e.g. sensations, rational insights, apparent memories, other beliefs) and to external facts (e.g. daylight or dusk, has recently ingested a hallucinogen or has not, suffers from severe dementia or not).

So I might have a plan to believe "all crows are black" whenever I have observed lots of black crows all over the world in different seasons and at different stages of maturity, while you might have a plan to believe the same thing if, and only if, your crystal ball says that all crows are black when you ask it. It seems that on Gibbard's account, it would be correct for each of us *to say* that we are justified in believing all crows are black. Further, if according to our respective plans these justified beliefs have been reliably produced by some process (and so are not "flukes"), then, if the belief is true, we will both know that all crows are black![14]

---

[12] "Knowing What to Do...", 225; see also 226.
[13] "Knowing What to Do...", 226.
[14] Of course, Gibbard will say that I will judge that you do not know that all crows are black because, according to my epistemic plan, you are not justified in believing all crows are black on the basis of consulting a crystal ball. Similarly, if, when asked, your

Given this general account of justification and knowledge, we can now ask what it would be for someone to be *intuitively* justified, or know *by intuition*, that something is true. When it comes to pain, Gibbard says that to *intuit* that pain is bad is to think it bad on no further grounds, that is, non-inferentially to think it bad, and,

> Thinking pain bad is thinking pain a thing to avoid, and thinking this amounts to planning, for any course of action open to me, to treat whatever painful prospects it carries as weighing against that course of action. To do this, and to do it on no further grounds, we can say, is to *intuit* that pain is bad. That's a technical label for this familiar psychic state that I'm in.[15]

To think anguish is bad is to plan to weigh it heavily against any course of action.[16] To think that *on the basis of intuition* is to think it non-inferentially, on "no further grounds." To *know* that anguish is bad *on the basis of intuition* is to have a justified true belief that it is bad, where the justification is based on intuition and the justification is "no fluke." For Gibbard, being "no fluke" will amount to being reliably produced, but for him "reliability is a normative [not a statistical] notion, an ought-laden notion, and ought thoughts consist in plans. To judge a process of coming-to-accept as reliable will be, in effect, to plan to rely on such a

crystal ball says that I am not justified on the basis of induction in believing all crows are black, then you will judge that I do not know that all crows are black. Who is right? Well, I think all Gibbard is entitled to say is, "I am right, according to my epistemic plan, and he is right, according to his epistemic plan. Each of us, because of the self-affirming and alien-condemning nature of our plans, will *judge* the rival plan *to be mistaken*, and even that we would be *mistaken* if we switched plans, and that's the end of it!" Parfit says that, "We may want our enemy to suffer whether or not we continue to have this desire," but then goes on to add that "this kind of non-conditionality doesn't amount, as Gibbard claims, to a kind of *objectivity*" (*OWM*, II, 406). Similarly, a norm's being self-affirming and alien-condemning is not sufficient for its being objective. Gibbard only offers a sort of quasi-objectivity, for we can sensibly ask, "Which self-affirming and alien-condemning plan is correct?" and not ask it from the standpoint of some plan we already accept.

[15] "Knowing What to Do...", 225.

[16] Gibbard says this in *Reconciling Our Aims: In Search of Bases for Ethics* (Oxford: Oxford University Press, 2008), 184.

process."[17] According to Blackburn, to say that you *know* pain is bad is to express confidence that your belief that it is bad will not easily change. Gibbard might also accept Blackburn's view about what it is *to say* that you know pain is bad, but he also tries to give a plan-relative, non-cognitivist account of knowledge when understood as non-accidentally justified true belief.[18]

People say that pain is bad, but they also say that it is long-lasting, unremitting, distracting, throbbing, etc. In these other cases a property is being attributed to pain. Badness seems to be just another property that pain can possess. Why think otherwise? Early on in *Wise Choices, Apt Feelings* Gibbard says that,

> According to an expressivist analysis, to call something rational is not in the strict sense to attribute a property to it. It is to do something else: to express a state of mind. It is, I'm proposing, to express one's acceptance of norms that permit the thing in question.[19]

Presumably he would say something similar about calling something bad, for he says that to think pain bad is to plan to weigh the prospect of pain heavily against any course of action. What is it that leads him to this odd view that normative judgments, judgments about what there is reason to believe or want or do, or evaluative judgments about what is good or bad, do not ascribe properties but instead express acceptance of norms or plans? Why does he think that all we can sensibly talk about is what it is *to think*, *judge*, *claim*, *call*, or *say* that there is reason to believe or want or do certain things? Why can't we sensibly talk

---

[17] Ibid., 226. My remark in brackets. It is hard to see how reliability can help solve the Gettier problem (the "no fluke" problem) if it is not given a statistical interpretation. Once you make reliability itself a normative notion it is connected to justification, and we know that justified true belief is not sufficient for knowledge.

[18] Blackburn also gives an account of knowledge in "Securing the Nots." He says, "we know something when we have exercised reliable judgement, and there is no chance of an improvement overturning our verdict" (87). His view of knowledge seems to be that it is reliably produced true belief plus "sensitivity," for the "no chance of improvement" requirement means that in nearby possible worlds where you believe the relevant proposition is true, it is true, which is what sensitivity amounts to.

[19] *Wise Choices, Apt Feelings* (Cambridge, MA: Harvard University Press, 1990), 9.

about whether a belief or desire or action has *the property* of being reasonable or rational?

Ultimately, Gibbard's answer is that we cannot make sense of normative disagreement if normative judgments ascribe properties. If we disagree about whether some coin has the property of being round, then, if we agree about all the empirical properties (other than roundness) that the coin has, we must either mean something different by "round" or one of us is trivially wrong. So if we disagree about whether some action (or desire or belief) is rational (or good or bad), despite agreeing about all the empirical properties of the action (or desire or belief), then we must either mean something different by "rational" or one of us is trivially mistaken. And if we mean something different, we will just be talking past each other, somewhat like two people who mean different things by "bank" and seem to disagree about whether it's a good idea to put your money in a bank! But Gibbard thinks that people need neither be talking past each other, nor need at least one be trivially mistaken, in cases of genuine disagreement. But how could that be? Gibbard's diagnosis is that our disagreement stems from different standards that we accept and then apply to the particular case about which we disagree. When I *say* that "keeping mum" is rational in a Prisoner's Dilemma situation, and you *say* that it is not, I am not claiming that this action has the property of being rational, and you are not denying that it does. Rather, I am expressing that "keeping mum" is permitted by the standards of rationality that I accept and you are expressing the opposite, that it is not permitted by the standards you accept.[20]

The realist has a different account of the disagreement. According to him, we are disagreeing about what "rational" means and so disagreeing about what property the word designates. People disagree about whether the Pope is a bachelor, but surely there is a property of being a bachelor.[21] They disagree about what that property is. Is it the property of being an unmarried male of marriageable *age* or the more general property of

---

[20] See *Wise Choices, Apt Feelings*, 13–18.
[21] In "Doubts about Conceptual Analysis," in *Reasoning, Meaning, and Mind* (New York: Oxford University Press, 1999), 140, Gilbert Harman cites work by Winograd and Flores in *Understanding Computers and Cognition* (Norwood, NJ: Ablex, 1986) to support his claim that, "Speakers do not consider the Pope a bachelor."

being an unmarried male of marriageable *status*? People disagree about whether a lie must be a falsehood or only something the person who tells it *believes* to be false. If I tell a beggar asking for change that I have none, all the while thinking I have change in my pocket, do I tell a lie if it turns out that, unbeknownst to me, the change has fallen out through a hole in my pocket? People disagree because they disagree about what the property of being a lie amounts to. People disagree about what words mean, and so sometimes, at least, about what exactly the property is that a word designates.

Epistemology is analogous to ethics, and it is clear that this sort of disagreement occurs there. Epistemologists ask, "What does 'S knows that P' mean?" Reliabilists think knowledge is reliably produced true belief, but those who think it is justified true belief plus some anti-luck condition disagree. Parfit says that a claim is substantive just in case we can learn something from it or people can disagree with it (*OWM*, II, 343, 349, 353 and *OWM*, II, 275 where he gives a similar account of "significant"). It is trivial just in case it is not substantive. Given this account of trivial, philosophical disagreements about what a term means are not trivial because we can learn something from the claims in such disputes (e.g. the conflicting claims about what "knowledge" means) and people can disagree with the particular claims that are made.

It's tempting to think that a claim that P means Q must be trivial because some are, say, the claim that "brother" means "male sibling." But we can see philosophical analyses as proposals about what something means, and they are not trivial. When Smith and Jones are disputing about what "rational" means, it doesn't matter whether Smith means X by it and Jones Y. We are not concerned with *what the speakers mean* by the term. If that were the concern, Gibbard's dilemma would be a sound argument: either both mean X or they do not. If both mean X, one is trivially wrong (at least if they agree about the relevant background considerations); if one means X and the other Y, they are talking past each other. Suppose the dispute over whether some type of action is rational, say, "keeping mum" in Prisoner's Dilemma situations, is at bottom a dispute over what "rational" means, not over what the speakers mean by "rational." Then that dispute can be substantive, not trivial. So there is no reason to adopt some form of non-cognitivism to explain the disagreement.

We have seen that Gibbard's non-cognitivist view in epistemology left open the possibility that a person could correctly *say* that she knew that all crows are black because her crystal ball told her they were. Since her justification plan, her plan of what to believe when, tells her to believe whatever her crystal ball says, relative to it, it is correct for her to *say* that she is justified in believing, and knows, all crows are black. Similarly, Gibbard's view of what it is to say that some action is rational, or that it is what there is most reason to do, leaves it open that, relative to someone's plan, it is correct for her to say that the envisaged acts in *Agony*, *Anorexia*, *Early Death*, *Revenge*, and *Burning Hotel* are rational, or are what there is most reason for the people to do.

Of course, quasi-realists like Gibbard and Blackburn will reply that their views do *not* allow them to say that other conflicting normative views, whether epistemic or practical, are *correct*.[22] For instance, if someone asks Blackburn if it would be wrong for an anti-Semite, who accepts different normative standards than we do, to kill Jews, he will hear this as a moral question and appeal to his own moral standards. When he does, he will say that it is wrong to kill Jews and that the anti-Semite's views that say it is not are *mistaken*. Of course, the anti-Semite, who is also a quasi-realist, will hear the question of whether it is wrong to kill Jews as a moral question, judge it not wrong, and judge Blackburn's views *mistaken*. This makes Blackburn's and Gibbard's view a form of relativism, not semantic relativism because for them "wrong" is not short for "wrong for someone," or "wrong relative to some standard or plan," but still, for them there is nothing that is wrong, period, not relative to some standard or plan. Similar remarks apply to "rational," "justified," etc., regardless of whether they are applied to beliefs, actions, or desires.

Words like "large" are relative in some sense. A baby elephant may be a large animal but a small elephant. If one person says that some baby elephant is large, and the other person denies it, they can easily reach agreement by making clear what comparison class they have in mind: other animals in the zoo or adult elephants. If Gibbard were right in thinking that ascriptions of wrong or rational are plan-relative, then, in principle, people should be able to reach agreement by making clear

---

[22] Note 14 is relevant here.

what standard or plan they are employing as a basis of their judgments. But fundamental epistemic and practical disputes do not seem to be standard- or plan-relative disputes that could be resolved once each party made clear what his standard or plan is. They are disputes over what the correct standard or plan is, where "correct" is a standard- and plan-neutral notion.

On Gibbard's theory intuitions have an epistemic role, and his appeal to them as a means of justifying some practical views and rejecting others *sounds* just like what cognitivists would say. But in the end, intuitions are not evidence of moral or practical truths for him, where such truths imply the existence of moral or practical properties. If they are evidence of truth, it is only truth in a deflationary sense. But isn't there a fact of the matter about whether induction or the crystal ball really is a basis of justification?[23] Isn't there a fact of the matter about whether the prospect of agony is a reason to avoid some course of action, regardless of whether I, or anyone else, is strongly committed to weighing that prospect in our plans about what to do? We have intuitions that there is a fact of the matter about these things, intuitions about what those facts are, and an intuition that those intuitions are evidence about what those facts are. Barring sound arguments to the contrary, we should accept what those intuitions say.

3. Disagreement

Disagreement in intuitions, whether they are about practical matters or not, is sometimes taken as reason to believe that they do not provide evidence for the propositions that are their objects. How could they since they must be unreliable? Not all of them can deliver the truth, and even if some do, we can't know which do and which don't. But

---

[23] My colleague, Lewis Powell, suggested to me that if the Crystal Ball Gazer (CBG) has the aim of believing truths and avoiding falsehoods, his method will not do as well as the inductivist's. However, suppose the CBG first asks his crystal ball whether he is in the Matrix. Suppose it answers "yes." The CBG then relies on induction for practical purposes to tell him what is likely *to appear true* in the future, and relies on his crystal ball to tell him important things about the supercomputers, how they came to have power, how they control humans, and the like. Then the CBG will have no reason to think that his method is not as reliable as the inductivist's.

what is important is not whether there is actual agreement in intuitions but what the best explanation is of whatever disagreement there is.[24] Disagreement that stems from distortions (due, say, to self-interest, stubbornness, or unfounded religious convictions), different meta-ethical beliefs (say, about whether moral obligations always provide reasons to act and whether reasons to act necessarily imply motivation to act), the imprecision of concepts, the consideration of borderline cases, beliefs about the relevant non-moral facts, etc., do not support the anti-realist's view that there are no moral facts because the hypothesis that there are no such facts is not the best explanation of such disagreement. The best explanation involves one or more of the listed factors. Nor does such disagreement support the view that intuitions that are had *in ideal conditions* (that is, *when such factors are absent*) do not provide reason to accept the propositions that are their objects.[25] In fact, convergence of views in ideal conditions could support moral, and practical, realism if the best explanation for such convergence is that people have come to

[24] Parfit has two strategies for handling disagreement: (1) arguing that there is less of it than first appears, for example, less between him and both Hume (*OWM*, II, 454–7, esp. 457) and Nietzsche (*OWM*, II, Ch. 35; on this see the essay by Andrew Huddleston in this volume), and less between Kantians, rule utilitarians, and contractarians than is commonly thought (*OWM*, I), and (2) arguing that only disagreement in "ideal conditions" would really support anti-realism. Why? I believe it is because a realist can hold that the factors (taken from Parfit) that I list below explain disagreement in a way that does not undercut his realism. If he can't explain disagreement when those factors are absent, that is, in what Parfit calls "ideal conditions," then there is reason to think that his intuitions do not put him in touch with some normative reality (cf. *OWM*, II, 548). Parfit does write of the best explanation of disagreement (*OWM*, II, 547) and says we can try to predict what would happen in "ideal conditions" on the basis of the best explanations of actual disagreements (*OWM*, II, 547 and 552). For more on this topic, see Parfit's Ch. 34 titled, "Agreement"; see *OWM*, II, 563 for his summary of the factors I list below that I think the realist can invoke to explain disagreement.

[25] Recently, there has been a lot of discussion in epistemology of what a reasonable person should do as regards adjusting his beliefs when he is aware of disagreement among his so-called epistemic peers, people who have all the intellectual virtues that he has and the same total evidence. Of course, that is a general problem that I cannot discuss here. Nor can I discuss how a reasonable person should adjust his beliefs when he becomes aware of the conflicting views of those who do not have all of his evidence, or perhaps lack some of his intellectual virtues. The latter might be relevant to determining what we should make of the results of experimental philosophy where non-philosophers sometimes disagree among themselves, and with philosophers, in their intuitive judgments.

grasp moral, and practical, truths once they were freed from distorting and corrupting influences.

Even if intuitions under "ideal" conditions provide evidence for the propositions that are their objects, why do intuitions that we have under *non-ideal* conditions provide evidence for those propositions? We all have come, upon further reflection, to no longer believe a proposition that at one time was the object of an intuition of ours. So we should all think that intuitions are fallible. The worry is that even if some intuitions have evidential weight not all do, and because we can't tell which do and which do not, we cannot rely on any of them for justification. To use Walter Sinnott-Armstrong's analogy, it is like knowing that some thermometers in a jar are reliable, that some are not, and not being able to tell the difference.[26] How could any of the thermometers provide evidence of the temperature in those conditions?

Perhaps Sinnott-Armstrong's analogy is not apt. Suppose I am a student learning how to add numbers. My teacher tells me that I do well on some problems, not so well on others. As it turns out, I do well adding small numbers—I get 2 + 2 = 4 and even 11 + 3 = 14 right—but I make lots of mistakes when it comes to adding many large numbers together. Because it seems so obvious to me that 2 + 2 = 4 is true, won't I be justified in believing that it is true and hypothesizing that I've been making errors on other sorts of problems? I think so, and I think the same could be said of intuitions that seem especially obvious, even though I know that sometimes my intuitions have caused me to have a false belief.[27] We all know that perception is fallible, too, but that does not mean that no perceptions provide reason to believe relevant propositions.

[26] Walter Sinnott-Armstrong, *Moral Skepticisms* (New York: Oxford University Press, 2006), 201. See also 210–11 where he compares being on a street *where we know there are lots of barn facades* to our situation where we know that moral intuitions often found false beliefs because they are often formed under conditions that render them unreliable.

[27] In "Intuition and the Autonomy of Philosophy," Bealer says, "But, if we limit ourselves to suitably elementary propositions, then relative to them we *approximate* ideal cognitive conditions" (219, his italics). Like Parfit, he thinks that intuitions had under ideal conditions provide evidence for the propositions that are their objects. Because of what he says above about approximation, he thinks that intuitions of *elementary propositions* also provide evidence even in non-ideal circumstances.

I have assumed that, barring arguments to the contrary, intuitions in epistemology have evidential weight. Because some of those intuitions are about what we are justified in believing, and that is a normative consideration, there is reason to think that intuitions about what we are justified in doing, or wanting, also have evidential weight. I might have appealed to the apparent evidential force of intuitions in other areas of philosophy, say, in discussions about the nature of causality or personal identity, but I chose to look at epistemic intuitions because of their greater similarity to moral and practical intuitions, which also have normative propositions as their objects.

4. Naturalism

There is an argument that anti-realists use against non-naturalists like Parfit who hold that moral and practical reasons are non-natural properties. It goes:

1. If there are moral or practical reasons in the realist's sense, then there are non-natural facts.
2. There are no non-natural facts; all facts are natural.
3. Therefore, there are no moral or practical reasons in the realist's sense.

Anti-realists then often have a positive view of reasons for action which links them necessarily to motivation and so founds reasons on either actual desires or desires a person would have if he had true beliefs and were ideally situated, where being so situated is describable solely in naturalistic, or procedurally rational, terms. Parfit thinks that reasons necessarily motivate *a fully rational person*, but what it is to be such a person cannot be described solely in naturalistic terms. He says,

> If we are aware of facts that give us certain reasons for acting, and we are *fully substantively rational*, we would be motivated to act for these reasons. But that does not imply that normativity in part consists in actual or possible motivating force. (*OWM*, II, 268, my italics: cf. 382)

He attacks the argument I offered above by arguing against the second premise. He accepts the first premise, but I do not think his arguments for it are sound, even if it turns out to be true.

For Parfit Analytical Naturalism (AN) is the view that normative, or moral, expressions *mean the same as* certain naturalistic expressions, where naturalistic expressions refer to natural facts and natural facts are the sort investigated by those working in the natural or social sciences (*OWM*, II, 265, 305). I will assume that natural facts are empirical facts, that is, facts whose presence or absence can, in principle, be determined by empirical means, since those are the sorts of facts that the natural and social sciences investigate. His argument against (AN) is that if it were true, then what intuitively seem to be *substantive* moral claims (or claims about what there is reason to do) would turn out to be *trivial*. For instance, on (AN), Act Utilitarianism, which tells us that, all things considered, we morally ought to maximize happiness, turns out to be the trivial claim that what maximizes happiness maximizes happiness or what we morally ought, all things considered, do is what we morally ought, all things considered, do! Recall from above (p. 244) that by a "substantive claim" Parfit means a claim that we can learn something from or with which people can disagree (see *OWM*, II, 343; also, 275, 349, 353). By "trivial" he means the opposite. But on this account, Act Utilitarianism can be a substantive claim, not a trivial one, even on (AN) because we can learn that this is what "morally obligatory" means and other people can disagree with that claim. So Act Utilitarianism might be a substantive claim on (AN) even if the other two claims are not.[28]

There are analogies in other areas of philosophy. We might come to learn that "knowledge" means "reliably produced true belief" or "justified true belief that is not essentially founded on any false beliefs," and other people can disagree that it means either of those things. And we might come to

---

[28] It is surprising that Parfit says that claims about the meanings of terms cannot be substantive, that they must be trivial, for he says, "People sometimes fail to understand, not only what other people mean, but even what they themselves mean" (*OWM*, II, 272; cf. 292–3). Because we don't fully understand what we mean by, say, "knows" and "reasons," we can come to learn what we mean, and others can disagree with us about whether that really is what we mean. For Parfit, those are the factors that make a claim substantive.

learn that "lying" means "telling something the person believes to be false with the intention of deceiving someone about what is said," and other people can disagree that it means that. So claims about what some term, or expression, means can be substantive even if closely related claims are not. The error in the argument stems from assuming that if "X means Y" is a substantive claim, then so are "X is X" and "Y is Y." The examples about "knowledge" and "lying" are counter-examples to this claim.[29]

Someone might think that even if Parfit's argument against (AN) fails, G. E. Moore's Open Question argument succeeds. But I do not think it does. Let a closed question be one that anyone who fully understands the question can answer solely on the basis of his understanding what the question asks. An open question will be just the opposite. So "Are bachelors unmarried?" will be closed but "Are bachelors unhappy?" will be open. Moore thought that for any naturalistic expression X, if "good" means X, then "Is X good?" will be open but "Is good, good?" and "Is X, X?" will be closed. Is that true? Do we know that *for all* X the question "Is X good?" will be open *if a person fully understands* the question, and so *fully understands the concepts involved*?

I do not think that many believe that a naturalistic analysis of "knowledge" *is impossible*, but a parallel argument could be used to show that it is. "Is reliably produced true belief knowledge?" seems open, but "Is reliably produced true belief reliably produced true belief?" seems closed, as does "Is knowledge knowledge?" Despite that, some think that "knowledge" does mean "reliably produced true belief." I think they are mistaken because of the counter-examples involving Truetemp and her offspring, and the Matrix. But I don't think the Open Question argument applied to knowledge shows that "knowledge" *could not* mean the same as some naturalistic expression. Further, the Open Question argument could be applied to the analysis of any concept, say, of causality or

---

[29] Parfit says that "concealed tautologies," such as "(3) illicit acts are wrong," can be deceptive because "they can *seem to be substantive*" (*OWM*, II, 276, my italics; cf. 362). He goes on to say, "But if I were using 'illicit' to mean 'wrong', (3) would be a concealed tautology whose open form would be (2) wrong acts are wrong." But how does that show that (3) is trivial? Further, some concealed tautologies may be trivial, some not. "'Knowledge' means 'reliably produced true belief'" may be what Parfit calls a concealed tautology, but if it is, it is substantive, not trivial. Cf. *OWM*, II, 287.

personal identity, to yield the conclusion that no naturalistic analyses of these concepts is possible. Assume that T is the term to be defined. The error in this type of argument stems from assuming that if "Is X, T?" is open, and T means X, then "Is X, X?" and "Is T, T?" are also open. That assumption might be true for a person who *fully understands* what X and T mean, but when "Is X, T?" *seems* open to us, we do not know whether to conclude that T does not mean X or that we simply *do not fully understand* T, or X, or both.

Parfit calls the other form of Naturalism that he argues against Non-Analytic Naturalism (NAN). According to (NAN), a normative and a naturalistic expression might introduce different concepts even though those concepts refer to the same naturalistic property. The analogy that is often invoked here deals with water and H2O. More precisely, "the stuff that is water" and "the stuff that is H2O" refer to the same stuff even though the concepts involved are different. So maybe "morally obligatory" and "what maximizes happiness" refer to the same naturalistic property (namely, to what maximizes happiness) even though the expressions do not mean the same.

Parfit tries to refute (NAN) by what he calls the *Fact Stating Argument*. His own analogy involves the following two statements:

1. Shakespeare is Shakespeare.
2. Shakespeare is the author of *Hamlet*.

He thinks that both statements assert the identity of the person referred to in the subject of the sentence with the person referred to in its predicate. However, (2) provides information that (1) does not. Why is that? According to Parfit, it is because the terms in the subject refer to a different property than the terms in the predicate.

He uses this example to motivate the following principle (though he does not explicitly state it): if an identity statement "X is Y" is informative, then X and Y must refer to different properties. Any claim that what there is most reason to do, or what is morally obligatory, is identical to some naturalistic property, N, is informative. So in any identity claim such as "what there is most reason to do is N" or "what is morally obligatory is N," the normative expression must refer to some property different from the property referred to by N.

However, the *principle* relied on in this argument is false. "One meter long" and "39.37 inches long" refer to the same property (namely, the property of being a meter long), yet the statement, "A meter is 39.37 inches long" is informative.[30] In his argument against (AN), Parfit covertly assumes that we cannot *discover* that two expressions *mean* the same. In his argument against (NAN), he covertly assumes that we cannot *discover* that two expressions that mean something different *refer* to the same property. It is this possibility of discovery that makes it possible for claims about identity of meaning or reference to be substantive and informative, not trivial and uninformative. Parfit's first objection, the *Fact Stating Argument*, is that for a claim to be informative it must refer to two different properties. However, Non-Analytical Naturalism (NAN) says that such claims refer to only one property and that some of them are informative. Hence NAN must be false. The example of the meter's being 39.37 inches long shows that an informative claim need not refer to two different properties. So Parfit's *Fact Stating Argument* rests on a false premise.

Parfit's second objection is what he calls the *Triviality Objection* (*OWM*, II, 343–4). Let (A) be the claim: when some act would maximize happiness, this act is what we ought to do. Parfit says that (A) is substantive and "*might* state a positive substantive normative fact" (*OWM*, II, 343, my italics). He says that claims are positive:

> when they are or imply that, when something has certain natural properties, this thing has some other, different, normative property. (*OWM*, II, 343)

According to NAN, normative claims refer to only one naturalistic property, not to two properties. So according to NAN, normative claims cannot be positive. So (A) *could not be* positive. But it *might be*. So NAN is false.

"Might" has at least two senses, one epistemic, the other logical. Goldbach's Conjecture says that every even integer greater than two is

---

[30] I thank my colleague Michael McKinsey for providing this example and for discussion of the nature of natural kind terms. What follows owes much to what I learned from him in conversation and e-mail correspondence.

the sum of two primes. When we say it *might* be true, we mean *for all we know, it's true*, that is, we don't know that it's false. However, if it's false, it *could not be true*, that is, it is logically necessary that it's false. So Goldbach's Conjecture *might be true* (for all we know it's true) even though it *could not be* (if it is in fact false).

In the same way, Parfit can say that (A) *might be positive* (for all we know, it is) even though if NAN is true, it *could not be* (it is logically necessary that it is false). This sounds like a contradiction, and so it sounds as though something must be given up. Given the choice, it looks like NAN must go. But it is not a contradiction. Some proposition that *might be true* in the epistemic sense of "might" can also be *necessarily false* in the logical sense. Parfit's *Triviality Objection* rests on an invalid argument because that argument equivocates on "might."

Of course, Parfit might claim that (A) *is* a positive substantive claim, not just that it *might be* (cf. OWM, II, 358 where he says this about a similar claim). Let's grant that it is substantive in Parfit's sense because we might disagree with it, or it might tell us something we did not already know. Still, why think that it is also positive, that is, that it says that actions that maximize happiness also have the *different property* of being what we ought to do? Because it could not be substantive or informative if it did *not* have that different property? But the example of the meter counts against that. All that Parfit is justified in holding is that (A) *might be* positive, but as we have seen, the argument from that possibility to the conclusion that NAN is false is invalid. The argument Parfit offers for his *Triviality Objection* either rests on a false premise or is invalid, depending, respectively, on whether it starts from the claim that (A) *is* substantive and positive or from the claim that it *might be*.

Despite the failure of Parfit's arguments against NAN, I believe it is false. NAN treats normative terms as if they were natural kind terms, terms like "water," "heat," "gold," and "horse." Parfit says that the pre-scientific meaning of "heat" is:

> the property, *whichever it is*, that [*in the actual world*] can have certain effects, such as those of melting solids, turning liquids into gases, causing us to have certain kinds of sensations, etc. (*OWM*, II, 301; my bracketed material)

We might say that the pre-scientific meaning of "water" is:

> the stuff, *whatever it is*, that *in the actual world* has the properties of quenching thirst, putting out certain fires, falling from the clouds as rain, filling the lakes and rivers, etc., on the planet on which we live. (cf. *OWM*, II, 335)

Treating our ordinary meaning of "wrong" in a similar way, we might say that our ordinary meaning of "wrong" is:

> the property of actions, *whichever it is*, that causes people *in the actual world*, when ideally situated (understood naturalistically), to disapprove of genocide, rape, slavery, torturing kids just to hear them scream, etc.

Here's the problem. When it comes to even numbers, we can know that some of them are the sum of two primes, for instance, that $12 = 7 + 5$. We can correctly say that, for all we know, there is *some* even number that is *not* the sum of two primes, but we can't correctly say that, for all we know, 12 is not the sum of two primes. However, if "wrong" were a natural kind term, we could correctly say that, for all we know, torturing children just to hear them scream, killing innocent people because of racial hatred, rape committed in order to humiliate the victim, and treating slaves as if they were objects of property with no interests worth considering, is *not* wrong in some other possible world.

Why? Because if "wrong" were a natural kind term, we would have to discover empirically what the property in the actual world is (say, being suboptimal or being done with the intention to humiliate or being done from a desire for sadistic pleasure) that causes people judging under ideal conditions to disapprove of that sort of torture, killing, rape, and treatment of slaves. We do not know if that property would attach to those acts in all possible worlds. So if "wrong" were a natural kind term, we would not now know whether those sorts of act are wrong in every possible world, that is, are *necessarily wrong*. However, we know a priori that they are wrong in all possible worlds. Insofar as NAN treats "wrong" and other normative terms as natural kind terms, it faces this epistemic objection.

Perhaps (AN) is false. I've only argued that Parfit has not shown that it is. My own view is that fundamental moral and practical claims are more like the claim that no object can be red and green all over at the same time, than like "bachelors are unmarried," or like "a meter is 39.37 inches long." In any case, moral intuitionism is an epistemological view compatible with the view that sees moral and practical claims as similar to the red-green proposition, as compatible with (AN), and compatible with Parfit's view, according to which fundamental moral and practical claims are necessary truths about non-natural properties. That is because moral intuitionism is a view about the nature of a priori evidence for non-deflationary moral and practical normative truths. As such, it is compatible with all three of those semantic and metaphysical views, though not with non-cognitivism, quasi-realism, NAN, and nihilism. Here I have argued against non-cognitivism and its offspring, quasi-realism, and NAN. I believe Parfit's criticisms of the arguments for nihilism are sound, and that examples of seemingly obvious moral truths make nihilism implausible if it is not backed up by argument. The viability of Analytical Naturalism remains an open question, as does Parfit's Non-naturalistic Cognitivism. In any case, moral intuitionism is compatible with both those views.

References

Audi, Robert. 1996. "Intuitionism, Pluralism, and the Foundations of Ethics," in *Moral Knowledge? New Readings in Moral Epistemology*, ed. Walter Sinnott-Armstrong and Mark Timmons. New York: Oxford University Press.

Audi, Robert. 1997. *Moral Knowledge and Moral Character*. New York: Oxford University Press. (See esp. Ch. 2, "Intuitionism, Pluralism, and the Foundations of Ethics.")

Audi, Robert. 2004. *The Good in the Right: A Theory of Intuition and Value*. Princeton: Princeton University Press.

Bealer, George. 1987. "Philosophical Limits of Scientific Essentialism," in *Philosophical Perspectives I, Metaphysics*, ed. James E. Tomberlin. Atascadero, CA: Ridgeview.

Bealer, George. 1992. "The Incoherence of Empiricism." *The Aristotelian Society Supplementary Volume* 66: 99–138.

Bealer, George. 1996a. "On the Possibility of Philosophical Knowledge," in *Philosophical Perspectives 10, Metaphysics*. Oxford: Basil Blackwell.

Bealer, George. 1996b. "*A Priori* Knowledge and the Scope of Philosophy" and "*A Priori* Knowledge: Replies to William Lycan and Ernest Sosa." *Philosophical Studies*, 81: 121–42 and 163–74.

Bealer, George. 1998. "Intuition and the Autonomy of Philosophy," in *Rethinking Intuition: The Psychology of Intuition and Its Role in Philosophical Inquiry*, ed. Michael DePaul and William Ramsey. Lanham, MD: Rowman & Littlefield.

Bealer, George. 2000. "A Theory of the *A Priori*." *Pacific Philosophical Quarterly*, 81: 1–30.

Blackburn, Simon. 1996. "Securing the Nots: Moral Epistemology for the Quasi-Realist," in *Moral Knowledge? New Readings in Moral Epistemology*, ed. Walter Sinnott-Armstrong and Mark Timmons. New York: Oxford University Press.

Blackburn, Simon. 1998. *Ruling Passions.* Oxford: Clarendon Press.

Blackburn, Simon. 2006. "Antirealist Expressivism and Quasi-Realism," in *The Oxford Handbook of Ethical Theory*, ed. David Copp. New York: Oxford University Press.

BonJour, Laurence. 1985. *The Structure of Empirical Knowledge.* Cambridge, MA: Harvard University Press.

BonJour, Laurence. 1998. *In Defense of Pure Reason.* Cambridge: Cambridge University Press.

DePaul, Michael R. 2006. "Intuition and Moral Inquiry," in *The Oxford Handbook of Ethical Theory*, ed. David Copp. New York: Oxford University Press.

DePaul, Michael R. and William Ramsey, eds. 1998. *Rethinking Intuition: The Psychology of Intuition and Its Role in Philosophical Inquiry.* Lanham, MD: Rowman & Littlefield.

Gibbard, Allan. 1990. *Wise Choices, Apt Feelings.* Cambridge, MA: Harvard University Press.

Gibbard, Allan. 2002. "Knowing What to Do, Seeing What to Do," in *Ethical Intuitionism: Re-evaluations*, ed. Philip Stratton-Lake. New York: Oxford University Press.

Gibbard, Allan. 2003. *Thinking How to Live.* Cambridge, MA: Harvard University Press.

Gibbard, Allan. 2008. *Reconciling Our Aims: In Search of Bases for Ethics*, ed. Barry Stroud: 11–88; reply to commentators: 147–88. New York: Oxford University Press.

Harman, Gilbert. 1999. *Reasoning, Meaning, and Mind.* New York: Oxford University Press.

Huemer, Michael. 2005. *Ethical Intuitionism.* New York: Palgrave Macmillan.

Kvanvig, Jonathan L., ed. 1996. *Warrant in Contemporary Epistemology: Essays in Honor of Plantinga's Theory of Knowledge.* Lanham, MD: Rowman & Littlefield.

Lehrer, Keith. 1996. "Proper Function Versus Systematic Coherence," in *Warrant in Contemporary Epistemology: Essays in Honor of Plantinga's Theory of Knowledge*, ed. Jonathan L. Kvanvig. Lanham, MD: Rowman & Littlefield.

Lycan, William G. 1996. "Plantinga and Coherentisms," in *Warrant in Contemporary Epistemology: Essays in Honor of Plantinga's Theory of Knowledge*, ed. Jonathan L. Kvanvig. Lanham, MD: Rowman & Littlefield.

Lycan, William G. 2006. "On the Gettier Problem Problem," in *Epistemology Futures*, ed. Stephen Hetherington. New York: Oxford University Press.

Russell, Bruce. 2001. "Epistemic and Moral Duty," in *Knowledge, Truth, and Duty: Essays on Epistemic Justification, Responsibility, and Virtue*, ed. Matthias Steup. New York: Oxford University Press.

Russell, Bruce. 2002. "Review of *Ruling Passions: A Theory of Practical Reasons*" by Simon Blackburn. *The Philosophical Quarterly*, 51: 110–14.

Russell, Bruce. 2007. "A Priori Justification and Knowledge," in *The Stanford Online Encyclopedia of Philosophy*.

Russell, Bruce. 2010. "Intuition in Epistemology," in *A Companion to Epistemology*, 2nd edn, ed. Jonathan Dancy, Ernest Sosa, and Matthias Steup. Malden, MA: Wiley-Blackwell.

Russell, Bruce. 2012. "Rock Bottom: Coherentism's Soft Spot." *Southern Journal of Philosophy*, 50: 94–110.

Russell, Bruce. 2013. "Moral Intuitionism," in *The International Encyclopedia of Ethics*, ed. Hugh LaFollette. Wiley Online Library.

Sinnott-Armstrong, Walter. 2006. *Moral Skepticisms*. New York: Oxford University Press.

Sinnott-Armstrong, Walter and Mark Timmons, eds. 1996. *Moral Knowledge? New Readings in Moral Epistemology*. New York: Oxford University Press.

Stratton-Lake, Philip, ed. 2002. *Ethical Intuitionism: Re-evaluations*. New York: Oxford University Press.

Stroud, Barry, ed. 2008. *Reconciling Our Aims: In Search of Bases for Ethics*. New York: Oxford University Press.

12

MORALITY, BLAME, AND INTERNAL REASONS

Stephen Darwall

In *On What Matters*, Derek Parfit mounts a strong challenge to internalist views, like Bernard Williams's, that seek to bring motivation, perhaps that resulting from procedurally ideal practical reasoning, into our understanding of normative practical reasons, or that maintain that an agent's motivational capacities constrain, either conceptually or metaphysically, what can provide normative practical reasons for her.[1] Parfit's main target is what he calls a "motivational conception" of normativity, according to which motivational capacities enter into the content of normative reasons claims and 'ought' claims in the "reason-implying sense" (*OWM*, II, 268). His leading example is *Analytical Internalism*, the view that

when we say that

(D) someone has decisive *reasons* to act in a certain way, or *should* or *ought* to act in this way,

we often mean something like

---

[1] Especially in Bernard Williams, "Internal and External Reasons," in *Moral Luck* (Cambridge: Cambridge University Press, 1981), 101–13; and Williams, "Internal Reasons and the Obscurity of Blame," in *Making Sense of Humanity* (Cambridge: Cambridge University Press, 1995), 35–45.

> (E) this act would best fulfil this person's present fully informed telic desires, or is what, after fully informed and procedurally rational deliberation, this person would be most strongly motivated to do, or would choose to do. (*OWM*, II, 270)

Analytical internalism contrasts with *Externalism*, which holds that "reasons" and "ought" in claims like (D) should often be understood in "simpler, irreducibly normative senses" (*OWM*, II, 270).

Analytical internalists and externalists are thus concerned with the analysis of normative reason claims and ought claims that imply them. Both can agree that *motivating* reasons have to do with agents' motivations, but they divide on the question of whether normative reasons and practical oughts that imply them do. Although an agent's reasons for having done something plainly concern what moved her to do it, what reasons there were *for* her do it, or even what reasons she had to do it, do not appear to, at least, not obviously. Externalism, which is Parfit's own position, holds that the concepts of normative reason and the practical ought are irreducibly normative.

There are good reasons to agree with Parfit about this. Williams coined "internal reason" to refer to considerations like (E), which involve an act's relation to an agent's "motivational set."[2] Philosophers since have come to refer to Williams's "internal reasons thesis" as the claim that the only normative reasons for acting are internal reasons or, in one formulation:

> R is a reason for A to φ only if A would, if ideally [procedurally] rational, be motivated to φ by believing R.[3]

But if analytical internalism is correct, the internal reasons thesis becomes an empty tautology. If its being the case that A would, if ideally procedurally rational, be motivated to φ by believing R is (part of) an *analysis* of the concept of R's being a reason for A to φ, then the internal reasons thesis is a trivial truth. Of course all reasons must be internal if being relevantly internal is what it means to be a reason.

---

[2] "Internal Reasons," pp. 101–2.
[3] Stephen Finlay, "The Obscurity of Internal Reasons," *Philosophers' Imprint*, 9/7 (2009): 5.

In his original article, Williams did say that his use of "internal reasons" and "external reasons" was "for convenience," and that, as in Parfit's formulations of analytical internalism and externalism, he was primarily concerned with internalist and externalist "interpretations" of normative reasons statements.[4] Understood in this way, the thesis that there are no external reasons is the thesis that, on an externalist interpretation, no normative reasons statements are ever true.

Philosophical discussion about the internal reasons thesis has tended to treat it as a substantive philosophical (meta-ethical) hypothesis rather than an empty tautology. Since there can be an intelligible question of whether internal reasons are the only normative reasons for acting, or whether there are also external reasons, only if the concept of normative reason has an externalist rather than an internalist analysis, it would seem that this discussion should follow Parfit and proceed on the assumption that the *concepts* of normative reason and the practical ought are irreducibly normative.

Once we agree that these concepts are irreducibly normative, however, it is still open to the internal reasons thesis to hold, indeed on broadly conceptual and philosophical grounds, that nothing can be a normative reason unless it is related in the right way to the agent's motivational capacities, for example, its being a consideration that the agent would be moved by through ideally [procedurally] rational deliberation. The external reasons theorist would deny this, but both would employ the same irreducibly normative concept of normative reason. Indeed, they would have to in order to disagree.

Let us proceed on this basis, reject the "motivational conception" of normativity, and assume that the concepts of normative reason and reason-implying practical oughts are irreducibly normative. What I would like to consider is whether, on broadly conceptual grounds, agents' motivational capacities might still constrain what can be normative reasons for them even so within, at least, one practical domain, namely morality.[5]

Parfit considers what he terms a "better," explicitly normative form that an internalist thesis about reasons might take (*OWM*, II, 288–9). Using an

[4] "Internal Reasons," p. 101.
[5] At least, as Parfit (and I) conceive it. See n. 20.

externalist, irreducibly normative concept of normative reason, it is possible to hold as a substantive normative thesis that we have reason to perform an act "just when, and because, this act would best fulfil our present fully informed desires, or is what after ideal deliberation, we would choose to do" (*OWM*, II, 289). This would be a *normative* internal reasons thesis.

The internalist thesis I want to consider, however, is conceptual rather than normative. And it concerns, again, not normative reasons or reason-implying practical oughts, in general, but the moral ought, even more specifically, indeed, the sense of moral "ought" that is analytically related to moral right and wrong. In this sense, it follows analytically from the proposition that someone morally ought to do something, either *pro tanto* or all things considered, that it would be wrong for her not to do it, either *pro tanto* or all things considered. What we morally ought to do in this sense is what we are morally required or obligated to do. It is what morality *demands*.

I maintain that the concept of moral obligation or demand is tied to that of moral *accountability*.[6] What morality demands of us is, as a conceptual matter, what we are morally accountable for doing. If this is so, it will follow on conceptual grounds that moral obligation, and the moral "ought" that expresses it, inherit whatever constraints accountability brings. Roughly, it can be the case that an agent morally ought to do something, in this sense, only if that agent could coherently be held accountable for doing it. Following a number of philosophers who have written on moral responsibility in the wake of P. F. Strawson's "Freedom and Resentment," I shall argue that this partly depends on the agent's motivational capacities, on whether she is capable of being aware of the reasons that might support or be implied by the relevant reason-implying moral ought and of being motivated by them.[7]

---

[6] I will argue for this claim presently, but a fuller defense can be found in Darwall, *The Second-Person Standpoint: Morality, Respect, and Accountability* (Cambridge, MA: Harvard University Press, 2006).

[7] P. F. Strawson, "Freedom and Resentment," in *Studies in the Philosophy of Thought and Action* (London: Oxford University Press, 1968); R. Jay Wallace, *Responsibility and the Moral Sentiments* (Cambridge, MA: Harvard University Press, 1994); Gary Watson, "Responsibility and the Limits of Evil: Variations on a Strawsonian Theme," in *Responsibility, Character, and the Emotions: New Essays in Moral Psychology*, ed. F. D. Schoeman (Cambridge: Cambridge University Press, 1987).

To be clear, my claim will not be that it would be *unfair* to blame or hold someone accountable were he to lack the relevant powers. Holding *on these grounds* that no one should be regarded as subject to moral demands that he lacks the powers to appreciate and be moved by would be a *normative* internalist thesis. My claim will be that understanding the "second-personal" character of accountability should lead us to conclude that there is a kind of incoherence that is involved in having attitudes like moral blame toward beings who lack the motivational powers to hold themselves responsible and enter into relations of mutual accountability (who lack "second-personal competence"). This is a conceptual rather than a normative claim.

Again, the kind of internalist thesis I want to consider and defend does not concern normative reasons or practical oughts in general, but the moral ought in particular. Indeed, it is narrower still. One thing we can mean when we say that someone morally ought to do something is that the action is one that moral reasons recommend, perhaps even decisively. I agree with Parfit that when we say that someone ought to do something in the sense in which failing to do it would be morally wrong, however, we normally mean something narrower than this. We mean that this is what morality requires or demands.

We can satisfy ourselves that the concept of what moral reasons recommend, even decisively, and the concept of what morality demands, of moral duty or obligation, are distinct concepts by noticing that it is a conceptually open question whether there is such a thing as supererogation. Suppose someone believes that there are good moral reasons, even morally decisive reasons, to perform an action, but that because of the level of sacrifice to the agent, there is no moral requirement or obligation to perform the action. This person thinks that even though the moral reasons to perform the action, say to save someone at great personal risk, are not undermined by the level of sacrifice (it wouldn't be foolhardy, say), any moral obligation is. He believes that the reasons in favor of making the sacrifice are, in Parfit's terms, "*morally-decisive reasons*" in the sense that they "morally outweigh any reasons that we may have not to act in this way" (*OWM*, I, 167). Making the sacrifice would be a morally good thing to do, this person acknowledges, but he denies that failing to make it would be morally wrong. In his view, the action would be supererogatory. Of course, someone else might disagree. An act consequentialist would hold that the fact that the sacrifice would be *the agent's* is morally irrelevant and that it would be wrong for the agent to do anything other than what would have the best consequences impartially considered. For an act consequentialist, there is no such thing as moral supererogation; anything morality decisively recommends, it requires.

Surely this is a substantive normative disagreement. Even if act consequentialism is the correct *normative* theory of moral right and wrong, there is no self-contradiction or conceptual confusion in the thought that some burdens are sufficiently high that morality does not require us to bear them in certain cases even if there are good moral reasons to do so. Without any conceptual confusion whatsoever we can think that what it would be best, from the moral point of view, for someone to do, is something that morality does not require him to do, that is not his moral obligation or duty. But if this is so, the concept of what moral reasons recommend, even decisively, must differ from the concept of what morality requires or demands, of what it would be morally wrong not to do.

"Morally ought" is thus ambiguous. I agree with Parfit that the sense that is normally in play in normative theories of right and wrong, whether act- or rule-consequentialist, Kantian- or Scanlonian-contractualist, or intuitionist, is the narrower notion of moral requirement or demand. My claim is that there is a conceptual connection between this sense of the moral "ought" and accountability, specifically, that it is a conceptual truth that an action is morally obligatory or wrong not to do, if, and only if, it is an action that it would be blameworthy not to perform were the agent to do so without excuse, where blame is understood, not as an action or a social practice, but as a(n impartial) Strawsonian *reactive attitude*.[8] Because this is so, this sense of the moral "ought" must inherit

---

[8] Strawson uses the term "impersonal" to refer to reactive attitudes that are felt as if from a third-party perspective. It is important to Strawson's argument in "Freedom and Resentment," as it is to mine in *The Second-Person Standpoint*, however, that all reactive attitudes are essentially "interpersonal" (in Strawson's terms) or "second-personal" (in mine) because they implicitly make (address) demands. Because all reactive attitudes are

whatever constraints motivational capacities impose on accountability and moral blame as a conceptual matter.

We should note that Parfit explicitly recognizes *"blameworthiness"* and *"reactive-attitude"* senses of "morally wrong" and the moral "ought." His preferred diagnosis is that the sense of moral "ought" and "wrong" we are now discussing is an indefinable concept expressible, respectively, by "must-be-done" and "mustn't-be-done" (*OWM*, I, 165–9). We shall consider these different possibilities in more detail below. The important point will be that whether or not moral wrong and "ought" are definable in terms of blameworthiness (lacking excuse), there is nonetheless a conceptual connection between them, in particular, that we can intelligibly think individuals subject to moral demands only if we take them to have the motivational capacities necessary to be held accountable for complying with them.[9]

Before beginning, we should note several preliminary points. First, although Parfit's position is steadfastly externalist, he does say that "normativity is closely related to motivation" (*OWM*, II, 268). What Parfit means by this, however, is that if something is a reason for someone to do something and if that person is aware of that fact and is "fully substantially rational," then she would be moved by it (*OWM*, II, 268). This does not mean, Parfit hastens to add, that the fact's being a reason is in any way a function of, or constrained by, its capacity to move the agent. The work is done by the idea of *substantive rationality*, which Parfit defines in terms of reasons responsiveness. What it is for an agent to be substantively rational is for her to be appropriately moved by normative reasons (*OWM*, I, 78). The close connection Parfit affirms between normativity and motivation thus runs from normativity to motivation, not the other way around. To be a normative reason is to be something that should move an agent, something failure to be moved by which manifests a defect of (substantive) irrationality in the agent. An agent's motivational capacities in no way constrain her normative reasons. What

essentially interpersonal in this sense, it seems better to call moral blame an "impartial" rather than an "impersonal" reactive attitude. The perspective from which we have the attitude is clearly nothing like Sidgwick's "point of view of the universe."

[9] Henceforth, I will use "moral ought" to express the idea of moral obligation or demand.

reasons there are for an agent to act are fully independent of whether she could be aware of these reasons or be motivated by them.

I shall argue that this is not the case with the reasons that flow from the moral ought. An agent cannot coherently be held accountable for doing something for reasons of which she could not be aware and by which she could not be motivated. Since this is so, we should conclude on conceptual grounds that what morality can demand of an agent, what she morally ought to do in this sense, is constrained by the agent's capacities to be aware of and motivated by reasons that could support and flow from the moral ought. Although there is nothing odd in the thought that there might be reasons for someone to do something of which that person cannot be aware and by which he cannot be motivated, it is not just odd, but incoherent, to think that someone could be morally responsible for doing, hence that it would be wrong for him not to do, something were he incapable of appreciating and being moved by the reasons that would make the omission wrong or by the wrongness of the omission.

Second, we cannot assume therefore that if something is true of normativity, normative reasons, and practical oughts in general, that it will also hold of the moral ought. At one point, having argued against naturalist and non-cognitivist analyses of normative reasons, Parfit remarks, "if Naturalism and Non-Cognitivism fail as accounts of reasons, these theories will also fail, I believe, when applied to morality" (*OWM*, II, 269). Whether or not Parfit is right that arguments against naturalist and non-cognitivist analyses of normative reasons in general transfer seamlessly to morality, I shall be arguing that this is not the case for at least one kind of internalist thesis. Even if we assume that the concepts of normative reasons and the moral ought are irreducibly normative notions, and even if we assume that nothing in the concept of normative reasons and practical oughts generally entails any motivational constraints, I shall claim that this is not the case for the moral ought.[10]

---

[10] It is worth noting a similar phenomenon with Jonathan Dancy's defense of "moral particularism" based on features of normative reasons in general. Even if normative reasons claims don't require general principles, this might not be true of moral requirements in particular. I make a similar argument against Dancy that the connection between moral demands and accountability provides some support to the idea that claims about moral requirements must be backed by general principles even if there is

Third, we will want to bear in mind a distinction Parfit makes between "reason-implying" and "rule-involving" conceptions of normativity. The latter might include positive rules and requirements of games, practices, and institutions that, in the more familiar philosopher's (reason-implying) sense, lack normativity because they do not entail any reasons for actions or for attitudes of any kind. It is a rule of baseball, for example, that once pitchers have begun their motion toward the plate, they must follow through. Otherwise, a balk is called, and runners are allowed to advance one base. But this rule of baseball entails reasons for acting only in conjunction with other premises about normative reasons, for example, reasons to be playing baseball in the first place. It is important that the normativity of morality is not simply rule involving (*OWM*, I, 145–9). Moral requirements differ from rules of baseball or even, Parfit argues, from legal requirements imposed by law (*OWM*, II, 308). The normativity of morality is reason implying rather than merely rule involving. The question will be how to understand the *distinctive* normativity of moral requirements if, as Parfit and I agree, it cannot be captured in the existence of moral reasons, even "morally-decisive reasons" (*OWM*, I, 167). I shall argue, again, that it must be understood as entailing moral accountability for compliance. To that argument we now turn.

1. *Moral Demands and Accountability*

"We do not call anything wrong," Mill famously remarked, "unless we mean to imply that a person ought to be punished in some way or other for doing it; if not by law, by the opinion of his fellow creatures; if not by opinion, by the reproaches of his own conscience."[11] Unless we think "blame" is warranted, Mill continues, we think, "it is not a case of moral

---

no reason to think, in general, that normative reason claims must be. Just as applicable public (general) law seems essential to criminal responsibility, so also might it be argued that publicly available general principles are necessary for the kind of accountability that is conceptually implicated in moral demands. For an argument of this kind, see Darwall, "Morality and Principle," in *Thinking About Reasons: Essays in Honour of Jonathan Dancy*, ed. David Bakhurst, Brad Hooker, and Margaret Little (Oxford: Oxford University Press, 2013), 168–91.

[11] John Stuart Mill, *Utilitarianism*, Ch. 5, ¶14.

obligation."[12] This claim is most plausible, I believe, if we understand "blame" and "reproaches of... conscience," not as sanctioning or blaming *actions*, but as *attitudes*, more specifically, as Strawsonian reactive attitudes. The idea is not that it is a conceptual truth that wrongdoing and wrongdoers merit the infliction of a harm or penalty of some kind, but rather that there is a distinctive kind of "holding accountable" attitude, the kind Strawson calls a "reactive attitude," that is conceptually tied to unexcused wrongdoing. Similarly, I argue, the ideas of moral demand and moral wrong are tied conceptually to that of actions that are blameworthy (lacking excuse).

It is crucial to Strawson's argument in "Freedom and Resentment" that reactive attitudes necessarily involve a distinctively "interpersonal" (or as I prefer to put it, "second-personal") way of regarding its object that implicitly *relates to* him or her. According to Strawson, reactive attitudes like moral blame implicitly address *demands* to their objects.[13] In this sense, the object of a reactive attitude is also its implicit addressee. Unlike "objective" critical attitudes, like contempt or disdain, that are not "participant" attitudes, and seek no particular response from their objects, reactive attitudes call for response. They come with an implicit R.S.V.P. They hold their objects to account by implicitly calling for their objects to account for themselves.

I shall argue that the implicit addressing, or second-personal aspect of reactive attitudes, which enables them to mediate mutual accountability, brings along with it necessary presuppositions of the addressee's powers (his second-personal competence) as what Watson calls "constraints on moral address."[14] We can only intelligibly hold someone to a moral demand if we assume that he is capable of holding himself to it. And this requires that he be able to access, appreciate, and be guided by the reasons that support the demand and that are implied by it.[15]

---

[12] Ibid.
[13] Strawson, "Freedom and Resentment," p. 85. For a fuller defense, see Darwall, *The Second-Person Standpoint*, Ch. 4; Wallace, *Responsibility and Sentiment*, p. 19, Watson, "Responsibility," pp. 263–4.
[14] Watson, ibid.
[15] This is what I call "Pufendorf's Point" in *The Second-Person Standpoint*.

It is important that reactive attitudes like moral blame don't seek merely to *impose* or to make a *naked* demand. They purport to address, rather, a putatively *legitimate* demand, one we have the authority to make of one another and ourselves as representative persons or members of the moral community. In holding their objects to account, reactive attitudes implicitly call on their objects not to give in or to defer to the demand, but rather to acknowledge its legitimacy and to hold themselves to it. In this way, they are a Fichtean "summons" that aims to direct an addressee's conduct through the addressee's own free practical reasoning rather than simply to force deference.[16]

In the next section we shall consider how presuppositions of second-personal address entail motivational constraints on being subject to a moral demand. Although there is nothing in the general idea of normative reasons weighing in favor of or against a course of action that the agent be capable of accessing, appreciating, or of being motivated by the reason, this is not the case with demands with which one can coherently be held accountable for compliance, hence with any reasons for acting that are implied by them.[17]

First, however, we should examine more carefully what Parfit says about "blameworthy" and "reactive attitude" senses of "wrong" and the moral "ought." As Parfit notes, philosophers often distinguish so-called "subjective" senses of these terms that apply to situations in which agents have only partial knowledge of morally relevant facts (*OWM*, I, 150–64). These are useful distinctions, since though an action might be morally obligatory if an agent knew all the morally relevant facts, it might not be given her actual beliefs or available evidence. Parfit starts from the assumption that there is a single, "ordinary" sense of wrong that people employ when they are considering "acts of people who know all the morally relevant facts" (*OWM*, I, 150). Various subjective senses can be defined in relation to this ordinary notion: for example, an act can be said to be wrong in the "*belief-relative* sense" if the act would be wrong in the ordinary sense if the agent's beliefs were true (*OWM*, I, 150).

---

[16] On this point, see *The Second-Person Standpoint*, pp. 252–7.
[17] In *The Second-Person Standpoint*, I argue that this is a general feature of what I call "second-personal reasons."

It will help to keep the simplifying assumption of the "ordinary" sense of "wrong." Let us suppose we are talking about cases in which the agent knows all the morally relevant facts. Notice, first, that although Parfit distinguishes between "blameworthiness" and "reactive attitude" senses of moral wrong, he does not say what he takes the difference to be:

in the *blameworthiness* sense, "wrong" means "blameworthy,"

in the *reactive attitude* sense, "wrong" means "an act of a kind that gives an agent reasons to feel remorse or guilt, and gives others reasons for indignation and resentment." (*OWM*, I, 165)

If "blame" refers not to any blaming or sanctioning action or social practice, but to the *attitude* such actions or practices are normally taken to express, it is hard to see what the difference is supposed to be between an action's being of a kind to warrant feelings of guilt, on the one hand, and blame, on the other. Recall the passages from Mill at the beginning of this section that tie "blame" and the "reproaches" of "conscience" together.

Surely it is a conceptual truth that an action is of a kind that makes feelings of guilt fitting for the agent if, and only if, it warrants blame. (We should note that the blameworthiness sense of "wrong" is better defined by saying that "wrong" means "blameworthy *lacking excuse*." In other words, an act is wrong if it is "of a kind" that warrants blame if it is done without a valid excuse. If an agent has an excuse, though he is no longer to blame, his action remains wrong nonetheless. If there exists, not just an excuse, but a *justification* for the action, then it follows that the action was not actually wrong.) As I understand it, moral blame is a Strawsonian reactive attitude having an implicit second-personal structure.[18] Unlike "personal" reactive attitudes, like guilt, which are felt as if from the perspective of a party involved in the situation under consideration, blame is an "impersonal" (better, impartial) reactive attitude that is felt as if from anyone's point of view, the perspective of a representative person or the moral community. But blame is fitting if, and only if, guilt would

---

[18] Cf. T. M. Scanlon, *Moral Dimensions: Permissions, Meaning, Blame* (Cambridge, MA: Harvard University Press, 2008), p. 227: "[B]lame, in contrast to a judgment of blameworthiness, is a second-personal attitude in the sense described by Stephen Darwall."

be warranted also. I will take it, therefore, that blameworthiness and reactive attitude analyses of "wrong" come to the same thing.

Note, next, that Parfit frequently implicitly relies on a conceptual connection between moral demand, wrong, and blameworthiness. When Parfit argues against a Non-Analytical Naturalist approach to moral properties like rightness and wrongness, the example he uses to make his point is the blameworthiness sense of "wrong." A term like "heat" can mean "the property, *whichever it is,* that can have certain effects, such as those of melting solids, turning liquids into gases, ..., etc." (*OWM*, II, 301) and so refer to the same property referred to by "molecular kinetic energy," even though these terms have different meanings. However, Parfit replies, "no such claim applies" with the "fundamental [moral] concept wrong." The "concept expressed by the word 'blameworthy' ... does not [analogously to "heat"] refer to some property indirectly, as the property of which something else is true. This property refers directly to the property of being blameworthy" (*OWM*, II, 301).

Parfit's most striking implicit reliance on the blameworthiness sense, however, is in his move from defending act consequentialism in *Reasons and Persons* to arguing for rule consequentialism in *On What Matters*. In the earlier work, Parfit in effect wrote the game plan for how consequentialists might maintain an act-consequentialist theory of right action while nonetheless agreeing that it might maximize the good for agents to accept and be guided by some nonconsequentialist theory closer to common-sense morality like rule consequentialism.[19] Even if, for example, there are good consequentialist reasons for agents to accept and be guided in their practical reasoning by rules that include an agent-relative prerogative to give their own interests and those of their near and dear greater weight, that doesn't mean that they morally should do anything other than what would have the best consequences impartially conceived.

In *On What Matters*, however, Parfit holds that act consequentialism "may be better regarded," not as a theory of morally right action in the "ordinary sense" at all, but as a theory of (impartial) reasons for action that is an "external rival to morality" (*OWM*, I, 168). It is worth quoting

[19] *Reasons and Persons* (Oxford: Oxford University Press, 1984), 24–62.

at some length what Parfit says about Sidgwick's famous "point of view of the universe" passage:

> When Sidgwick claims that he *ought* not to prefer his own lesser good, he does not seem to mean that such a preference would be blameworthy, or unjustifiable to others, or that such an act would give him reasons for remorse and give others reason for indignation. Sidgwick seems to mean only that, when assessed from an impartial point of view, his reason to give himself some lesser good is weaker than, or outweighed by, his reason to give some greater good to someone else. (*OWM*, I, 168)

Parfit then concludes, "this kind of Consequentialism may be better regarded, not as a moral view, but as being like Rational Egoism, an external rival to morality" (*OWM*, I, 168).

This is a remarkable change in view. Parfit now thinks that rather than being a contending theory of morally right action, much less the leading contender, act consequentialism may be better regarded as a theory of impartial reasons for action (*Impartial-Reason Act Consequentialism*) that is an "external rival to morality." It is "much closer to morality" than Rational Egoism, but Parfit adds that that makes it "in some ways, a more serious rival" (*OWM*, I, 168). Someone might accept Impartial-Reason Act Consequentialism and "not even have moral beliefs" in the "ordinary" sense. "They may be doubtful whether any acts are duties, or mustn't-be-done, and doubtful about blameworthiness, and about reasons for remorse and indignation" (*OWM*, I, 168).[20]

If it is a conceptual truth that actions that are morally wrong are blameworthy lacking excuse, then it is clear why rule consequentialism would have to be a better theory of morally right conduct than act consequentialism. Owing to its second-personal character, holding someone accountable through moral blame, even privately in one's heart, bids for reciprocal recognition in a way that assumes a common space

---

[20] Note that Parfit takes moral right and wrong in the "ordinary" sense to be definitive of morality. I think he is right about this, and defend the claim in "Morality's Distinctiveness," in *Morality, Authority, and Law: Essays in Second-Personal Ethics I* (Oxford: Oxford University Press, forthcoming).

of public reasons. Sidgwick's idea that act consequentialism is best con-ceived as an "esoteric morality" is precisely that it is ill fitted to serve as a standard that people hold themselves accountable to, including through reactive attitudes like moral blame.[21] One cannot intelligibly hold someone accountable for complying with a standard he wouldn't want her to share.

As I mentioned earlier, Parfit's own proposal is that the core "ordi-nary" notion of wrong and the entailed moral ought is an "indefinable sense" expressible "with the phrase 'mustn't-be-done'" (*OWM*, I, 169). I doubt, however, that this can be sufficient. Pitchers in baseball must not interrupt their motion toward the plate once they have begun it, and a doctor may truly say that her patient must stop smoking. There seem to be many appropriate uses of the phrase "mustn't be done" that have nothing to do with moral demands and right or wrong. Mill's diagnosis enables us to see why they don't. Any warrant to blame a pitcher for a balk, for example, can come not simply from the rules of baseball, but from some fact such as that his team is counting on him.

However, it doesn't really matter for our purposes whether Parfit's proposal is correct, since he agrees that it is a conceptual truth that an act is wrong if, and only if, it is blameworthy (lacking excuse). Parfit says that the blameworthiness and reactive attitude senses might be claimed to appeal implicitly to his indefinable sense since these attitudes might all "involve the belief that some act is wrong" in this sense (*OWM*, I, 169). Whether or not that is right, there is a clear difference between the belief that an act is wrong, or even the belief that an action is blameworthy, and the attitude of blame itself. For one thing, as with other attitudes, one can (irrationally) blame someone for an action one does not believe to be blameworthy. Just as one can believe there is nothing to fear and still fear flying, so one can have the attitude of blame where one thinks there is nothing to blame.

In any case, all we need in order to proceed is that it be a conceptual truth that an action is wrong, something one has a moral duty or obliga-tion not to do, if, and only if, performing the action would be blamewor-thy, were that to be done without valid excuse. Before we proceed though,

---

[21] Henry Sidgwick, *The Methods of Ethics*, 7th edn (London: MacMillan, 1967), 489–90.

we should note that blameworthiness is itself a normative notion, albeit a distinct one from moral wrong. To be blameworthy is for an action to provide normative reasons for the attitude of blame (and for guilt from the agent and resentment from the victim). The reasons must, however, be of the "right kind." They must be what Parfit calls "object given" rather than "state given."[22] They must show, not just there are, for example, pragmatic reasons to bring it about that one has the attitude, but reasons that show the object to be a "fitting" object of the attitude.[23]

2. *Blame, Second-Personal Competence, and Motivation*

Although Williams's original argument for his internal reasons thesis was based on closely tying rational justification to explanation—roughly, that any normative reason must be a potential motivating reason, something the agent could act on and that could be *the agent's reason*—he returned to the topic in a later paper in connection with a discussion of blame.[24] Blame "operates in the mode of ought to have," as Williams puts it.[25] When we blame someone for not having done something, we presuppose that there was reason for her to have done it—and not just "from the moral point of view," but *period*. It is incoherent to express blame to someone for not having done something and then add, "but you had, nonetheless, good reason not to do it." Neither does the incoherence result from an excuse that renders blame inappropriate while leaving the act's wrongness intact. One would be admitting, rather, that the agent had a *justification* for her action and so it could not have been wrong.

As it happens, Williams believes that we sometimes blame agents who lack internal reasons in his relatively restricted sense of subserving their

---

[22] I discuss the "wrong kind of reason problem" in relation to reasons of the right kind for blame and other second-personal attitudes in *The Second-Person Standpoint*, e.g., pp. 15–17.

[23] As discussed in the work of D'Arms and Jacobson. Justin D'Arms and Daniel Jacobson, "The Moralistic Fallacy: On the 'Appropriateness' of Emotions," *Philosophy and Phenomenological Research*, 61 (2000): 65–90; and "Sentiment and Value," *Ethics*, 110 (2000): 722–48.

[24] "Internal Reasons and the Obscurity of Blame."

[25] Ibid., p. 40.

actual "motivational set." So he takes it that blame involves a kind of fiction. Since we cannot blame someone without presupposing the relevant normative reasons, when these reasons are not internal, we treat the agent as though they were nonetheless. Sometimes our doing so functions proleptically, for example, via "the desire to be respected by people whom, in turn, one respects."[26] But when people are sufficiently distant motivationally so that the blaming person's motivating reasons can get no purchase, even by empathy, Williams concludes, blame is no longer appropriate.[27]

The reason, I submit, is because blame implicitly involves second-personal address. Just as it makes no sense to ask a question of someone in a language she cannot understand, or worse, of a being who lacks any language and concepts of questioning, so it makes no sense to address putatively legitimate demands to someone who lacks the requisite second-personal language, concepts, and attitudes to understand these.

Imagine a being who is substantively rational, in Parfit's sense, with regard to considerations of impartial good, but who, like Parfit's Impartial Act Consequentialist, is blind, conceptually and motivationally, to the moral ought in the "ordinary" sense, that is, to moral obligation, demand, and blameworthiness. Such a being would be moved by considerations of impartial good to desire and bring about maximal impartial good. Suppose that on act consequentialist grounds, this being performs an impartial-good-maximizing act that we believe to be gravely wrong, like Harman's case of the doctor who kills a patient to distribute his organs to five needy others.[28]

As we are imagining it, the being would lack the Strawsonian reactive attitudes essential to "second-personal competence." In other words, although he forms desires for states of affairs from an impersonal, third-person's perspective, he lacks the capacity to take a second-personal perspective toward himself and others and form implicitly demanding, holding accountable attitudes. When he considers a world in which everyone follows a rule that requires doctors to forgo killing

---

[26] Ibid., p. 41.
[27] Ibid., p. 43.
[28] Gilbert Harman, *The Nature of Morality* (New York: Oxford University Press, 1977), 16.

for the purpose of organ distribution, even when that would be optimific, he sees that such a world would be better than one in which doctors were guided by Act Consequentialism as a public rule for the
familiar reasons. If patients had to fear organ-distributing killings, that
would undermine their trust in doctors, and so on. So he desires the
former world in preference to the latter. But he doesn't see the relevance
of this desire to the deliberative situation that confronted him. He was
not in a position to bring about either of those worlds. The best thing he
could do was to bring about the most impartial good in his situation,
and that meant killing the one healthy patient and distributing his
organs to the needy five while keeping his actions secret so that doctor/
patient trust wouldn't be undermined.

Suppose, however, that his action comes to light. This being might
then well understand his being sanctioned or imprisoned to help secure
public trust, and desire this from an impartial point of view. But lacking
reactive attitudes, he would be blind to others' *blame* and incapable of
holding himself accountable through feeling guilt. So although there
would be nothing incoherent or otherwise untoward about incarcerat-
ing him, it would be incoherent to think that in doing so we were holding him accountable, that our actions could intelligibly be seen as
expressing blame to him.

When we address a putatively legitimate demand through the attitude of blame, we assume that the object of our blame is capable of
appreciating and accepting the legitimacy of the demand and of guiding herself by it. The appropriate response to blame is guilt, an implicit
acknowledgement that blame is warranted, and that the demand to
which one is being held is legitimate. If we are convinced that someone
we would otherwise be inclined to blame lacks the second-personal
competence to take the reciprocal second-personal attitude of guilt
toward herself, it makes no sense to blame her. The point is not, again,
that various defensive or even aggressive actions or sanction might not
make sense or that blame would be unfair; it is that the distinctive
(second-personal) attitude of blame would not be comprehensible in
its own terms. Such a being would be incapable of R.S.V.P.-ing in the
way necessary to enter into relations of accountability and be subject to
moral demands.

In *The Critique of Practical Reason*, Kant famously discusses the case of someone whose prince demands "on pain of…immediate execution, that he give false testimony against an honorable man whom the prince would like to destroy under a plausible pretext." Whether this person would refuse to do such a thing, Kant writes, "he would perhaps not venture to assert." But once he sees that it would be *wrong* to do so, Kant writes, he "must admit without hesitation that it would be possible for him" not to do so. This is Kant's "fact of reason":

> He judges, therefore, that he can do something because he is aware that he ought to do it and cognizes freedom within him, which, without the moral law, would have remained unknown to him.

One cannot coherently make a moral demand of oneself that one believes one cannot possibly be motivated to comply with. To hold oneself to the demand is already to accept the demand as legitimate and to be moved by it.

The reciprocal point holds with blame. When we blame someone, we presuppose that they are capable of accepting the legitimacy of the demand and of being motivated to comply with it. If we become convinced that they are incapable of the motivation that would reciprocate our blame—prospectively, the sense of obligation, or retrospectively, guilt—then having the attitude of blame toward them is no longer intelligible.

3. Morality and Objectivity

If, as I have been arguing, the "ordinary" concept of moral ought or demand is tied to that of accountability conceptually, it follows that beings who lack the motivational capacities necessary for accountability cannot be subject to moral demands, and so cannot have any normative reasons for acting that derive from these. When you or I are morally obligated to do something, this fact is a normative reason for us to do it (one Parfit calls a "*deontic reason*") (*OWM*, I, 201, 448–51).[29] But if someone lacks the

---

[29] I argue for this, and against "buck-passing" views of moral wrongness, in "But It Would Be Wrong," *Social Philosophy and Policy*, 27 (2010): 135–57. Also in *Moral Obligation*, ed. Ellen Frankel Paul (Cambridge: Cambridge University Press, 2010).

motivational capacities necessary to be subject to moral demands, he will lack deontic reasons for acting. Many wrong-making considerations may still be normative reasons for him. The fact that it would require him to take a human life is in no way undermined as a reason for our demand-blind being not to distribute the patient's organs to the five. By lacking the capacity for moral blame, however, the being lacks the capacity to appreciate what wrongness and thus wrong-makingness are. So he is not subject to moral obligations in the way you or I are.

But if moral demands, and so deontic reasons, are subject to motivational constraints in this way, doesn't that make them unacceptably subjective?[30] This is a larger subject than we can possibly enter into here, but it might help to point out that morality on the view I am proposing is better characterized as purporting to be *intersubjective* rather than impersonal or objective. When we hold one another and ourselves to moral demands, we take up a standpoint we suppose impartial between us, and from which we assume anyone is authorized and competent to address demands *to* one another. It is an impartial (or third-*party*) version of a second-*person* standpoint. And we assume a form of common reasoning from this point of view that anyone subject to moral demands is thereby capable of engaging in, and through which they can appreciate the demand's legitimacy and be motivated by it.[31]

I have been arguing that Parfit himself implicitly replies upon this view of morality and its demands in the shift from *Reasons and Persons*' defense of act consequentialism to *On What Matters*'s view that act consequentialism may be an external rival to morality and its defense of rule consequentialism instead. In so doing, I have argued, Parfit has acquired a justification for an internalist constraint on moral obligations and on the deontic reasons for acting that derive from them.

[30] In a sense about which Parfit is concerned at, e.g., *OWM*, I, 102.
[31] Parfit's defense of the "Triple Theory" might be seen as a nod to this idea, since Kantian and Scanlonian contractualism and rule consequentialism can be interpreted as providing forms of reasoning in which moral agents can engage to determine the deontic status of acts.

13

PARFIT ON OBJECTIVITY AND "THE PROFOUNDEST PROBLEM OF ETHICS"

Katarzyna de Lazari-Radek and Peter Singer

1. Introduction

The late Victorian philosopher Henry Sidgwick concluded his major work, *The Methods of Ethics*, on a note of failure. He had set out to find rational grounds for answering the question "What ought I to do?" but instead his arguments led to an "ultimate and fundamental contradiction in our apparent intuitions of what is Reasonable in conduct." In the first edition of *The Methods* he put this failure in dramatic terms:

> the whole system of our beliefs as to the intrinsic reasonableness of conduct must fall... the Cosmos of Duty is thus really reduced to a Chaos, and the prolonged effort of the human intellect to frame a perfect ideal of rational conduct is seen to have been foredoomed to inevitable failure.[1]

---

[1] Henry Sidgwick, *The Methods of Ethics*, 1st edn (London: Macmillan and Company, 1874) 473; this passage is quoted by Parfit in *OWM*, I, 143.

In later editions this language was toned down to some extent, but Sidgwick still felt forced to admit that "the apparently intuitive operation of the Practical Reason, manifested in these contradictory judgments, is after all illusory." And if we are not thereby required to "abandon morality altogether," we will at least have to abandon "the idea of rationalising it completely."[2] Sidgwick calls this problem "the dualism of practical reason" and says that it is "the profoundest problem of ethics."

In *On What Matters*, Parfit describes Sidgwick's *The Methods of Ethics* as "the best book on ethics ever written."[3] If the conclusion of the best book ever written on ethics is that some of our apparently most solid and carefully examined intuitions about practical reason are illusory, this poses a serious problem for anyone who, like Parfit, defends the view that we can know some ethical judgments to be objectively true because they are based on reason. Hence Parfit's response to Sidgwick's "profoundest problem of ethics" is of particular significance. In our view, his response leaves much of Sidgwick's problem untouched.

One of the arguments that Parfit considers, in defending the objectivity of ethics, is that our normative beliefs are the outcome of a process of natural selection in which our ancestors did better if they came to hold normative beliefs that helped them to survive and reproduce. But whether the normative beliefs help us to survive and reproduce has nothing to do with whether they are true, and we have no empirical evidence, nor any other grounds, for believing them to be true. Hence we are not justified in believing that the normative beliefs we hold are true.[4] Parfit calls this "the *Naturalist Argument for Normative Skepticism*." It has recently been pressed in a particularly forceful form by Sharon Street.[5] In this essay we respond to it in a manner that is similar to Parfit's response, but goes further in one important respect. This leads us to a surprising result: the best method of vindicating the objectivity of ethics against this argument for normative skepticism leads to a resolution of the dualism of practical reason that overcomes the disadvantages of Parfit's approach to that "profoundest problem of ethics."

[2] Sidgwick, *The Methods of Ethics*, 508.
[3] Parfit, *OWM*, I, xxxiii.
[4] *OWM*, II, 511–13.
[5] Sharon Street, "A Darwinian Dilemma for Realist Theories of Value," *Philosophical Studies*, 127/1 (January 2006): 109–66.

2. The Dualism of Practical Reason

Parfit presents Sidgwick's view of the dualism as follows:

> [T]he Dualism of Practical Reason: We always have most reason to do whatever would be impartially best, unless some other act would be best for ourselves. In such cases, we would have sufficient reasons to act in either way. If we knew the relevant facts, either act would be rational.[6]

This is, Parfit thinks, closer to the truth than either rational egoism or universal benevolence (which Parfit calls "rational impartialism"). Rational egoism is false because it asserts that we could not have sufficient reason to do what is worse for us. But I would have sufficient reasons, for example, to suffer an injury in order to save the life of a stranger. Rational impartialism is false because it maintains that we could not have sufficient reasons to do what would be impartially worse. But I would have sufficient reasons to save my own life rather than the lives of several strangers.

This leads Parfit to what he calls:

> [W]ide value-based objective view: When one of our two possible acts would make things go in some way that would be impartially better, but the other act would make things go better either for ourselves or for those to whom we have close ties, we often have sufficient reasons to act in either of these ways.[7]

The inclusion of the word "often" in the statement of this view marks a significant difference between his position and Sidgwick's. On Parfit's view, it would not be rational for me to do something that would be only very slightly better for me, but very bad impartially. For instance, it would not be rational to save myself from one minute of discomfort if doing so meant that a million people would die or suffer agony. Our

---

[6] *OWM,* I, 131.
[7] *OWM,* I, 137.

self-interested reasons can be outweighed by impartial or moral reasons. Nevertheless, because the relative strength of these different kinds of reasons is very imprecise, there is a wide range of cases about which Parfit agrees with Sidgwick that it is not irrational to do what is in one's own interests, and also not irrational to do what is impartially better. This would include, for instance, a case in which I have to choose between an injury to myself or saving the life of a stranger, whether the injury were losing one finger, or losing both legs; similarly it would include a case in which I have to choose between saving my own life or saving the lives of strangers, whether the number of strangers whose lives are at stake were two or 2,000.

Despite this wide range of imprecision in the guidance reason can give us, Parfit says that Sidgwick's famous despairing remarks about the damage that the unresolved dualism does to the rational basis of ethics are "overstatements." He defends this assessment by pointing out, first, that Sidgwick believes that in most cases, duty and self-interest do not conflict, but more significantly, Parfit denies that our whole system of beliefs of what is reasonable in conduct would fall "if we concluded that, when duty and self-interest conflict, we could reasonably, or rationally, act in either way." On the other hand, he concedes: "But it would be bad if, in such cases, we and others would have sufficient reasons to act wrongly. The *moralist's problem*, we might say, is whether we can avoid that conclusion. And it would be disappointing if, in such cases, reason gave us no guidance."[8]

Parfit then reformulates Sidgwick's dualism in terms of two questions: "What do I have most reason to do?" and "what ought I morally to do?" Parfit accepts that if the two questions often had conflicting answers, so that we often had decisive reason to act wrongly, morality would be undermined. "For morality to matter," he writes, "we must have reasons to care about morality, and to avoid acting wrongly." We could try to claim that though it is rational to act contrary to morality, these acts would still be wrong, and hence morality would not be undermined. But this would make morality trivial:

[8] *OWM*, I, 143.

It could be similarly claimed that, even if we had no reasons to follow the code of honour, or the rules of etiquette, this code and these rules would not be undermined. It would still be dishonourable not to fight some duels, and still be incorrect to eat peas with a spoon. But these claims, though true, would be trivial. If we had no reasons to do what is required by the code of honour, or by etiquette, these requirements would have no importance. If we had no reasons to care about morality, or to avoid acting wrongly, morality would similarly have no importance. That is how morality might be undermined.[9]

This sets up a problem to which Parfit is unable to give a compelling answer. He claims that for morality not to be undermined we must have reasons to care for morality and to avoid acting wrongly. But are sufficient reasons to avoid acting wrongly enough? Parfit writes: "Morality might have supreme importance in the reason-implying sense, since we might always have decisive reasons to do our duty, and to avoid acting wrongly." A few lines later he says: "we can plausibly assume that we do have strong reasons to care about morality, and to avoid acting wrongly." The use of "strong" rather than "decisive" is significant. Parfit does not defend the claim that we always have decisive reasons to act morally. He writes:

> We might have sufficient reasons to act wrongly, for example, if some wrong act was our only way to save from great pain or death, not ourselves, but our close relatives, or other people whom we love.[10]

In a personal communication, Parfit has offered an example of what he has in mind.[11] Suppose a man saves his own life and that of his two children by stealing medicine from a stranger who, as the man knows, needs the medicine to save her own life and that of her four children. Parfit agrees that this man's act would be wrong, but he finds it hard to accept that this man would be acting irrationally. Parfit also holds, of course,

[9] *OWM*, I, 147.
[10] *OWM*, I, 143.
[11] Emails to PS, 15 January 2010, and to PS, 13 August 2012.

that this man also has sufficient reason to act morally and not steal the medicine.

If, however, we have sufficient but not decisive reasons to act morally, morality may still be undermined. As we have seen, Parfit himself has said that "it would be bad" if, in cases in which duty and self-interest conflict, "we and others would have sufficient reasons to act wrongly." Now Parfit concedes that in some cases—and perhaps in many cases, for the imprecision of comparisons of these different types of reasons makes it hard to say how often such cases would occur—we do have sufficient reasons to act wrongly. We might say that nevertheless morality is important because we always have sufficient reasons to act in accordance with it. If I always choose to act wrongly, however, and in so choosing I am doing nothing contrary to reason, the importance of morality is seriously diminished. We therefore conclude that any form of the dualism of practical reason, whether it is Sidgwick's original version of it or Parfit's modified version, undermines morality to a significant degree. If we want morality to have the importance that it is often believed to have, we need to be able to overcome the dualism completely.

3. *Street's Darwinian Dilemma*

Sharon Street has argued that a "Darwinian Dilemma" faces those who hold a realist theory of value. The defining claim of realism, as Street uses the term, is that at least some evaluative facts or truths hold independently of all our evaluative attitudes, so Parfit is a realist in Street's sense. Street starts from a premise that we fully accept: "Evolutionary forces have played a tremendous role in shaping the content of human evaluative attitudes."[12] She then argues that those who defend objective moral truth face a choice between two uncongenial possibilities. The first possibility is that evolutionary forces have no tendency to lead to the selection of beings who hold objectively true evaluative attitudes. In this case, objectivists will have to admit that most of our evaluative judgments are unjustified. The second possibility is that evolutionary forces did favor the selection of those who are able to grasp objective moral

---

[12] Street, "A Darwinian Dilemma," 109, 122.

truths. But this, Street argues, is contrary to a scientific understanding of how evolution works.

To take the first horn of the dilemma and accept that evolutionary forces have no relation to objectively true evaluative attitudes means, Street suggests, that our prospects of having evaluative attitudes that lead us to moral truths are like the prospects of sailing to Bermuda while allowing our boat's course to be determined by the winds and tides. We would be incredibly lucky to reach Bermuda, and if we did, it would be a remarkable coincidence. Barring such a coincidence, however, the realist has to accept what Street considers a "far-fetched skeptical result," namely that "most of our evaluative judgments are off-track due to the distorting pressure of Darwinian forces."[13]

Those taking the second horn of the dilemma fare no better. They make a claim that is unacceptable on scientific grounds. Street offers a list of some of the judgments we make, which includes, for example: "We have greater obligations to help our own children than we do to help complete strangers."[14] Such judgments are conducive to reproductive success, so it is easy to see how evolutionary forces would lead us to make them. It is not so easy to see how evolutionary forces would lead us to make only judgments that are objectively true. Why should the truth of a judgment be something that evolution favors? As Street says, it is more scientifically plausible to explain human evaluative attitudes as having evolved because they help us to survive and to have surviving offspring, than because they are true.

To show how evolution could shape our evaluative judgments, Street asks us to suppose that we had evolved as a different kind of being. Social insects, for example, have a stronger orientation towards the welfare of the community than to their own individual survival, and male lions kill offspring that are not their own. Assuming that in some way we could be intelligent, but with reproductive patterns more like those of social insects or lions, we would, she claims, have different basic evaluative attitudes that would lead us to make different reflective evaluative judgments. Since not all these judgments could be true, wouldn't it be a

[13] Ibid., 109.
[14] Ibid., 115.

remarkable coincidence if we just happened to have evolved as the kind of beings that make true evaluative judgments?[15]

In responding to such doubts about our evaluative attitudes, utilitarians are at an advantage over those who hold moral views that are based on our commonly accepted moral rules or intuitions. Utilitarians seek to maximize utility in the circumstances in which we find ourselves. If therefore we find ourselves in very different circumstances, perhaps as intelligent sentient social insects, or as lions, with their modes of reproducing and surviving, the specific acts that will be right or wrong in those circumstances will be very different from the specific acts that are right or wrong for us as we are now, but it will still be true that we ought to maximize utility. Hence it is quite possible for a utilitarian to accept what Street describes as the "far-fetched skeptical result" that "most of our evaluative judgments are off-track due to the distorting pressure of Darwinian forces." Given that evolutionary forces operate at the level of the gene or the individual, or at most the community, rather than at the level of the species (and certainly not at the level of all sentient beings), it is quite plausible that these evolutionary forces have produced evaluative attitudes that fail to conduce to ultimate moral truths such as "Maximize the utility of all sentient beings." We can therefore reject any particular judgments based on these evolved evaluative attitudes, while maintaining the validity of the more general principle that we should do what is best for the well-being of all.

This position avoids Street's dilemma by accepting its first horn, for many of our common moral judgments. Street would no doubt then try to press her argument against the ultimate principle. How do we reach it, if it has no relation to our evolved basic evaluative attitudes? Was it sheer coincidence, like our drifting boat reaching Bermuda? When it comes to an ultimate principle like that of doing what is best for the well-being of all, however, rationalists like Sidgwick and Parfit have a good response. They can say that we come to understand such principles by the use of our reason.

At this point rationalists can take the second horn of Street's dilemma. Street focuses on the question whether evolution is likely to lead us to

---

[15] Ibid., 120.

have a capacity to recognize objective moral truths. If our moral beliefs are evolutionarily advantageous, then the advantages they confer on us in surviving and reproducing have nothing to do with their truth. So why would evolution have led us to have a capacity to recognize moral truth? Street correctly points out that a specific capacity for recognizing moral truths would not increase our reproductive success. But as Parfit points out, a capacity to reason *would* tend to increase our reproductive success:

> Because we can respond to epistemic reasons, we are able to form many other kinds of true belief, especially beliefs about the further future, and the possible effects of different possible acts. The ability of early humans to form such true beliefs had evolutionary advantages, by helping them to survive and reproduce. Natural selection slowly but steadily gave later humans greater cognitive abilities. Just as the faster cheetahs and taller giraffes tended to survive longer and have more offspring, who inherited similar qualities, so did the humans who were better at reasoning validly and responding to reasons.[16]

Moreover, once we have this capacity to reason, it may lead us to other true beliefs, some unrelated to survival and reproduction. These beliefs may be about physics, such as beliefs about black holes, or about higher mathematics, or about valid proofs. They may also, Parfit has suggested, be normative epistemic beliefs, for instance, the belief that, when some argument is valid and has true premises, these facts give us a decisive reason to believe this conclusion. Parfit argues that this normative claim, about what we have decisive reason to believe, is not itself evolutionarily advantageous, since to gain that advantage, it would have been sufficient to have the non-normative beliefs that the argument is valid, and has true premises, and that the conclusion must be true. Hence

[16] *OWM*, II, 494. Colin McGinn suggested this explanation of why evolution has not eliminated moral behavior in "Evolution, Animals and the Basis of Morality," *Inquiry*, 22 (1979): 91. One of us has defended a similar view in Peter Singer, *The Expanding Circle* (Princeton: Princeton University Press, 2011, first published 1981), Ch. 5, and also in Peter Singer, "Ethics and Intuitions", *The Journal of Ethics*, 9/3–4 (2005): 331–52.

this and other normative epistemic beliefs are not open to a debunking argument.[17] This may also hold for some of our moral beliefs. Parfit suggests the Golden Rule, which in his formulation requires us to "treat other people only in ways in which we would be willing to be treated by others, whether or not these others treat us in these ways." As Parfit points out, natural selection cannot easily explain our widespread acceptance of the Golden Rule.[18] A similar example would be Sidgwick's axiom of universal benevolence.[19]

It may be objected that if some aspects of our capacity to reason conferred an evolutionary advantage, while other aspects were disadvantageous in that respect (perhaps because they lead us to act more altruistically than we would otherwise have done) then these other aspects would have been selected against, and would have disappeared. (They might also have disappeared even if they were merely neutral, neither advantageous nor disadvantageous, because of evolutionary drift, but obviously the more a trait or capacity disadvantages the being who possesses it, the more rapidly it is likely to disappear.) It appears to be the case, however, that we have retained capacities to reason that do not confer any evolutionary advantage, and may even be disadvantageous. How can that be? A plausible explanation of the existence of these capacities is that the ability to reason comes as a package that could not be economically divided by evolutionary pressures. Either we have a capacity to reason that includes the capacity to do advanced physics and mathematics and to grasp objective moral truths, or we have a much more limited capacity to reason that lacks not only these abilities, but others that confer an overriding evolutionary advantage. If reason is a unity of this kind, having

---

[17] Parfit, *OWM*, II, 492, and Parfit, email to the authors, 16 August 2011.

[18] *OWM*, II, 537. For the widespread acceptance of the Golden Rule, see *The Analects of Confucius*, also known as *The Selected Sayings of Kongfuzi*, XV, 23; *Mahabharata*, Anusasana Parva 113.8; for Buddhism, see *Samyutta Nikaya* v.353. The words of the *Mahabharata* are especially clear on the distinction, to which Parfit refers, between self-interest and concern for others: "One should not behave towards others in a way which is disagreeable to oneself. This is the essence of morality. All other activities are due to selfish desire." For a comprehensive list of such ideas in many different texts and civilizations, see Howard Terry, *Golden and Silver Rules of Humanity*, 5th edn (West Conshohocken, PA: Infinity Publishing, 2011).

[19] *The Methods of Ethics*, 382.

the package would have been more conducive to survival and reproduction than not having it.

Street discusses the objection that our capacity to grasp objective moral truths could be a by-product of some other evolved capacity. She argues that this capacity must be a highly specialized one, "specifically attuned to the evaluative truths in question."[20] Therefore those who make this proposal face the Darwinian dilemma once again, this time with respect to the relationship between the specialized capacity to grasp objective moral truths and the other more basic evolved capacity. Either there is no relationship between the evolution of the basic capacity and the independent moral truths—in which case it is a remarkable coincidence that the basic capacity had, as a by-product, a capacity to grasp objective moral truths—or there is some relationship between the evolved basic capacity and the capacity to grasp independent moral truths. We have taken the second horn of this dilemma. Those who take this course, Street says, must claim that the evolved capacity "involves at least some *basic* sort of ability to grasp independent evaluative truths, of which our present-day ability to grasp evaluative truths is a refined extension, in much the same way that our present-day ability to do astrophysics is presumably a refined extension of more basic abilities to discover and model the physical features of the world around us." She then adds: "But at this point the realist has to give some account of how this more basic sort of ability to grasp independent evaluative truths arose."[21] Indeed, that is true: but given that philosophers like Sidgwick have long said that it is our capacity to reason that enables us to grasp moral truths, and given that we can explain why a capacity to reason would have been evolutionarily advantageous, it is odd that Street does not directly confront the idea that the capacity to grasp moral truths is simply an application of our capacity to reason, which enables us to grasp a priori truths in general, including both the truths of mathematics, and moral truths. For if the ability to grasp moral truths is an aspect of our ability to reason, and to respond to reasons, it is easy to give an account of how it arose.

[20] Street, "A Darwinian Dilemma," 143.
[21] Ibid., 144.

4. Which Moral Beliefs Survive the Evolutionary Critique?

The Golden Rule and the axiom of universal benevolence contradict the very evaluative attitudes that Street offers as examples of judgments that are likely to lead to reproductive success, such as "We have greater obligations to help our own children than we do to help complete strangers." Evolutionary theorists have long had difficulty in explaining how pure altruism is possible. They tend to explain it in terms of more limited forms of altruism, such as altruism toward kin, and reciprocal altruism, that is, altruism toward those with whom we are in a cooperative relationship. Some theorists also accept the possibility of altruism toward one's own group. It is, however, difficult to see any evolutionary forces that could have favored universal altruism of the sort that is required by the axiom of rational benevolence. On the contrary, there are strong evolutionary forces that would tend to eliminate it. In the absence of an appeal to our evolved capacity to reason as the basis for our ability to grasp moral truth, therefore, it is difficult to see what plausible evolutionary explanation there could be for the idea of equal concern for the interests of complete strangers who do not belong to one's own group.[22]

On the other hand, an evolutionary understanding of the origins of our ethical judgments does seem to undermine some of our ethical judgments, at least to the extent of suggesting that we should not take them for granted merely because we intuitively judge them to be sound. Parfit offers the example of incest.[23] Among our ancestors, for millions of years, such sexual relationships probably increased the proportion of abnormal offspring, and hence diminished prospects of reproductive success, as compared to sexual relationships between those who were not so closely related. Hence our negative evaluative attitude towards incest—which is less universally held when the degree of consanguinity, and hence the risk of abnormal offspring, is reduced—is easily explained as part of our evolutionary heritage. This is also a debunking explanation, since today it is possible to separate sex and reproduction, so this

---

[22] For further discussion of this point, see Katarzyna de Lazari-Radek and Peter Singer, "The Objectivity of Ethics and the Unity of Practical Reason," *Ethics*, 123 (October 2012): 9–31.

[23] *OWM*, II, 536.

reason for rejecting incest in the circumstances described is no longer always applicable. Thus the judgment that incest is always wrong—even, for instance, when it is between adult siblings—can be seen to be the product of a cause that, in at least some cases, produces judgments likely to be in error.[24]

Parfit also suggests a more significant example of a moral belief that can be debunked by an evolutionary explanation: "the beliefs that, rather than following the Golden Rule, we ought to give, or may give, strong priority to the well-being of people who are members of our tribe, nation, or race, or followers of the same religion." As Parfit points out, these beliefs may have helped some communities to conquer or destroy others, and could have been evolutionarily advantageous, not only at the genetic but also at the social or cultural level.[25]

Parfit is surely right about such forms of tribalism; but we think that the same line of thought applies also to another moral belief which, as we have already mentioned, Street uses as an example of how our judgments coincide with intuitions likely to lead to reproductive success. This is the judgment that, in Street's words, "We have greater obligations to help our own children than we do to help complete strangers." We saw earlier, in discussing Parfit's reformulation of Sidgwick's dualism, that Parfit accepts that the fact that an act "would make things go better either for ourselves or for those to whom we have close ties" gives us sufficient reason for doing it. This alleged reason for action is subject to the same kind of evolutionary explanation as the belief that we may give priority to members of our tribe, or other group to which we belong. The widespread belief that this judgment is true may be the result of the fact that those who accept it would be more likely than those who do not accept it to leave surviving offspring to carry on their genes. Why are families not just like tribes, in this respect?

This is not to say that the judgment that we have greater obligations to help our own children than to help strangers cannot be justified, but

---

[24] Cf. Jonathan Haidt, "The Emotional Dog and Its Rational Tail: A Social Intuitionist Approach to Moral Judgment," *Psychological Review*, 108 (2001): 814–34, citing Jonathan Haidt, Fredrik Björklund, and Scott Murphy, "Moral Dumbfounding: When Intuition Finds No Reason" (unpublished ms).
[25] *OWM*, II, 537–8.

rather that if it is to be justified, it needs a form of justification that does not start from the idea that because we strongly feel that it is right, it must be true. For instance, it may be the case that our nature is such that the most reliable way of raising happy, well-adjusted children is to raise them in a close, caring family, united by natural ties of love and affection. If so, then this would provide an indirect justification of the judgment that we have greater obligations to our own children than to the children of strangers. Given the kind of creatures we are—mammals with children who are dependent on us for many years—loving our own children and helping them more than we help the children of strangers would, on this view, be justified in terms of a more ultimate principle, for example that it is good to do what is best for the well-being of all.

5. *The Dualism Resolved*

Now that we have prepared the ground, it is not difficult to see the implications of our argument for Sidgwick's "profoundest problem." It is, Sidgwick believes, "in accordance with common sense to recognize—as Butler does—that the calm desire for my 'good on the whole' is authoritative; and therefore carries with it implicitly a rational dictate to aim at this end."[26] This may indeed be in accordance with common sense, but here common sense seems likely to have been formed by the evolutionary influences we have been discussing. Since the claim that egoism is rational clashes with the Golden Rule and with the principle of universal benevolence, and the principle of egoism is subject to a debunking evolutionary explanation, while the impartial principles are not, we have grounds for supporting the impartial principles rather than the egoistic one. If the rationality of egoism can thus be put in doubt, we can tentatively conclude that all reasons for action are impartial, and the dualism that led Sidgwick to fear "an ultimate and fundamental contradiction in our apparent intuitions of what is Reasonable in conduct" can, at least on the level of rationality, be dissolved.

This may seem too paradoxical to take seriously. Utilitarians face a similar issue when defending the impartiality of utilitarianism. Sidgwick's

---

[26] Sidgwick, *The Methods of Ethics*, 112.

response was to point out that although utilitarianism is impartial at the level of theory, in practice there are various factors that limit the extent to which we should try to act impartially, including our greater knowledge of how to bring about our own happiness—which is of course a part of the general happiness—as compared with the difficulty of knowing what will increase the happiness of strangers. Sidgwick also notes that we are better able to increase the happiness of others when we are happy ourselves.[27] In a similar manner, the common view that it is rational to act self-interestedly may gain plausibility because acting in one's own interest, broadly conceived, is often in harmony with doing what is in the best interests of all. Nevertheless, this harmony is far from complete. In a world with a wide gulf between rich and poor, and many opportunities for the rich to help the poor, impartiality remains highly demanding for the rich.

Some of the remaining air of paradox around the idea that all reasons for action are impartial stems from the assumption that a reason for action must provide the person for whom it is a reason with a motivation for acting. Denying the rationality of egoism leaves reason detached from our strongest sources of motivation, namely our desires to further our own interests and those of our family. If, however, we follow Parfit—as well as Thomas Nagel, Thomas Scanlon, and Jonathan Dancy among many—in distinguishing normative reasons from motivating reasons, the paradoxical nature of our claim is reduced.[28] On this view, normative reasons are independent of our present desires, wants, and beliefs. A normative reason can be a motivating reason when we act for this reason. But we may also have a motivating reason without having a normative reason. Parfit gives the example of someone who acted in order to get revenge. We may say: "His reason was to get revenge, but that was no reason to do what he did."[29] A discussion of motivating reasons is, Parfit believes, relevant to why people act as they do, but not to how they ought

[27] Ibid., 431.
[28] See Thomas Nagel, *The View From Nowhere* (New York: Oxford University Press, 1986), Ch. 8; T. M. Scanlon, *What We Owe To Each Other* (Cambridge, MA Harvard University Press, 1998), Ch. 1; Jonathan Dancy, *Practical Reality* (Oxford: Clarendon Press, 2000); Parfit, *OWM*.
[29] Parfit, *OWM*, I, 37.

to act. The distinction is vital for Parfit's defense of objective reasons for action, because it allows for a conception of practical reason that is free of Hume's assumption that reasons for action must be based on desires. We can have normative reasons for action, irrespective of whether we like them, agree with them, or desire to act in accordance with them.

Given Parfit's insistence on the normative rather than the psychological nature of practical reason, our argument suggests that he could have gone further and rejected what he refers to as personal and partial reasons. Why then does Parfit accept the validity of personal and partial reasons, rather than say that they are very common *motivating* reasons, but—as with the desire for revenge—not *normative* reasons? The explanation might seem to be that, like so many contemporary moral philosophers, he accepts the model of reflective equilibrium made popular by John Rawls, and this leads him to be reluctant to reject too many of our common moral judgments. But Parfit interprets reflective equilibrium widely, so that the process of reaching an equilibrium takes into account both scientific theories and normative theories. As he puts it: "When we try to achieve what Rawls calls reflective equilibrium, we should appeal to all of our beliefs, including our intuitive beliefs about the wrongness of some kinds of act."[30] Among the scientific theories to be taken into account is evolutionary theory, along with the argument that it undermines the credibility of some of our most widely shared moral intuitions. Parfit, in particular, is well aware of this, for he stated it with his usual clarity in *Reasons and Persons*:

> ... if some attitude has an evolutionary explanation, this fact is neutral. It neither supports nor undermines the claim that this attitude is justified. But there is one exception. It may be claimed that, since

[30] *OWM*, I, 367. Street, too, refers to the "widespread consensus that the method of reflective equilibrium, broadly understood, is our sole means of proceeding in ethics." Street's acceptance of this model may have led her to neglect the possibility of defending moral realism that we have adopted, namely that of accepting that many of our common moral intuitions are false, while defending at least one fundamental principle that we reach by the use of our reason. If we can grasp some moral truths by the use of our reason, while we hold others only because their acceptance enhanced our evolutionary fitness, it would be a mistake to assume that the best normative view is the one that holds these two kinds of beliefs in reflective equilibrium.

we all have this attitude, this is a ground for thinking it justified. *This* claim is undermined by the evolutionary explanation. Since there is this explanation, we would all have this attitude even if it was not justified; so the fact that we have this attitude cannot be a reason for thinking it justified. Whether it is justified is an open question, waiting to be answered.[31]

Parfit, and other proponents of reflective equilibrium, widely interpreted, could therefore draw on evolutionary theory, as well as on Sidgwick's normative arguments in order to reject many widely-shared moral intuitions, while retaining the principle of universal benevolence. Although those who make use of reflective equilibrium in normative and applied ethics typically assume that they should try to achieve an equilibrium between a plausible normative theory and most, or at least many, of our commonly accepted moral judgments, there is no need for them to make this assumption. They could reject the commonly held view that it is rational to do what is in one's own interests (even though people may have strong motivating reasons to act in this way) and accept that when one of two possible acts would make things go impartially better, that is what we have decisive normative reason to do.

6. Conclusion

At the beginning of this essay we agreed with Parfit that for morality to be important we have to have reasons to care about it and to avoid acting wrongly. We did not, however, agree that this requirement will be satisfied as long as we have sufficient reasons to do what is moral. For morality to have its full importance we have to have decisive reasons to avoid doing what is wrong. I may have sufficient reasons to watch a football match and at the same time have sufficient reasons to go to an exhibition of old master paintings. Sufficiency of reasons for choosing the exhibition does not undermine the value of going to the football. If I really cannot decide what to do, because I have sufficient reason for either

[31] Derek Parfit, *Reasons and Persons* (Oxford: Clarendon Press, 1986) 186; we owe this reference to Kahane, "Evolutionary Debunking Arguments," 110.

choice, I can simply toss a coin. In such situations, either both things matter to roughly the same extent, or neither of them matters at all. But the choice between right and wrong is not like the choice between going to the football or to an art exhibition. If we lack decisive reasons to do what is right, the significance of morality is seriously diminished.

For Sidgwick the dualism was between partiality and impartiality. The argument we offered against Street's critique of realism had, as a by-product, a way of overcoming that dualism. Street thinks that a sound scientific understanding of evolution shows that our moral judgments are highly unlikely to be objectively true. We agree that this evolutionary debunking does apply to many of our common moral judgments, and this includes all kinds of partial moral judgments. Partiality, where it cannot be given an impartial justification, is the domain of what Street calls "evolutionary forces." It can be understood and explained in terms of our natural capacities or desires, and it has been incorporated into what can be called common-sense morality. Reason, on the other hand, is independent of natural forces and presents us with rules or principles that are impartial. Moral acts, understood as acts that are justifiable from an impartial perspective, are not only rational to undertake but, given the debunking of partial reasons that count against impartiality, are rationally required.[32]

[32] Katarzyna de Lazari-Radek and Peter Singer thank the Polish National Science Center for its financial support of this project.

INDEX